WOODWORKING FOR WOMEN 101

How to Speak the Language, Buy the Tools, & Build Fabulous Furniture From Start to Finish

Marilyn MacEwen

LARK BOOKS

A Division of Sterling Publishing Co., Inc.
New York

EDITOR:
Aimé Ontario Fraser

COPY EDITOR:
Chris Rich

ART DIRECTOR:
Megan Kirby, Kathy Holmes

COVER DESIGNER:
Barbara Zaretsky

PROJECT COORDINATOR:
Linda Kopp

DEVELOPMENTAL EDITOR:
Deborah Morgenthal

ASSISTANT EDITOR:
Rebecca Guthrie

ASSOCIATE ART DIRECTOR:
Shannon Yokeley

ART PRODUCTION ASSISTANT:
Jeff Hamilton

EDITORIAL ASSISTANCE:
Delores Gosnell

ILLUSTRATOR:
Melanie Powell

PHOTOGRAPHER:
Keith Wright

Library of Congress Cataloging-in-Publication Data

MacEwen, Marilyn, 1953-
   Woodworking 101 for women: how to speak the language, buy the tools, & build fabulous furniture from start to finish / Marilyn MacEwen.— 1st ed.
         p. cm.
   Includes index.
   ISBN 1-57990-608-7 (pbk.)
  1. Woodwork.   2. Woodworking tools.   3. Furniture making.   I. Title.   II. Title: Woodworking one hundred and one for women.
TT180.M18 2006
684'.08082—dc22

2005036774

10 9 8 7 6 5 4 3 2 1

First Edition

Published by Lark Books, A Division of Sterling Publishing Co., Inc.
387 Park Avenue South, New York, N.Y. 10016

Text © 2006, Marilyn MacEwen
Photography © 2006, Lark Books unless otherwise specified
Illustrations © 2006, Lark Books unless otherwise specified

Distributed in Canada by Sterling Publishing,
c/o Canadian Manda Group, 165 Dufferin Street
Toronto, Ontario, Canada M6K 3H6

Distributed in the United Kingdom by GMC Distribution Services,
Castle Place, 166 High Street, Lewes, East Sussex, England BN7 1XU

Distributed in Australia by Capricorn Link (Australia) Pty Ltd.,
P.O. Box 704, Windsor, NSW 2756 Australia

If you have questions or comments about this book, please contact:
Lark Books, 67 Broadway, Asheville, NC 28801
(828) 253-0467

Manufactured in China

ISBN 13: 978-1-57990-608-5
ISBN 10: 1-57990-608-7

For information about custom editions, special sales, premium and corporate purchases, please contact Sterling Special Sales Department at 800-805-5489 or special-sales@sterlingpub.com.

WOMEN, WOOD, AND TOOLS

Learn to think like a woodworker.

Women, wood, and tools. Why is it that when you put these words in the same sentence, the world seems to tilt on its axis and continents drift apart? The once familiar world divides and everything seems uncertain. Where once you stood your familiar ground, now you gaze across a chasm to a new world.

That new continent is a realm where machines dot the landscape, tools hang ready for deployment, and the inhabitants speak in terse technical jargon. On the opposite shore, you see men busily at work building the world, tearing it down, crunching numbers, structuring economics, and drawing up plans for the next era of war and peace. This new world is a man's world with its own language and customs; to women it often seems strange and foreign.

This hasn't always been so. During World War II, America's women stepped into that world and filled the vital industrial and technical jobs left by the men who'd gone off to battle. By war's end, Rosie the Riveter had proven that women possess the physical, intellectual, and technical abilities to not only survive but to thrive in the formerly male territory.

Despite Rosie's trailblazing, once the war was over few women traveled to the other side. Instead, women were encouraged to stay at home with the kids and the laundry. With her technical skills no longer needed, Rosie's self-confidence seemed to drain away with each rinse cycle.

Yet now you find yourself standing before a bridge to that land, looking at the territory ahead with longing. You might have arrived at this point via any number of roads. Perhaps you saw the latest episode of "Building Furniture for Yourself," where

Of course you can build beautiful furniture that fits your home, your life, and your style. Pursue your happiness!

Norm Neanderthal perpetrated his latest woodworking wizardry. You thought, "I *could* do that, but I *won't*. I'm going to build my *own* furniture."

Perhaps you saw an exhibit of studio furniture or a book on design. Maybe you're sick of the corporate world and long to build something honest and real. Or maybe you're acknowledging an elemental force that inextricably draws you to woodworking, as it did me.

Am I able?

You're thinking the territory looks like an interesting place to sojourn, but you pause. It's scary to leave your comfort zone and enter a foreign land. You've done enough research to realize it's not going to be easy getting there. The sheer amount of information you need to learn about woodworking can be daunting. You wonder, "Where do I start? What tools should I buy? After all, I've never had a shop class, and my father didn't want me around when he was working in the garage on his projects. Perhaps I'm not even capable of learning to build furniture."

Nonsense. Don't buy into what I call "The Declaration of Inability." The ability to work wood is not a birthright. It's something every woodworker—man or woman—earns over time by gathering information and experiences. Though the culture of woodworking may be biased toward men's strengths, every woman has skills and traits that are directly applicable to woodworking. Patience, adaptability, multitasking, intuition, problem solving, and endurance are but a few. If you have any experience with cooking or needlework, you can add to the list things like measuring, organizing sequence, planning outcomes, and high-level hand-eye coordination. You can do woodworking. Pursue your happiness!

Woodworkers are made, not born. As a beginner, even the author had to overcome her doubts and fears. Her mantra was "Mistakes are just information."

Don't fear tools; respect them.

I'll come right out and say it now so you don't have to: Woodworking tools can be scary. Wood is a tough material, and you need sharp and powerful tools to work it. Used wrongly, these tools can do some serious damage. Make it your mission to learn how the tools work, and always use redundantly safe setups and procedures, and you will have nothing to fear.

Yet banishing this fear is often easier said than done. It's not uncommon for woodworking machines to become a kind of psycho-emotional magnet for a woman's vague fears and self-doubts. You may find that constructing furniture involves, at least at first, deconstructing the person you believed yourself to be.

When I took my first formal woodworking class (circa 1978), I was the only woman and the only person with no woodworking experience. It made for a very charged atmosphere. I'm not sure which was more intimidating—the roar of big machines or the mumbling of the men who didn't want me there. In any event, a life's worth of fears and doubts decided to attach themselves to the table saw. I couldn't approach the machine without tensing up, which only made it more difficult to operate it with confidence.

It took me weeks to work through it. By practicing cuts on the table saw, I was at last able to rip away the rough edges of my fears and produce proper material from which I built a solid image of myself as a woodworker. Now I am at one with the table saw, and I get a secret joy when guys visit my shop and admire my table saw and its setup.

Setbacks happen

Such emotionally-based woodworking conundrums are much more common for women than for men. Most men cheerfully blunder onward in the face of setbacks, eager to learn something new. Women, on the other hand, tend to interpret setbacks as signs that they lack some personal virtues required for woodworking success.

It's been my aim in writing this book to provide you with information and guidelines to prevent you from falling into these pits of despair and frustration. So each page of this book is a step across the bridge, leading you in a logical progression to the ultimate destination—building furniture.

When those moments do occur (and they will), keep them in perspective. Cry if you must, but know that the feeling is not "The Truth"—it will soon pass. Hold on to your determination to learn woodworking, even when you feel as if you'll never succeed. Have patience and perseverance, and those feelings will rapidly diminish, replaced by the satisfaction of foreseeing a problem and preventing it. Or perhaps by finding a creative solution that turns a "mistake" into a design element.

Crossing the divide

Learning a new language can be scary, too. Woodworking is a complex body of knowledge that crosses the borders of many disciplines. Each has its own special language and way of thinking that woodworkers put to daily use. Metallurgy, for example, offers an understanding of the steels used in tools and how to sharpen them. Electrical engineering helps us to understand motors and how machines work. Biology informs us about trees, how they grow, and why wood looks and acts the way it does; and chemistry defines how and why finishes and adhesives work. Materials science includes the study of the strength of materials and fastenings, and why and how joints hold; physics is involved in manipulating, setting up, and using tools properly; and you'll use mathematics for measuring and designing. While this vast quantity of information enables us to turn ideas into furniture, it can present a special set of learning problems for women.

The technical, linear, and detail-loving orientation we see in woodworking and its subdisciplines is common among those for whom the left hemisphere of the brain is dominant. Generally speaking, left-brain dominance is a male trait. It's what makes so many of those clichés about male characteristics true. Men love details, hate to talk, aren't much interested in feelings, want things laid out in sequences, prefer nonfiction to fiction, are good at math and numbers, and want to make fine distinctions that prevent the sort of generalization that I'm making right here. Women tend to be right-brain dominant—the big picture is what matters to them. Women are into connections, and feelings are important because feelings are what make everything in some way interconnected.

Of course, men use their right brain and women use their left. The two hemispheres are connected by a thick bridge of nerve fibers called the corpus callosum, which gives access to the whole brain. Some studies have shown that the bridge is generally thicker in women than in men, suggesting that women are more adept at accessing both sides of the brain. So with a little practice, you should be able to cross to the realm of the technical more readily than most men can cross to your familiar emotional territory.

If you're ready to cross the bridge, woodworking can provide you with a route to new ways of thinking about yourself and the world around you. No longer is a chair just a chair; a table is no longer a mere table. You'll start thinking about each chair's particular form and function, and noting how that table differs from all others. You'll find yourself on bended knee, looking at the backs, interiors, and undersides of all kinds of furniture, figuring out how it was built. When you find yourself engag-ing in this peculiar activity, you'll know you've crossed the bridge and are at home in the new world.

Women, wood, and tools. Why not?

HOW TO USE THIS BOOK: LEARNING TO THINK LIKE A WOODWORKER

If you flip through this book and look for how space is divided among the various topics, you'll get a clear pic-ture of how a woodworker thinks.

The first topic is wood, and a moderate amount of space is devoted to the subject. Wood is the medium in which we work, and its color, texture, heft, feel, and smell are the means by which we express ourselves.

The tools section is a relatively small percentage of the whole. While it's easy for woodworkers to get wrapped up in tool specs and focus on minutiae, a fraction of horsepower is insignificant compared to how well you set up and use that tool. Therefore, the section on how to use the tools is the largest portion of this book. It's a collection of detailed photos and step-by-step instruc-tions covering every major woodworking process. If you learn all the techniques, you'll be thinking, plan-ning, and even moving like a woodworker.

The techniques section is designed to stand alone, but it's also an encyclopedia of the processes you'll use to build the projects. For example, milling lumber four-square is covered in detail in the techniques section, but barely mentioned in the projects. The book refers you to the place in the techniques chapter that describes the process in detail. Read each section until you understand it well enough to explain it to someone else. Then practice each technique. Take the time and do the job as well as you'd do it if you were making the project.

All the projects start with a materials list showing the fin-ished dimensions of the various component pieces. Review the list to figure out the quantities and dimensions of rough lumber you'll need to yield those results. Just what you buy will depend on the species of wood you choose, the machine tools you have for milling, and what's available locally.

A set of drawings comes after the materials list, collected in one place for easy reference. Each project has a front view, a side (or top) view, and an exploded view. Some projects also have bottom views, back views, cutaway views, and detailed drawings of important or more com-plex parts. By comparing the views, you can visualize each part and how it fits into the whole.

Your first job as a woodworker is to study these draw-ings, comparing views back and forth until you under-stand exactly how each part is made and how it fits together to construct the whole. Keep looking—what may be hazy in one view will become clear after comparing it to others.

After your first perusal of the drawings, read the "How to Build" section to get the big-picture view of the building process. Go back to the drawings if necessary for any clarification. Then read the step-by-step instructions, referring to both the drawings and the techniques section as necessary.

By the time you actually start building, you'll be thinking like a woodworker. You'll know what you're doing, and you'll make the project your own—not only because you built it, but also because you understand it.

WOOD

Choose wisely, and start your projects right.

Not too long ago, a builder friend called. He had, to use one of my favorite vernacular expressions, "A Big Situation," after installing a mantel in a new home. It was a massive piece of air-dried hickory, fully 4" thick and 64" long, bolted to the wall. While carefully built to begin with, it had cracked down the center and morphed into a ridiculous, twisted shape of nature. It had become a science project on the wall.

Hickory is a beautiful but deceiving wood, known for twisting out of shape with the changes in humidity that come with the change of seasons, even after thorough kiln drying. Glaring at the demon mantel I remarked, "Hasn't anyone told you hickory is possessed?" He teetered between laughter and tears as I assured him that I could fix his mantel. "That evil piece of hickory will make a good anchor for a box I'll build of nice kiln-dried lumber to shroud it."

The moral to this story is that wood is not a static material. It's constantly shrinking and swelling with changes in local humidity, and if you don't understand the relationship between wood and water, you'll face one "Big Situation" after another.

Wood and water: We've got a situation

Think of trees as gigantic conduits for water, every cell working to provide the necessary fluid and nutrients to sustain these marvelous living organisms. The cells are saturated with water, and the moisture content of a newly felled tree is something like 80 percent (the actual percentage varies by species). At the mill, the green logs are rough sawn into boards and placed in a kiln for drying.

The kiln environment is carefully controlled to drive the moisture from the wood, but not completely. The boards come out of the kiln with an 8 percent moisture content, and slightly smaller dimensions because wood cells shrink as they dry.

If the board could maintain that 8 percent moisture content, it would stay exactly the same size and shape that it was when it came out of the kiln, but the moisture content changes, and the board undergoes some dimensional changes.

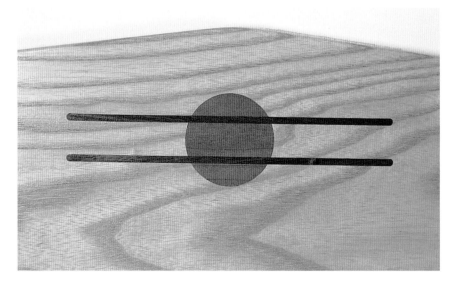

Wood is the medium. Its color, texture, heft, feel, and smell are how we express ourselves as woodworkers.

The moisture content—and therefore the dimensions—of a board are directly related to the humidity level of the air around it. The higher the humidity, the higher the moisture content of the wood. As the moisture content increases, the cells reabsorb some of the water they lost in drying, and swell. The converse is also true. As humidity decreases, so does moisture content. The board shrinks.

The shrinking or swelling occurs tangent to the growth rings—in a typical board that means across its width. Exactly how a board's dimensions change depends on how the grain runs, which in turn depends on the board's position in the log before sawing (see fig. 1).

Rough sawn boards left outdoors (and properly stacked) will eventually dry to around 15 percent moisture content. It takes about one year of air drying per inch of thickness to reach this level. Without that drying-out period in the kiln, air-dried lumber can be unruly and unpredictable. Don't expect it keep on the straight and narrow. It seems hell-bent on thwarting any plans you might have for it, and sometimes contorts into unbelievable forms.

Figure 1

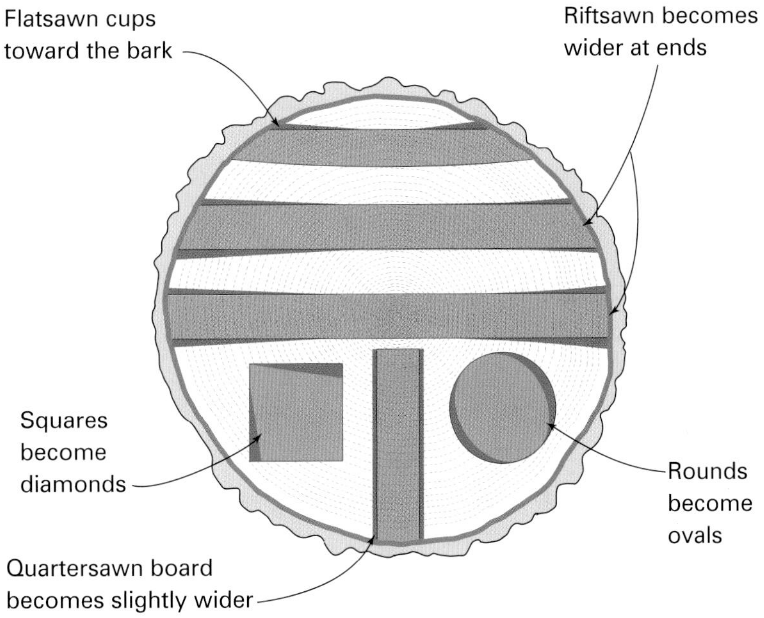

Flatsawn cups toward the bark

Riftsawn becomes wider at ends

Squares become diamonds

Rounds become ovals

Quartersawn board becomes slightly wider

Wood shrinks and swells roughly tangent to the growth rings. Exactly how this affects dimensional changes depends on the board's location relative to the center of the tree from which it came.

This is what happened with the big hickory mantel. It was air dried outdoors in high humidity, and its moisture content was at least 15 percent. Since it was so thick, the moisture content was probably even higher in the middle of the board. Once installed indoors, where humidity levels are considerably lower, the wood rapidly lost moisture, causing it to crack and twist.

When building furniture, use only kiln-dried lumber. Its 8 percent moisture content is comparable with indoor humidity levels and its big shrinking days are over. It will remain fairly stable, but be prepared for the occasional minor binge during times of extreme humidity. An unusually long rainy spell can cause swelling, and a very cold, dry winter will cause some shrinkage.

Designing and building for changes

Knowing that your wood will change with the seasons makes it possible for you to design and build your furniture so it can gracefully accept those changes.

Take for instance the top of the Table for Two (see p. 90). It's 27 1/2" wide. Interpolating from figure 2, you can expect a total of about 3/8" of change in width with changes in humidity (indoors only). When you fasten the top to the aprons, you must allow for that movement, or the top will pull itself apart. There are many ways to fasten a tabletop, but the easiest is to drill oversize pilot holes for the screws and put washers under the screw heads (see fig. 3).

I rarely do any kind of calculations. In the summer, my shop is very humid. If I'm hanging doors on a cabinet, I know to leave only a 1/16" gap between them. That way, when winter rolls around and the cabinet is in a heated space, the doors will shrink slightly, leaving a visually pleasant amount of space.

Reputable lumber dealers typically sell only kiln-dried lumber—if you want air-dried wood, you'll have to search a bit to find a supplier. Rarely will you encounter improper-

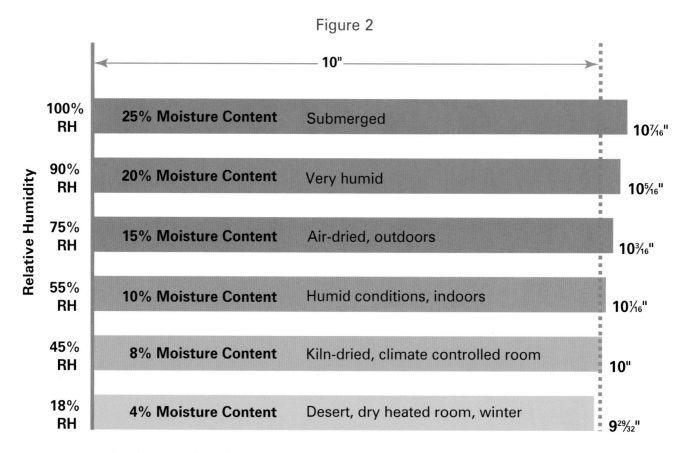

Figure 2

Relative Humidity		
100% RH	25% Moisture Content — Submerged	10⁷⁄₁₆"
90% RH	20% Moisture Content — Very humid	10⁵⁄₁₆"
75% RH	15% Moisture Content — Air-dried, outdoors	10³⁄₁₆"
55% RH	10% Moisture Content — Humid conditions, indoors	10¹⁄₁₆"
45% RH	8% Moisture Content — Kiln-dried, climate controlled room	10"
18% RH	4% Moisture Content — Desert, dry heated room, winter	9²⁹⁄₃₂"

Wood changes dimension with changes in local humidity. This chart shows how a board ripped to 10" wide at 8 percent moisture content will vary in size depending on the humidity. This is a generalization; each species of wood is affected to a different degree.

ly dried wood, so it isn't necessary to arrive at the yard with any suspicions. However, improper storage can increase moisture content. Kiln-dried lumber stacked outside in the weather is functionally the same as air-dried lumber.

If you do have any doubts or curiosity about the moisture content, there's usually a moisture meter floating around the yard somewhere. Don't hesitate to ask someone for verification if something feels fishy.

The plywood question

Substituting plywood for solid wood can also help prevent a problematic wood/water situation. Plywood is made by gluing up several thin layers of wood under high pressure, and it undergoes virtually no dimensional changes, no matter what the humidity is. Building with plywood can make things a lot easier—you don't have to worry about making complex joints that can withstand dimensional changes.

Another advantage of plywood is that it's sold in 4' x 8' sheets. Rather than going through the rather involved process of jointing and edge gluing narrow boards to achieve wide panels, all you have to do with plywood is cut the sheet to whatever dimensions you want. You will need to cover the unsightly substrate that shows at the cut edges, an added step that becomes part of the process of working with plywood. Everything has a trade-off.

Plywood has a reputation for cheapness (with all its unsavory connotations), but quality plywood is an excellent material for building furniture. I use it mainly for built-ins like kitchen cabinets and bookcases. I sometimes use it for building drawers, and I use it extensively for cabinet backs and drawer bottoms.

Figure 3

27" wide top has approx. 3/8" total seasonal movement

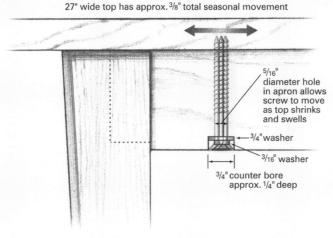

5/16" diameter hole in apron allows screw to move as top shrinks and swells

3/4" washer

3/16" washer

3/4" counter bore approx. 1/4" deep

Design for changes in dimension. When fastening a top to a table, you must allow room for the top to shrink and swell.

MOISTURE METERS

Just in case you are wondering, and I hope you are, moisture meters measure the electrical conductivity of the wood. A small electrical impulse travels easily through cells filled with water, which the meter shows as higher moisture content. Drier wood doesn't conduct electricity as well, giving a lower reading. Though useful, a moisture meter is not an essential tool. I use mine only rarely.

Knowledge is power

My debut at the lumberyard, some 20 years ago, was such a difficult experience that I walked off the stage vowing never to enter that theater of men again. I found myself in a rough and tumble world, a male bastion if ever there was one. To put it mildly, I wasn't greeted with open arms—it was more like bristled fur. I did manage to buy a few boards that day, only to figure out later that there was a "mistake" in the calculations.

After returning home and indulging in a good cry, my stubborn self decided to arise and assess what went wrong. My conclusion—I was simply unprepared on all fronts. I needed information, and lots of it! Here's some of what I've learned over the years, and I offer it in the hope that you'll have a more successful debut.

As you enter into the world of lumber, don't expect to find a pleasant, inviting place with soothing music and complimentary tea. Do expect to encounter some pretty rough-looking characters, possibly unaccustomed to or uncomfortable with women entering their domain. Learning to speak the language of lumber will help immensely.

Choosing Hardwords

Lumber for making furniture is typically purchased from hardwood suppliers (as opposed to home centers or builders' suppliers, though these may carry a limited selection of locally popular hardwoods). Stock varies from region to region and even from dealer to dealer, but most small yards carry a standard variety of domestic hardwoods. In most places, you can get red oak, white oak, hard and soft maple, hickory, cherry, walnut, poplar, birch, and ash. There's a growing market in fancy domestics selected for exceptional grain patterns, with names like curly, strong, flame, and bird's eye, and many yards will have at least a limited selection of such boards.

Most hardwood dealers will have some mahogany and other common imported woods like Brazilian cherry, rosewood, wenge, or teak. For anything rarer, you'll need to find a company that specializes in exotics.

If you need softwoods for your furniture projects, check with your hardwood dealer first. Unlike what you'd find at the builders' supplier, a hardwood yard will sell softwoods that are clear-grained, and properly stored and dried.

Buying hardwood lumber is a little different from purchasing softwood lumber from a builders' supplier or home-improvement store. Builders want standardized lumber dimensioned to industry standards for thickness, width, and length. These are the familiar 2 x 4s, 1 x 6s, and 2 x 12s used in home construction and sold by the linear foot. Since builders aren't too concerned with moisture content, this lumber is usually dried to about 15 percent moisture content and stored outdoors with little or no protection from the elements.

Hardwoods are sawn to get the best boards of a given thickness from a log—not necessarily the most boards. As a result, the boards vary in width and length. They also vary a bit in thickness.

NOMINAL DIMENSIONS

The more familiar lingo of 2 x 4s describes the construction-grade lumber used to build houses. If you've ever built anything with this kind of lumber, you know that a 2 x 4 is not 2" thick and 4" wide. It's actually $1\frac{1}{2}$" thick and $3\frac{1}{2}$" wide. When you talk about a 2 x 4, you're talking about nominal dimensions, not actual dimensions. A 2 x 4 was probably 2" x 4" when it went into the kiln, but after drying it was milled straight and flat, and the corners were heavily rounded to reduce splintering. It ends up smaller. To figure the actual dimension, just subtract $\frac{1}{2}$" from the nominal dimension. This works fine until you get to boards with a nominal dimension of 8" or wider. Then the actual dimension is $\frac{3}{4}$" narrower.

Understanding Boards

When you specify the thickness of a rough sawn board, you talk about quarters of an inch. In this lingo, a rough sawn board about 1" thick is referred to as "four quarter," written as 4/4. When the board was sawn from the log, the sawyer made it a bit more than 1" thick to account for shrinkage during drying. The board is probably a little more than 1" thick along most of its length, but since it's rough sawn on both sides, there's a strong possibility that could be less than 1" thick in places.

It's a time-honored convention that a 4/4 rough sawn board yields a flattened and planed board that's 3/4" thick. Sometimes you can get as much as 7/8", but don't count on it. Similarly, a 5/4 board yields 1". Most yards also sell 8/4 lumber, and 10/4, 12/4, or even 16/4 boards in some species.

Because every hardwood board is a little different in length and width, you pay for hardwoods not by the linear foot, but by volume. Oddly enough, the unit of volume is called a board foot.

You're not expected to tally your lumber purchase, but understanding board feet and how they work makes it easier to evaluate the boards you have to choose from. I've made up a stick that serves as a simple board-foot calculator (see p. 16). This way I can at least estimate the cost of each board, which helps me evaluate its suitability for the project.

The lumber industry has a baffling system that grades boards according to their quality. If you're buying a boxcar of lumber sight unseen, this is important, but for a one-woman shop, it's almost a non-issue. If it comes up, you want FAS grade, which stands for firsts and seconds. The industry specification for this says such lumber must be at least 5 1/2" wide and 8' long and that it can have a few troublesome defects. You could also get the grade called Select & Better, but you'll pay a premium for it. If you're milling the lumber yourself, you can easily deal with the few defects in FAS and save some money. The grade called No. 2 Common & Better costs less, but the specification allows for up to one-third of each board to contain defects that make it hardly worth your time. With so much waste, it may end up costing you more.

FUN WITH BOARD FEET

One board foot is the volume of wood in a board that's 1" thick, 12" wide, and 12" long. Multiply those three together, and you get the volume of said board—144 cubic inches. But we're not talking about cubic inches, we're talking about board feet. And to get that unit, you must divide the volume in cubic inches by 144. To calculate the cost of a board, just multiply the price per board foot by the number of board feet.

Here's the math:

Board Feet = (Thickness x Width x Length) (in inches, not feet))/144

Here's how it works in the yard. You're looking at a 4/4 board that's 6" wide and 10' long.

Board Feet = (Thickness x Width x Length)/144

= (1 x 6 x (10 x 12))/144 = (6 x 120)/144 = 720/144 = 5.06 bf

It works the same for thicker boards. This time let's assume we have an 8/4 board that's 6" wide by 10' long.

Board Feet = (2 x 6 x (10 x 12))/144 = (12 x 120)/144 = 1440/144 = 10 bf

CARRY A BOARD-FOOT STICK

Lumbermen don't like customers using their expensive board-foot rules, and I've spent too much time standing around lumberyards waiting for someone to tally up my lumber to see if I've pulled more than I need from the rack. I finally got smart and made my own easy-to-read board-foot stick.

It's a combination width ruler and board-foot chart on a piece of plywood. Along the top edge. I've measured out widths from 4" to 14", in 2" increments. The second row (labeled "8" in the photo below) shows the number of board feet in an 8' board at each width. The third row shows the board feet in a 10' board, and the fourth tallies a 12-footer. For 8/4 lumber, I just double the readings. There's a similar table for 5/4 lumber on the other side.

I used a waterproof marker and made the numbers big enough so I can see them without my glasses. Now I can easily keep a running board-foot total as I select boards. The yard guys think it's kind of geeky, but I think it's great.

A shop-made board-foot stick is a quick way to figure out how many board feet are in a prospective purchase. It roughly measures width, and tells you the board feet in a given length.

Choosing Plywood

Plywood is sold in 4' x 8' sheets (or sometimes the metric equivalent thereof). The most commonly available thicknesses are 1/4", 1/2", and 3/4".

For utilitarian projects or jigs, I use what's called shop-grade plywood. The veneers on the front and back are decent looking (usually birch), but the interior plys of shop-grade plywood can have knots or voids, which weaken the material.

For quality work, specify veneer-core plywood (they'll call it VC at the yard) and stick with A1 or A2 grade. The letter A refers to the quality of the front veneer, and A grade looks good enough to coat with clear finishes (lower grade B or C faces are only suitable for painting; higher grade AA faces use veneers chosen and matched for exceptional grain patterns). The numbers refer to the quality of the veneer on the back face. Back grade 1 has no major defects, but it's not as good-looking as an A face.

Most hardwood dealers offer these higher grades of plywood with a variety of species for the outer veneers. Birch, oak, maple, luaun (similar in appearance to mahogany), walnut, and cherry are usually easy to find, and virtually any species of wood is available as a special order.

All dressed up
and no place to go

On a number of occasions, people have given me exquisite handmade journals. I love holding these tiny works of art, flipping the pages, looking at the construction, thinking about what I will write in them. What pen shall I use? Should I include small sketches? Should I write the date each time I make an entry? I feel myself starting to tighten up, and I get concerned that my writing won't be worthy to blot those sacred pages. The book ends up on a shelf or table, where I simply look at it, my urge to write stymied by the entity of the journal in its perfection.

The same thing can happen with exquisite woods. You think more about the wood than what you are making from it. Maybe the money thing comes up, and you start calculating the cost of a mistake. Or you think the wood is so beautiful it deserves only perfect workmanship. Before you know it, your determination to do the wood justice has made you tense and brittle. You make the inevitable mistake or miscalculation, which makes you feel even worse. Setbacks happen, and when you're wound up tight, the accumulated errors can easily bring the project (and you) to the brink of implosion!

One of the things I remember most vividly about my early woodworking days was becoming enamored with fancy, highly figured woods. It developed into a little obsession and became a habit that was hard to support financially. Worst of all, every time things didn't go according to plan, it was as though Mr. Fancy Wood kept telling me I was not worthy. He seemed to sneer, "You've ruined my outfit with those sloppy joints!"

I remember being intrigued with an exotic wood called purpleheart (it really is purple, dense, and as hard as can be). I got the bright idea of making a dovetail box as a gift. Chopping out those dovetails was a nightmare; they didn't come out as well as I had envisioned. And as if that weren't bad enough, some months later I discovered that my beautiful purpleheart had oxidized to a dull brown.

It took some time, but I finally learned that beautiful woods can't save you from poor design or lack of technique. I came to prefer a plain but skillfully crafted piece to a poorly executed, ill-conceived piece constructed out of fancy woods.

Learn from my experience and make it easy on yourself. Start with relatively inexpensive Plain Jane woods like poplar, basswood, and soft maple. They're easy to work using both machines and hand tools, and they're excellent for chopping out joints, especially dovetails. With these woods, a mistake doesn't seem so catastrophic. Plain Jane just seems to say, "I'm not a fancy dresser. It's the overall effect that matters. This is no big deal. Let's get over it and move forward."

Ignore the lure of Mr. Fancy Wood and listen to Plain Jane for a while, eventually broadening the circle of conversation to include cherry, walnut, oak, and maple. Listen and you'll understand that each wood speaks a little differently. Learning the nuances is part of the fun. You'll hear how the conversation flows between them and how their looks can complement one another and enhance your design.

Eventually, you'll be ready to understand what Mr. Fancy and his fashionable friends are talking about. But get familiar with them slowly; start using them as accents to the outfit. If you really want to get all dressed up, make sure you have a place to go!

Stack your lumber against the wall where air can circulate around all sides.

Let's go shopping

You've done your homework; it's time to enter "Lumber World." I hope you encounter competent people who appreciate your business, but don't take it personally if the reception doesn't feel too warm. Just put on your lizard skin and get right down to business.

Before you negotiate with the natives, make up a shopping list that states the number of boards you need of a given thickness, width, and length. Don't get intimidated if the people there start slinging arcane lingo. Just explain that you need boards that will finish to a certain thickness and width and length, and they'll help you get the right wood. It never works out that they have exactly what's on your list—usually the boards are wider or narrower or longer or something else that your list doesn't account for. You'll have to think on the fly, but always err on the side of extra

wood. Nothing is more frustrating than running out of wood in the middle of a project.

Lumberyards are busy places. Stacks of wood levitate by forklift, and trucks arrive to load and unload materials; be watchful of all that's going on around you and assume that those drivers are not aware of your presence. Customers and yard hands are sifting through stacks and bins of lumber, pulling out boards for scrutiny. Watch out for things strewn about the floor like metal banding, reject boards, and maybe even an occasional blob of tobacco spit.

Some companies plane lumber or make moldings on site, so there could be a giant machine roaring incessantly in the background. Bring some earplugs.

You'll need to go through stacks of lumber to select your boards, so bring a tape measure,

your board-foot stick, and some gloves to prevent splinters. The best kind are the rubber-coated ones sold in the garden department. They fit better than leather gloves and have a lot of gripping power.

First, look for obvious defects. I start by sighting the board from end to end. You want to avoid boards that appear twisted or greatly curved. Check both sides of a board for defects such as cracks or knots, and pay close attention to any area of the board that has stains. Stains are usually the result of water damage from improper storage somewhere along the line. Stains often go deep into the wood itself, so planing may not completely remove them.

Most of the boards in a pile are flatsawn or riftsawn. Flatsawn boards show the growth rings as arcs on the ends of the boards (see fig. 1 on p. 11). They have the familiar cathedral grain on the face and a straight run of grain on the edges. Riftsawn boards' end grain shows the growth rings running diagonally. The grain appears fairly straight. These boards are more stable than flatsawn wood but less stable then quartersawn boards, in which the growth rings appear on the end grain as vertical lines. If you find a couple of random quartersawn boards in the pile, grab them; they're the most dimensionally stable and beautiful. Most of the time, quartersawn boards are segregated into another pile, and you'll pay a premium for them.

If the boards you purchase are 10' or longer, you can have the yard cut them to shorter lengths that are easier to transport and unload. Most places do this at no extra charge, even for sheets of plywood. This is no time to get fussy or indecisive. I usually just ask that they cut the boards in half, and I rarely ask them to make more than one cut per board. Think of this as a convenience only; don't assume the cut is in any way accurate, especially on plywood.

After you get the lumber back to your shop, it's a good idea to let it acclimate to the environment before you start to work, giving it a few days to reach moisture equilibrium with your shop's humidity level. Don't ever lay your lumber directly on the shop floor for any reason, where it could pick up grit or even extra moisture. I usually stack my newly purchased lumber against the wall, with air space between the boards.

Minimize moisture loss with finishes

A good finish serves three purposes: It helps to slow the moisture exchange between the wood and the air around it, thereby reducing the amount of shrinking and swelling; it protects the surface from wear and tear; and it improves the appearance of the wood. What constitutes an improvement is a matter of opinion.

Each project has different finishing requirements depending on what it's made from, and how and where it will be used. In my shop, planning any project includes a sanding and finishing strategy— often decided before the cutting begins. There are many things to consider, including sequence—contrary to what you might think, finishes often need to be applied before parts are assembled.

Sanding and finishing are inextricably linked; how well you sand is a determining factor in how well your finish will look at the end (see Surface Prep for Finishing on p. 79).

There are hundreds of different brands of finishing products, which can make things a bit confusing. I try to stick with those that are durable, easy to use, and relatively low in toxicity.

Take the time to read the labels on any finishes you use and follow the manufacturer's directions and warnings. Thin with the specified solvent. Store used solvents in appropriate cans and don't mix solvent types together. Consult your local government about safe disposal of old finishes and solvents. Never pour used finishes into a septic or sewer system, or even into the ground.

OIL-RESIN FINISHES

This family consists of Danish oil, varnish, polyurethane, linseed oil, tung oil, and the like. The two solvents for all of these are paint thinner (mineral spirits) or turpentine, which is quite pungent.

Danish oil is perhaps the most common type of finish, and the easiest to use. However, it is somewhat messy and smelly. When the weather is warm enough, I like to apply it outside. Despite the old-world, hand-rubbed mystique surrounding this type of finish, there's no big mystery. All Danish oils are the same—a mixture of linseed or tung oil, alkyd resin, and mineral spirits.

Apply it by flooding the surface with a foam brush, let it penetrate for 30 minutes or so (directions may vary slightly among brands), flood again, let dry 45 minutes or so, and wipe off the excess. Wiping off— that's where the hand-rubbed part comes in. Buy a Danish oil brand that is locally available to avoid shipping costs. Sometimes there are extra shipping charges associated with solvent finishes.

Danish oil is excellent for enhancing the natural tone and grain of woods such as oak, cherry, and walnut. But I think its slightly yellow cast isn't attractive on a light wood such as hard maple.

Because of its somewhat flat appearance, I think of Danish oil as a way of initially enhancing and sealing the wood. After at least 78 hours of drying time, you can apply other finishes on top for more pizzazz and protection. For items that don't generally receive a lot of wear, such as a table base, paste wax may be all that's required. For a bit more substance, polyurethane gel finish will improve appearance and protection. For tabletops, especially dining tables, I like to go the extra mile with three coats of water-based polyurethane. If you're applying water-based finish over oil, make sure the oil finish has had at least a week to cure.

I don't bother with straight linseed oil; it doesn't harden on its own. Nor do I mess with tung oil. I dislike the smell, long drying time, and short shelf life.

Of late, I have enjoyed great success with gel varnishes. Application couldn't be easier—just wipe on three or four coats with a soft cotton cloth. Shelf life is an issue with these finishes, as well, so I use an oxygen blocker when storing them.

Brushed on varnish finishes, if done well, require a little more work than most other finishes. The results certainly justify the effort. A successful varnish finish has excellent durability and visual appeal. I like this finish for wide surfaces such as tabletops and headboards.

For your first efforts, it's best to start small; save the 8' dining tabletop for another day. You'll need to apply at least three or four coats (with 24 hours drying time between them), sanding lightly with 220-grit paper between coats. Cleanliness is important with a high-gloss, slow drying finish. Work in an environment that's as free of dust as possible, and use lint-free rags for best results.

There are only a few companies producing high-quality, furniture-appropriate varnishes. You can pretty much rule out home-store-variety polyurethane and spar varnishes, which tend to be too soft and flexible. A good varnish has less oil and more resins, making it harder and more brittle—much better for achieving good results.

I don't have much use for straight polyurethane or spar varnish finishes; these are too soft and flexible for furniture. They're great for exterior doors and the like, where temperature and moisture extremes require a flexible finish. However, I use them as a base for what I call "3-2-1 Oil." This traditional recipe is similar to Danish oil but is thicker and easier to build up to a greater sheen. Mix three parts paint thinner, two parts polyurethane varnish, and one part linseed oil. Flood the piece with oil using a foam brush, wait until it becomes slightly tacky, then wipe it off. Let it dry overnight and repeat the process two more times. After a few days of drying time, you can buff and/or wax the surface with 0000 steel wool.

SHELLAC

I am very fond of shellac. I use it most often on cabinet panels, drawer interiors, and small projects. It takes only about 30 minutes for one coat to dry, so you can build a beautiful three- or four-coat finish in no time flat. A coat of paste wax at the end adds a nice touch.

Shellac comes in two forms; premixed in a can or as flakes that you dissolve as needed in the appropriate amount of denatured alcohol. I used to buy the flakes but have lately switched to premixed. Overall, the results are about the same, but without the mixing hassle and shelf-life problems associated with flakes. Flakes do have the advantage of a few more color selections, whereas canned shellac is available in only amber or clear.

Shellac is best applied with a high-quality brush that's made for shellac application only. Since shellac dries so quickly, I don't

The proper finish seals out moisture, protects the wood from wear, and enhances its appearance.

always clean the brush between coats—I put it in a tightly sealed plastic bag. For final cleaning, change the alcohol at least three times or until it's clear. Store the contaminated alcohol in a metal can for later disposal.

WATER-BASED POLYURETHANE

These clear finishes are relatively new to the finishing scene and seem to be improving all the time. They give off very little odor when drying, are easy to apply, and are durable enough to protect tabletops. I like to use them on maple, where I want the grain to show through without the yellowing effect of oil-based finishes.

Most of the time I use a foam brush to apply water-based poly, and sometimes a high-quality synthetic brush. Its low odor/toxicity level is a real plus, and cleanup couldn't be easier—just use a little soap and water.

LACQUER

I mention this finish in the hope that you will avoid it, especially if you have any chemical sensitivity issues. This highly flammable and toxic finish is frequently used in the furniture-making industry. However beautiful the finish and excellent its spraying characteristics, small shops are generally not equipped to use this finish in a safe manner. An explosion-proof fan is necessary to evacuate fumes, and you'll need a respirator that provides a continual supply of fresh air. Some local air quality and fire regulations simply do not

permit its use. Ironically, lacquer finishes are readily available.

ADDING COLOR

Afraid of color I am not, nor am I a "purist" when it comes to wood. Au naturel can be beautiful, but it's often desirable to create more balanced tones on wood that is swirling with sapwood and heartwood variations, such as walnut. And sometimes it's nice to add a dash of color here or there.

Rarely do I use ready-mixed stains; their appearance is too generic. I don't ever seem to find the exact tones I want. The stains all look murky and generic to me, like those on pieces of factory-built furniture. Instead, I find aniline dyes to be an excellent way to alter the color of wood without obscuring the grain. These easy-to-use products are mixed with water and applied with a foam brush. You can get a subtle range of color and tone by mixing various colors before application or by applying each color in turn. Aniline dyes come in a variety of colors and are amazingly colorfast.

Seal in the color with a few coats of shellac, and apply a final coat of water-based polyurethane. If you're using an oil-based varnish, you can skip the shellac.

An array of color awaits you at the local art store—artist's oils or acrylic paints in a tube work perfectly well on wood. Though this may seem elementary, use like with like—don't mix oil with water. Use oil-based paints with Danish oil as a

medium to flow on the color, and apply it with a soft cotton cloth. Acrylics can be used to tint water-based poly finish. Don't be afraid to experiment; that's how you will find the answers.

Just for fun, I once applied an earthy orange artist's oil paint to an unfinished pine tabletop. Using oil as a medium, I simply flowed the color on with a cloth. Then I applied a coat of black over the orange, using cheap brushes to create streaks and graining effects. The result was an unusual and exotic-looking table. Without fail, visitors to my shop are intrigued and ask what species that wild looking wood is.

Using milk paint is yet another way to add color to your work, but it's not subtle. Milk paint has a thick, solid, flat appearance. The off-the-shelf colors tend to be in the primary zone, but they can be mixed to create variations. Pitch black is excellent for ebonizing parts. If you want some sheen, apply three coats of gel varnish.

Sometimes I am not in the mood for the fuss of mixing milk paint for ebonizing. Then I head straight for the local drug store and pick up some black leather shoe dye. I apply two coats with the foam applicator on the bottle or with a foam brush, sanding lightly between each coat. Three coats of water-based poly provide protection and shine.

TOOLS

What you need—and when and how to get it.

Like many woodworkers, I enjoy the process of finding and procuring tools. But the process can be both confusing and even a little addictive considering the huge variety of tools and the growing number of supply sources—catalogs, retail stores, the Internet, and the like. How does anyone sort through this maze and know what to buy? Putting a few things in perspective might help.

Let's start by dividing tools into four main categories: small handheld power tools, machinery, hand tools, and clamping devices. At every stage of woodworking, you'll be using tools from each of the categories. A small shop will have fewer, simpler, and more generalized tools; a larger shop will have these tools, too, but they'll be larger and more powerful, and will often be specialized to optimize their use for specific functions.

A typical home center or hardware store, for all its variety, can provide you with only a small portion of the woodworking tools you'll need to do quality work. While such stores have good prices and selections of commodity items like handheld power tools, clamps, and garden-variety machinery, they don't usually stock the high-quality, specialty hand tools that furniture makers rely upon. For those tools, your best source of supply is a specialty woodworking supplier. Don't rule them out for commodity items either; they often have higher quality and a larger selection to choose from—especially in machinery. You might be lucky enough to have such a place nearby. If not, check out a woodworking magazine or the Internet to find the names of reputable catalog retailers.

There is a certain overlap among tool catalog retailers. You really don't need 50 catalogs arriving at your door each month in order to outfit your shop. I rely on only two or three suppliers for tools and about the same number of finishing and general suppliers, and I keep only a couple of hardware catalogs. The best companies not only sell a lot of quality products and provide good service; they also have trained staff to answer any technical questions. Eventually you'll find the suppliers who sell the tools you need for your style of woodworking and whose style of business suits your personality. Here's a trick I've learned that can prevent a catalog avalanche: When requesting information for the first time, ask them to hand address your copy. That

Protect your edge tools by storing and transporting them in boxes.

way, you won't get into their perpetual mailing loop until you actually order something.

Other woodworkers are a great source of information about tools and suppliers. Ask around and visit some shops—of amateurs as well as pros. Gather as much information as you can, but think in terms of what you'll be doing in your own shop. The expert who makes her living doing built-ins says she couldn't do woodworking without her five-horsepower table saw and industrial-size mortising machine, but that doesn't mean your shop requires either one. Pay the closest attention to people with similar woodworking ideas and a genuine willingness to share information. You can safely ignore those who are on ego trips about the size of their tools or their celebrity status in woodworking.

Though it happens to me less than it used to, sooner or later you're likely to have what I call "A Rooster Encounter." Roosters are those guys who just can't seem to get it that you're buying tools for yourself and not for a husband or boyfriend. As difficult as it may be, scratching a line in the sand is often the only way to deal with these birdbrains. It can be quite effective to remind the offensive rooster of his position in the roost—the realm of tools is a crowded barnyard indeed. Make it known that you have plenty of other options. If he's not capable of hearing you or shifting attitude, it's time to fly the coop.

Handheld power tools

This vast category of tools contains everything from drills and sanders to biscuit joiners and circular saws. Look at a catalog and you'll be astonished at the variety of what's available. Some of these tools are essentials—the first things a beginning woodworker should buy. Others are nice to have because they save time, while some are so job specific you might never need one.

Here's a list of the handheld tools I consider an essential foundation for doing good work.

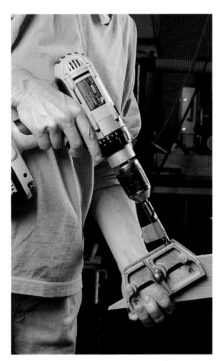

You'll use a battery-powered drill/driver for more than just boring holes. Get one that's at least 14 volts, with a 1/2" chuck.

DRILLS

A battery-powered drill/driver is sufficient for most shops. I recommend getting one that's at least 14 volts and capable of handling a 1/2" bit— with an extra battery included. You'll use it for boring holes and driving screws. If you're drilling a lot of holes (especially large diameter holes), a corded electric drill is useful.

Since you'll be using your drill a lot, you want one with good balance, one that feels right in your hands. Each brand and model is unique, so this is one tool you should get your hands on before you buy.

JIGSAW

You can make straight cuts with a jigsaw, but they're best at cutting curves. You'll use it to cut curves in solid wood or plywood (in lieu of a band saw) and for rough cutting lumber. And even if you do have a band saw, occasionally you'll need a jigsaw to make a cut that the band saw just can't handle.

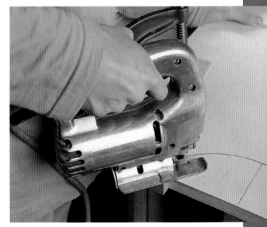

A jigsaw cuts curves. You'll need one for rough work, or as shown here, when the piece is too large for your band saw.

Use a circular saw to crosscut lumber to manageable lengths as the first step in milling.

CIRCULAR SAW

Widely used in the construction trades, woodworkers tend to limit their circular saw use to cutting down sheets of plywood that are too large or unwieldy to put on the table saw, and for crosscutting lumber to rough length.

Biscuit joints are both strong and easy to make. This biscuit joiner cuts the perfectly sized and shaped slots that make this joint possible.

BISCUIT JOINER

A biscuit joiner allows you to make a special kind of joint, called (surprise) a biscuit joint. The biscuit is a football-shaped wafer made of pressed wood. It's glued into special slots that are cut into the mating edges of the boards with a tool called a biscuit joiner. The biscuit spans the joint, making it significantly stronger.

ROUTERS AND ROUTER TABLES

The router is one of the most versatile tools in the shop. Fitted with the right bit, it can flatten, profile, or cut a complex joint. (See Router Bits on the next page.) You'll want both a fixed base router and one with a plunge base. A plunge base is a fairly complex spring-loaded affair that lets you raise and lower the bit while the router is running, giving you better control over the depth and location of certain types of cuts. They're important for many joinery operations such as mortising and making stopped cuts.

A $1^1/2$ horsepower motor is the minimum I suggest. You can buy one router motor with both a fixed and a plunge base, or you can buy two different routers. If you go that route, I recommend getting a plunge router with more horsepower.

Put your router into a router table, and it's even more versatile. Used with the right jigs and fences, the router can make complicated joints, moldings, and decorative profiles. It's easy to get overwhelmed by the sheer number of router table designs out there. I wouldn't bother with any that didn't have aluminum tables at least $1/4$" thick. They stay flat and aren't as bulky and difficult to deal with as wood composite tables. Sold as a set, they usually come with a fence and insert accessories.

The router is perhaps the most versatile tool in the shop. Fitted with the right bit, it can be used to profile an edge, cut joints, make inlay, or produce identical parts from a template—among other things.

ROUTER BITS

When you see your first router-bit display or catalog, try not to panic! It can be overwhelming at first—there are literally hundreds of bits and accessories to choose from.

To help sort things out, keep in mind that router bits fall into three basic categories: those for cutting profiles; those for making grooves, rabbets, mortises and other joinery-related operations; and those for pattern cutting (sometimes called template routing).

The **profile bits** I use most often are the roundover, chamfer, cove, ogee, and astragal.

Bits used for joinery, rabbets, dadoes, and grooves are usually **straight bits** and come in a variety of diameters from 1/8" to 1". For cutting mortises with a plunge router, **spiral bits** work best.

Template routing bits feature tip- or shank-mounted bearings that roll along the edge of a pattern; the bit cuts an accurate duplicate in the process.

Carbide bits cost more initially, but they're worth it. They'll cut cleaner and without burning far longer than high-speed steel bits. Whenever it's an option, I recommend buying bits with 1/2" shanks rather than 1/4" shanks. The extra metal makes them more rigid—they'll deflect less during cuts.

profile bits

A chamfering bit on the left and a roundover on the right

straight bits

A rabbeting bit with several bearings can cut a wide variety of widths and depths.

spiral bits

A spiral bit works best for removing material in most plunge-cut situations.

template routing bit

This template routing bit with a shank-mounted bearing will follow the plywood template to cut the edge of solid wood below so that it's exactly flush with the template.

FINISH SANDERS

Most of the time, a random orbit sander is the tool of choice for finish sanding. It's aggressive enough to save time, but not so aggressive that it leaves unsightly scratches. Just about the only time you shouldn't use a random orbit sander is when the edge of the disk might touch an adjoining surface. If it does, it'll probably abrade a nice little notch. When this is a possibility, use an oscillating sander. Either square or rectangular, they're designed to hold quarter- or half-sheets of standard sandpaper in such a way that they can go up to an adjoining surface without marring it.

A random orbital sander offers just the right combination of aggressive material removal and smooth finish. Shown here is a 5" pneumatic sander, powered by compressed air delivered through the yellow hose. An electric-powered random orbit sander works just as well.

Machinery

Sometimes when I'm running a pile of boards through the planer, I reflect on the fact that all of that work used to be done entirely by hand. The amount of human labor woodworking once required is stupefying. Thankfully, in the modern world we're spared hours of repetitive physical labor—woodworking machines are plentiful and relatively inexpensive. With a few basic machines, you can easily crank out all the dimensioned lumber you need to make unique creations from wood.

One thing about machinery is that you must always think in the plural. It's not practical to buy just one machine at a time; there are interdependent relationships among the various tools' functions. At the very least, you'll require a jointer, planer, band saw, table saw, crosscut saw, and drill press. Add to these as you please; that's part of the fun.

Another thing about machinery is that you get what you pay for. Beware of bargain pricing—some-

MACHINE LEARNING

Woodworking machines are used by hundreds of thousands (perhaps millions, even) of people each day without mishap. Manufacturers don't want anyone getting hurt using their products, so by design, woodworking machines (especially newer ones) have a lot of built-in safety features. You may not recognize or even see them, but they're working for you every time you turn on the switch. Why some people remove things like blade guards is beyond me. Use the safety equipment that comes with the saw, or upgrade it with aftermarket versions.

It's important to read the manual and fully understand how the machine operates and how to keep it tuned. Take the time to practice with the machine before you start work on a project.

While in theory you're more vulnerable to an accident at the beginning of the learning curve, a high percentage of accidents befall experienced operators. For them, the problem is complacency, or perhaps you could call it overconfidence. Most accidents occur when the operator knowingly engages in an unsafe activity but simply doesn't want to take the time to set up the machine to make the cut safely.

Don't take on a machining operation if you're not in good mental, physical, and emotional condition. Brain fog is a serious problem around heavy machinery. Fast-moving blades will not forgive a moment's inattention. If you're preoccupied with a problem; feel angry or upset; are suffering with a cold or the flu (especially if you're taking medication—even over-the-counter medication); or are behind on your sleep, find something else to do in the shop that doesn't require your undivided attention.

MACHINES ON WHEELS

If you have a small shop, keep in mind that any machine can become mobile, even a big table saw. Most manufacturers sell custom-fitted mobile bases for the tools in their line, and several companies sell generic bases in sizes that fit most tools. I sometimes make my own bases from wood and add big locking casters that I purchase from catalog suppliers.

An accessory sliding table makes working with big, heavy sheets of plywood q breeze.

MAINTAINING MACHINERY

Well maintained machines work better and are safer to use. It's that simple. Here are some things to keep in mind:

Switches and power cords. Worn cords and switches cause erratic on/off behavior. Keep them clean and in good working order.

Motors and fans. Sawdust is quite abrasive and will shorten a motor's life. Use a compressor and/or vacuum cleaner to keep these areas clean.

Tables. Dirty or rusty tables increase friction. Remove rust with fine sandpaper, steel wool, plastic scrubbing pads, or any number of proprietary products made for the purpose. Use paint thinner to remove any sticky residue. When the table is clean, apply a few coats of household paste wax to protect it from moisture (and incidentally to make it more slippery).

Foreign objects. Don't use your machines as extra horizontal space for storing tools or other items. Though they seem substantial, heavy woodworking machines are surprisingly delicate. A heavy object stored even for a short while on the edge of a table saw or jointer table can cause misalignment. A small item inadvertently left on the table could contact a spinning blade on start-up and cause all kinds of problems to the tool and the surrounding area.

Drinks. Whether it's your morning cup of coffee, a can of soda, or a bottle of water, don't put it on the machinery, where it could spill or leave a ring of rust.

BUYING USED MACHINERY

People often ask me about buying used or reconditioned machines. It's tempting, especially when the deals are for older American-made machines, which are considered desirable. But I usually find it too difficult to trust the stories behind old machines. It takes a discerning eye to see how a machine may have been mishandled. You may end up with less than you bargained for, and face a complicated process to get the machine properly adjusted. I don't recommend buying used or reconditioned unless tinkering with machinery is something you like to do almost as much as woodworking.

An onerous task becomes simple with the right machinery. Rounding the end grain of a board is slow work with files and rasps, but takes only seconds on a stationary belt sander.

thing that sounds too good to be true probably is. Quality woodworking machines are heavy and accurate; building and transporting such things is not cheap (see Maintaining Machinery on this page).

Some hallmarks of high-quality machines follow: Tables are flat and without hairline cracks; fences are flat and easy to calibrate and position; adjustment levers and wheels move smoothly and accurately; and access to frequently changed parts (such as blades, knives, etc.) is easy. A reputable maker also has good tech service by phone, quick turnaround on parts, and a gracious return policy if all else fails (see Buying Used Machinery, to the left).

TABLE SAW

A proper woodworking shop simply can't operate without a table saw. It's amazing just how many tasks this saw can perform, from cutting intricate joinery to ripping lumber and cutting plywood. Perhaps no other tool is as important or as critical for doing good work. For that reason, you want to invest in the best table saw you can afford.

With table saws, the more horsepower the better. An underpowered saw will bog down when cutting 8/4 lumber. If the motor gets too hot, it'll shut itself down completely, forcing you to wait until it cools enough resume your work. Don't bother with less than a 1 1/2 hp motor, the size found in a typical contractor's saw. A three horsepower cabinet saw is infinitely better in terms of power and accuracy, but the price is considerably more.

The table saw fence is almost as important as the motor. A good fence system slides smoothly and locks securely. It should also be easy to calibrate, since a misaligned fence can cause dangerous kickbacks. Several companies offer aftermarket fence systems, and some are significant improvements over the original fences.

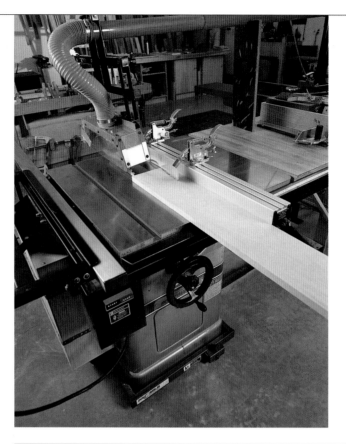

A three-horsepower cabinet table saw fitted with a mobile base, an overhead blade guard/dust collector, an aftermarket fence, end hold-downs to make ripping safer and more accurate. The original fence remains on the saw, on the left of the table, for occasional use.

TABLE SAW ACCESSORIES FOR SAFETY

Most table saw accidents occur when the wood binds between the fence and the back edge of the blade. If the wood can't travel past the blade to complete the cut, there's a good chance the blade (turning at more than 100 MPH) will pick up the workpiece and hurl it back at you with surprising force.

This should never happen when crosscutting because you always use a miter gauge or a similar device for this operation. Without one, it's simply not possible to hold a piece of wood steady enough to eliminate any possibility of twisting it slightly at the end of the cut and causing it to bind. New table saws come with miter gauges. (Given their critical safety importance, it would seem that manufacturers have a moral if not legal obligation to provide them.) But you should look into aftermarket miter gauges, crosscut sleds, and sliding tables. They offer significant improvements in accuracy and ease of use.

You can make ripping safer by using a hold-down device that keeps your hands well away from the blade at all times. With it, you can let go of the material if need be and walk around to the back to pull the piece through (this works especially well with plywood). The yellow rollers in the photo above have served me well for more than 15 years—nothing hurled, nothing lost.

BAND SAW

Though many people think them less important than table saws, in my book, band saws are right up there. You need one for cutting curves and making quick cuts safely (if not terribly accurately). More importantly, you need one capable of heavy-duty use in milling rough lumber to dimension. You can't use a table saw on rough lumber—in many cases the band saw is your only means to prepare a board for the jointer.

Band saws are sized according to the distance between the blade and saw frame (which dimension also happens to be the diameter of the wheel). A 14" saw is just about the minimum size suitable for serious work; bigger is better. A larger saw is more powerful for ripping and resawing, and the larger throat distance lets you work with wider

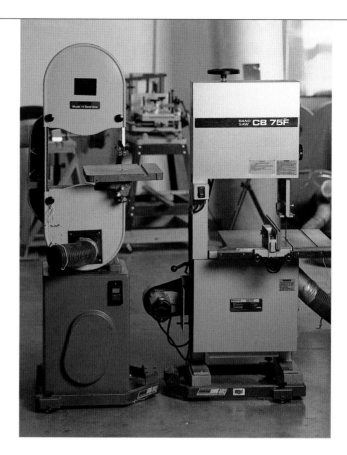

Ideally, a shop should have two band saws. The 18" resawing band saw on the right is for heavy ripping and resawing, while the 14" band saw on the left is used for finer work and cutting curves.

BAND SAW BLADES

Saw performance has a lot to do with choosing the right blade for the job. Dull blades or those with too many teeth for the job cut slowly, requiring you to push the wood quite forcefully to achieve a cut. The blade overheats, ruining its temper and burning the wood. Eventually the blade breaks from the stress.

For cutting curves and all-around duty, I keep a 1/4"-wide blade on my 14" band saw. I use a skip tooth blade with 4 TPI (teeth per inch). It's capable of making tight cuts and is aggressive enough for slicing through thick pieces of wood. I like bimetal blades—they cost a bit more than regular steel blades, but they stay sharp much longer.

Larger saws can handle wider blades, so I keep a 1"-wide blade on my 18" saw. It, too, is a bimetal blade, with the 4 TPI stick-tooth pattern.

panels. I have two band saws: an 18" saw set up for ripping and resawing, and a 14" saw that I keep for finer work. If I had to choose only one band saw, I'd pick the bigger one. In the long run, it's more versatile.

JOINTER

Think of the jointer as the foundation machine—the one that creates the initial flat and straight reference surfaces from which all other work derives (see Milling Lumber Four-Square on p. 43). The width of your jointer determines the width of the widest board you can mill. A 6" jointer is a good place to start, but a wider jointer lets you work with wider boards. Unfortunately, the price jump between a 6" jointer and an 8" jointer is significant. Just get the widest jointer you can afford.

PLANER

The planer runs more than any other piece of machinery in the shop. It is by far the hardest working machine and possibly the loudest, creating a whining roar as it shaves a board down to finished thickness (see Get a Thickness Sander ASAP, at right).

In recent years, a number of small, affordable portable planers have come on the market, and they work very well. They can handle boards up to 12" wide (conveniently twice the width that a 6" jointer can handle), and work fine in a nonproduction situation. Stepping up the next size planer, about 15" wide, more than doubles the price and weight. As with most machines, the extra weight is a good thing—it increases stability and helps the machine run more smoothly with fewer vibrations. The 15" planer is, in the long run, a better investment.

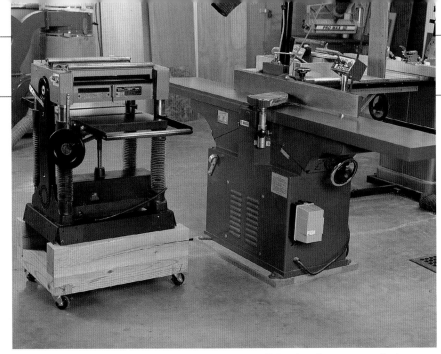

The jointer (on the right) is the first tool used to mill lumber four-square. Its long table flattens and straightens the faces and edges of boards. The planer (on the left) mills boards to the desired thickness.

GET A THICKNESS SANDER ASAP

A planer does a great job of removing material quickly but has its limitations. Some woods (notably maple) are nearly impossible to plane without literally tearing small chunks out of the surface, and the more figured the wood, the more likely it is to tear out. Nor do planers work well on really thin pieces.

A thickness sander picks up where the planer leaves off. Instead of using knives to chip away material, it uses a sandpaper-covered drum to sand the surface smooth. Fitted with a coarse abrasive, it quickly gets to the bottom of tear-out and other defects. You can thickness boards to less than 1/8", and you can thickness sand some pieces that would be too small to run through the planer safely. Switch to a finer abrasive (150 or 180 grit), and the machine leaves a remarkably smooth surface. You'll still need to do a final hand sanding prior to applying a finish, but a thickness sander can save countless hours of orbital sanding.

I suggest you make getting a thickness sander a priority, no matter how small your shop.

You can do your thickness sanding any time after planing, but do it before cutting to final length. An improperly adjusted sander can snipe the end of a board just as easily as a planer can. Keep in mind that the entire sanding process, from 80 grit through 180 grit, removes about 1/16" of material. You'll have to factor that into your milling process so you don't end up with boards that are nice and smooth, but too thin.

Though not as efficient as a planer, a thickness sander leaves a smooth surface on even the most tearout-prone woods.

DRILL PRESS

Handheld drills are great, but when you need accuracy and/or power, you need a drill press. It's the only way you can make sure the hole you're drilling is exactly 90° to the surface, or exactly 32° if that's what you need. Fitted with a fence and stops, this machine can drill holes in exactly the same location in multiple workpieces. It's capable of turning much larger bits than a hand drill, and by changing the drive belt configuration, you can control the rpm—a handy feature that makes certain operations (like drilling metals) easier. Turn a sanding drum instead of a drill bit, and you have a great means of shaping contours and curves.

I suggest you get a floor-mounted drill press. Bench-top models have limited power and capacity; a floor model is far more convenient to use and offers more drilling options. I wouldn't consider buying any drill press that didn't have rack and pinion adjustment for the table height.

A floor-mounted drill press provides the power and accuracy you need for joinery. It can also turn into a small sanding drum for shaping contours and curves.

SLIDING COMPOUND MITER SAW

The ability to get accurate, square crosscuts is critical to any project. Without it, things start on the wrong foot and get cumulatively worse as the project progresses. The sliding compound miter saw, originally developed as a job-site tool for trim carpenters, is designed for one thing: making smooth accurate crosscuts.

This saw can crosscut an end perfectly square to the edge or miter the ends at a wide range of angles. It can also cut a bevel on an end (a bevel is a cut made at an angle other than 90° to the face). Since you can set it up to do both of these at once, it's called a compound miter saw. The word "sliding" refers to the fact that the blade slides back and forth on rails to crosscut wide boards.

I suggest you get a 12" sliding compound miter saw. It can cut boards up to 12" wide or 6" thick. It's more expensive than a 10" saw, but you'll be glad you have the extra capacity. Treat it like a stationary tool, and bolt it to a bench, and build an accurate fence with a stop system for repetitive cuts.

Radial arm saws once filled the crosscut niche in many shops, but various idiosyncrasies, notably their tendency to wander out of square, render them inferior to modern sliding compound miter saws. I do keep a radial arm saw in my shop, but I use it only for rough crosscutting, a job for which it is well suited, given its powerful motor. If you have the space, I think it's worth having a radial arm saw for this task alone.

Use a 12" sliding compound miter saw to cut boards to final length with square ends, mitered ends, or with a bevel as shown here. For maximum accuracy, bolt the saw down to a bench and provide it with a sturdy fence.

STATIONARY BELT/DISC SANDER

Not to be confused with portable belt sanders (though some of the functions are the same), belt/disc sanding machines are extremely useful for many tasks, from fine-tuning a joint or shaping parts to sanding joints flush (such as dovetails or stile-to-rail connections on cabinet doors). Both bench and floor models are available, with disc sizes ranging from 6" to 12". It's well worth owning one of these handy machines, no matter what size you can afford.

A belt/disc sander is invaluable for all kinds of smoothing and shaping jobs. Here the author uses the belt portion to smooth the head of a mallet. The sanding disc shows in the left foreground.

DUST COLLECTION

Machines make dust and chips. A lot of dust and chips. Some of it goes on the floor, some of it goes in the air, and pretty much all of it's a problem. Machines simply can't operate well if chips and debris accumulate around the blades and motors. Nor is the shop environment healthy or safe with piles of chips on the floor and dust floating around.

Get some kind of dust collection system for gathering dust and chips at the source. Your machines will operate better, your cleanup will be faster, and you'll protect your respiratory system from harmful wood dust.

There are many good dust collectors on the market. Designs vary somewhat, but all rely on an impeller fan and a fairly large motor to pull waste into a collection bag or canister. A two-stage filter exhausts cleaner air, but even a simple one-bag system is capable of capturing particles as small as one micron.

For a one-woman shop, a dust collection system with a one-horsepower motor system is adequate. If you plan on running more than one machine at a time, get the next larger size. Don't be tempted to use your dust collector as a vacuum cleaner. Sucking up small objects like screws or small chunks of wood does serious damage to the impeller blades and shortens the life of the machine.

For general cleanup duty, get a heavy-duty shop vacuum. It's designed to handle the kinds of stuff you'll clean up in the shop—gritty particles, chunks of wood and metal, and all kinds of chips and dust. When I buy a shop vacuum, I focus on the quality of the hose and how it's attached to the machine, as well as to the accessories (cleaning brushes, extension tubes, etc.). These are often irritatingly underdesigned.

Finally, invest in an air filtration unit and hang it high on the ceiling where the fine dust lingers. Though many people consider it an optional piece of equipment, I consider it an important part of healthy woodworking. The very fine dust that dust collectors and vacuum cleaners miss can lodge in the nasal linings and lungs, increasing your susceptibility to allergies and respiratory infections. Keep in mind that long-term exposure to wood dust at very high concentrations (the kind of exposure that full-time workers in heavy industrial environments experience) has been deemed carcinogenic.

At the minimum, run the air filter whenever you run a machine, engage in a dusty activity like sanding, and sweeping, or cleanup. Studies have shown that it takes fine dust a few hours to settle, so keep the unit running for two or three hours after you complete the dust-generating activity.

Hand tools

This category comprises a wide variety of different tools, such as planes, saws, chisels, marking tools, and measuring devices—all of which are operated by body power and finesse (see Moving Your Axis on p. 42).

When getting started, you don't need hundreds of hand tools—just a few good-quality ones. As your skill level increases, you'll discover and appreciate a never-ending array of useful tools to add to your collection. Since this category is so vast, my goal is to help you narrow down the selection and focus on the tools you'll use most, not the ones that will end up just sitting on a shelf.

As a rule, hand tools are your most delicate tools, so store them with care. Left strewn on a bench top, tools get pushed around. They can collide and nick each other, roll off the bench, or get bumped to the floor. A tool won't always survive a crash to the floor. If it hits just right, it can be damaged beyond repair.

Find places for each of your hand tools so they can sit or hang in safety in convenient drawers, tool boxes, or cabinets. Protect blades with leather or any suitable material that is convenient to take on or off—old socks work well.

I have slots on some of my workbenches to hold chisels. You can also use magnetic bars. Just find a place where the tools you're currently using are safely out of the way yet readily accessible—and where they won't damage the workpiece.

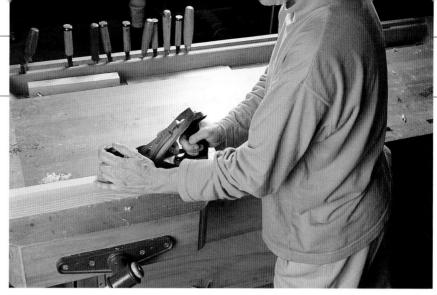

A slot on the back edge of the workbench keeps chisels out of the way but right at hand.

HAND PLANES

I use both Japanese hand planes and the more familiar planes of the European tradition (often called Western planes when differentiating them from the Asian varieties). Modern Western planes typically have metal bodies and work on the push stroke. Japanese plane bodies are made of wood and are designed to cut as you pull the plane toward you.

Western planes are easier to adjust and understand, so I suggest you learn to use them first. Once you understand the principles of planing and sharpening, you'll be in a better position to deal with the Japanese plane's rather finicky tune-up operations and the difficulty of correctly fitting the plane body to the cutting iron. To make

From left to right: Bronze block plane, shoulder plane, Japanese plane, smooth plane, wooden block plane, jack plane. Resting the front of a plane on a slip of wood keeps the blade off the bench and prevents damage to the cutting edge.

The Japanese plane works on the pull.

the transition a little easier, I suggest taking a class or a few private lessons from someone who understands Japanese tools.

Western planes have a curious nomenclature, which can be somewhat confusing to beginners and professionals alike. The common bench plane, used for edge and surface planing, comes in various sizes, with names like smooth, jack, and jointer.

A smooth plane is about 9" long. It's used for final smoothing of a board that's already flat. A jack plane is around 15" long and is an all-purpose plane—a jack of all

trades, so to speak. A jointer plane is something like 22" long and is used for getting surfaces truly flat so joints fit perfectly.

You'll also need a block plane for working end grain and a shoulder plane for joinery.

I don't have an extensive collection of hand planes. I seem to meet all my planing needs with three bench planes (smooth, jack, and jointer); two block planes (one made of metal and one made of wood); and two Japanese planes (similar in size to a jack plane and block plane). See Buying Planes below.

The blade on a shoulder plane extends all the way to the edge. This is the perfect tool for cleaning up tenons and grooves since you can plane right up to the shoulders.

A metal bench plane is easy on the hands for long planing sessions.

BUYING PLANES

If you've shopped around for Western planes, you know that the price for the same size plane can vary widely. The difference lies in the quality of materials and manufacture. An inexpensive plane can work as well as a very expensive one, but it's more likely that cutting corners to lower the price will result in some performance problems. A quality plane has a truly flat sole, good machine work in the body, and a good blade.

Many people look for good deals on planes at flea markets and antique shops, but in my experience, such places rarely have planes that are worth the bother. To get them up and running often requires a trip to a machine shop for flattening, a new blade, and a replacement handle. Unless the plane is of vintage character, I'd rather spend that money on something new.

You'll need a variety of chisels and chisel-like tools to build the projects in this book. From left: a set of five Japanese chisels, a wooden-handled bench chisel, a plastic-handled chisel, a skew chisel (good for cleaning out dovetails), another bench chisel, two dog-legged chisels for cleaning out the bottoms of dadoes and grooves, and two gouges for carving.

CHISELS

Start your woodworking practice with a couple of sets of butt chisels. They're the tools you'll reach for first. Buy a medium-priced set of four or six chisels to use in rough jobs like cleaning up glue, and a more expensive set for finer tasks. Stay away from low-end chisels; they're probably made from inferior steel. They won't sharpen properly, won't hold an edge, and are prone to break.

My Japanese butt chisels are by far my favorites, and I reach for them when doing any fine joinery or paring work, especially when making dovetails. Japanese chisels are made by laminating a layer of hard steel around an inner core of softer steel. The hard outer layer sharpens to a keen edge, but it's also somewhat brittle. It takes a little extra finesse to sharpen and use a quality Japanese chisel, so I recommend you gain some basic chisel experience before buying a set.

Explore catalogs and become familiar with the many types of chisels available. Someday you'll run into a problem that a specialty chisel can solve. Two specialty chisels you'll need sooner rather than later are a dogleg chisel and a mortising chisel or two. The dogleg lets you get down into the bottoms of mortises, grooves, and dadoes to fine-tune a fit. Mortising chisels are made for heavy pounding; they're heftier than ordinary chisels and have a steeper cutting angle.

It is better, in my opinion, to strike chisels with wooden mallets. This is true even for Japanese chisels, which are said to be designed for striking with special metal hammers. I think a wooden mallet is more pleasant to use and easier to control. Never use a carpenter's claw hammer for striking a woodworking chisel.

SHARPENING SUPPLIES

Sharpening is an integral part of woodworking and is something you need to master as soon as possible. It's a simple process, but the details are important; the details can make it seem more complicated than it really is.

With only a few good water-stones and a simple holding jig, achieving a good, sharp edge on plane and chisel blades is well within your grasp. In fact, the ability to sharpen is tantamount to reaching a higher level of wood-working skill.

Using stones to sharpen and refine an edge is called honing and involves five stones ranging in grit

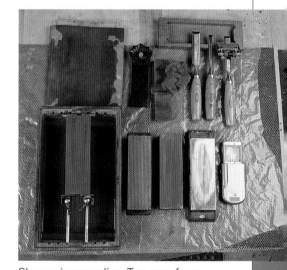

Sharpening supplies. Top row, from left: wet/dry sandpaper on a sheet of glass, device for setting the angle of a honing jig, rust erasers, steel wool, and chisels—the last one set up in a honing jig. Bottom row, from left: pond for storing and holding Japanese water-stones (coarse stone held atop the metal bars), extra-coarse diamond stone, medium-grit waterstone, fine waterstone, and magnifying glass. A sheet of plastic protects the bench.

from 220 to 6000. You probably won't use all five stones every time you hone an edge. Use only as coarse a grit as necessary. For instance, removing a small nick and an edge can be a lot of work, so you want to start with a coarse 220-grit stone to remove material as quickly as possible. On the other hand, touching up an edge that's in pretty good shape might require only a few passes on a 6000-grit stone. With practice you will learn to intuit what is required; it's not really all that complicated.

Rather than trying to hold the blade at the correct angle, I suggest you get a jig to hold the blade at a consistent angle during honing. There are a number of jigs on the market, and in this case the more expensive ones aren't necessarily better.

If your blade gets a bad nick, using a grinder can save a lot of time. A coarse wheel removes a lot

Japanese saws. From top: kataba ripping saw, kataba crosscut, ryoba saw with rip and crosscut edges, ryoba azebiki saw with rip and crosscut edges.

of metal in a hurry, but keep a light touch—it's easy to overheat the blade and ruin its temper.

I suggest a slow-speed grinder to reduce the likelihood of overheating, and I prefer ones with a wheel that turns in a water bath. I get such great results with my water-bath grinder that I now look forward to grinding.

JAPANESE SAWS

Once I started using Japanese saws, my Western saws became wall ornaments. Their pull-stroke design, razor-sharp teeth, and thin blades make cutting wood by hand almost effortless. These saws are well suited for women because they don't require nearly as much muscle power as push saws—making it possible to focus on precision rather than endurance.

A slow-speed grinder with a water bath makes quick work of removing nicks in the edges of your blades. The water keeps the steel cool, preventing the overheating that can cause a blade to lose its temper.

A honing guide holds the blade at a fixed angle, making it possible to get a sharp edge quickly and easily, every time.

Shaping tools, from left: spokeshave, large triangular file, small triangular file, fine wood file, coarse patternmaker's rasp, fine patternmaker's rasp, metal file, round grater-style rasp, medium-sized grater-style rasp, large two-handed grater-style rasp, carving knife, and small axe.

Be patient with your first saws; they take a little getting used to. The steel in Japanese saws is very hard and brittle, so you must take care not to bend or stress the blade beyond its capacity. It's all in the stance and grip. When you're holding the saw properly, sawing is easy (see Using Japanese Saws on p. 53).

There are many different types of Japanese saws, but for general woodworking you only need to concern yourself with two basic styles: ryoba and kataba. Ryoba saws have two different cutting edges, one with teeth set for ripping and one for crosscutting. Kataba saws have only one cutting edge. Within these styles, you'll find all kinds of saws with varying shapes, lengths, and tooth styles—each intended for a specialized task.

To start out, a general purpose ryoba saw will serve well for ripping, crosscutting, dovetailing, cutting angles, and cutting tenons. I like saws with replaceable blades because I don't have to bother resharpening them.

Another handy saw, the azebiki, is useful for starting cuts in the middle of material, making stopped cuts, cutting grooves, and even creating end rabbets. The kugihiki is fine toothed and has no set to the teeth. It's excellent for flush cutting protruding dowels and the like without scratching the surface. Finally, there's a hefty saw called anahiki, which is used for rough crosscutting and is so effective that it's often more to convenient than taking lumber over to the radial arm saw, or finding and plugging in a circular saw.

SHAPING TOOLS

In woodworking, we frequently wander off the straight and narrow—situations where we want curves and edges that aren't perpendicular. Then we must rely on hand tools to help shape things up. Woodworkers who incorporate extensively shaped parts in their furniture often have arsenals of tools, both hand and power, to accomplish their tasks. Sculptural woodworking is a labor-intensive proposition. But adding texture and form with a few curves, some low relief areas, and profiles is easily accomplished with just a few simple hand tools.

Rasps and Files

Files are made for working both wood and metal, but they're not interchangeable. Metalworking files are much less coarse and don't work very well on wood. Wood files are best for finish-shaping work. Rasps look like files, but the tooth pattern cuts more aggressively. I like patternmaker's rasps, which have relatively fine, sharp teeth and cut wood quickly and cleanly. Rasps that aren't flat are called rifflers, and they're useful for smaller detail work.

Files and rasps are usually sold without handles, and you can use them that way. You'll find it a lot more comfortable if you also purchase the special wooden file handles made to fit the ends of these tools. Keep your rasps and files free of dust and debris. Use a file card to scrub the teeth clean, and store these tools carefully so the teeth aren't dulled by contact with other metal objects.

Spokeshaves

You don't need a fancy designer spokeshave; just get a run-of-the-mill, metal-bodied version and learn to use it. A spokeshave works best on outside curves and profiles, but it will take some practice to get the feel of using it. You've got to hold it at just the right angle to cut properly. Chatter is the big problem with spokeshaves, and you can reduce that problem somewhat by replacing the blade with a thicker one. You'll need to enlarge the blade opening slightly, but that's easily accomplished with a metal worker's file.

MEASURING, MARKING, AND LAYOUT TOOLS

Accurate measuring and marking is a critical part of woodworking. At first, you're likely to find the whole measuring/marking/accuracy thing a little daunting. You may have a few mind blocks surrounding fractions, measuring, or just dealing with numbers in general.

Most adults are a little rusty with fractions. They're not things most people use on a daily basis, and as with a foreign language, fluency is quickly lost without practice. In woodworking we're normally concerned with fractions $1/16"$ and larger; get out a tape measure or ruler and reacquaint yourself what these measurements mean: $1/16"$, $1/8"$, $3/16"$, $1/4"$, $5/16"$, $3/8"$, $7/16"$, $1/2"$, $9/16"$, $5/8"$, $11/16"$, $3/4"$, $13/16"$, $7/8"$, and $15/16"$. For easy addition and subtraction, it helps to memorize the decimal equivalents of the more common fractions ($1/8"$ = .125", $1/2"$ = .5", and so on). Until it comes easily, keep a fraction/decimal conversion chart handy.

At this point, you might need some reassuring. Don't worry, your woodworking needn't be bogged down with numbers. They're just a way to convey information. If the increments are too small to see, such as 32nds or 64ths, I dispense with them all together and figure out another way to solve the problem.

Measuring Devices

Perhaps the most basic of all woodworking measuring devices is the tape measure. You probably have a few lying around, but if they're old and hard to read, get a new one. You don't need a 25' tape if you're

Measuring, marking, and layout tools, from left: dial caliper, saddle squares, wheel-type marking gauge, sliding bevel, engineer's protractor, marking knife, 24" metal rule, 6" metal rule, 6" combination square, 12" combination square, and No. 2 pencil.

building furniture. You rarely need the length, and it's awkward to hold and too bulky to keep in a tool apron. A 16' tape is perfect.

A few metal rules will be helpful in the shop. I always have a 6" rule in my tool apron for quick access, and a 24" rule nearby. I prefer rules marked in increments of $1/16"$ and $1/32"$ on one side and 1 mm and 0.5 mm on the other. The metric system is handy on occasion.

Though many people associate it with metalworking, I find a dial caliper very handy around a woodworking shop. It's an easy way to measure the thickness of wood as it comes out of the planer, and to measure the insides of mortises and the outsides of tenons, and it serves as a depth gauge as well. Woodworking calipers don't need to be as precise or as expensive as

machinist's calipers. Look for a pair made for woodworking, with a dial graduated in fractions of an inch. My favorite caliper gives readings in three units: fractions of an inch, decimal inches, and millimeters.

Squares

Possibly no other tool in the shop is more often used and relied upon than the combination square. Don't scrimp here. A cheap square simply won't cut the mustard. I recommend both a 6" and a 12" square. You need the larger one frequently, but the smaller one fits in your work-apron pocket and will be your constant companion.

Marking perfectly square lines on both the face and edge of a board can be difficult with a square, so I suggest purchasing a set of saddle squares to make this job much easi-

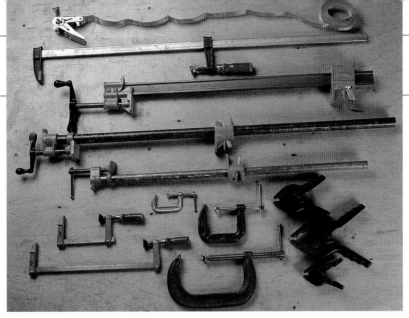

Clamps, from top: strap clamp, long light-duty bar clamps, heavy bar clamp, heavy-duty pipe clamp, light-duty pipe clamp, light-duty bar clamps, C-clamps, and spring clamps.

er. Saddle squares have a lot of surface area, so you don't have to balance the square with one hand while you mark with the other. A set of saddle squares should include a 90° saddle square and two others to mark standard dovetail angles.

Pencils and Knives

Elementary as it may seem, the right pencil is important for accurate woodworking. More often than not, students arrive in my classes with those big, square carpentry pencils meant for marking 2 x 4s for house construction. They're worthless for fine work. A crisp narrow line is what you need—a line you can cut to with a fine-toothed Japanese saw.

You might think a mechanical pencil would be ideal, but the lead breaks almost instantaneously on wood. The best thing is a common No. 2 pencil. Keep it nice and sharp (I use an electric pencil sharpener). It leaves a line that's dark enough to see, fine enough to cut to, and soft enough not to dent the wood under any lines you may need to erase later.

Sometimes even a pencil line is too wide. When you're cutting dovetails (or tenons), being off by a pencil width is too much. In those situations, mark with a knife line. It leaves a tiny kerf that you can find by feel to start the saw cut, or pare to with a chisel. Any woodworking marking knife is fine for this job, as are surgical knives.

Marking Gauge

A marking gauge is a way to make a long knife cut without a ruler. You adjust the gauge against the edge of the wood so the knife is positioned just where you want it. Rather than an old-fashioned kind that uses an

actual knife, I prefer the kind that uses a wheel. They make very clean and distinct lines.

Take care to store this tool in a box or protective cover, as a nick in the wheel will render it useless. Wheels can also come loose from stems; tighten them periodically so you won't have wobbly marks.

Tools for Angles

If you're only dealing with 90° or 45° situations, a combination square will serve you well. But for other angles, you'll need to enlist a few more tools.

A sliding bevel gauge with an adjustable arm lets you measure and transfer angles from layout to workpiece to machine, as necessary. You don't need a fancy one—this is one case where an inexpensive home-center tool will work fine.

A drafting protractor will come in handy from time to time, as will a 6" steel engineer's protractor. From time to time, you'll need a larger 10" adjustable protractor. These are usually clear plastic and have two arms that you lock at the appropriate angle with a knurled knob.

Clamps

You can't do woodworking without clamps. Integral parts of everyday life in the shop, they're used for gluing pieces together and as holding devices. Woodworkers often lament that they never have enough clamps.

For gluing up wide surfaces such as tabletops, you will need pipe or bar clamps. Pipe clamp fixtures come as a set (head and tail piece) that grip any length of $3/4$" (or $1/2$" for lighter-duty applications) black pipe from a home or plumbing-supply store. Bar clamps are purchased as complete units, and it's a good idea to have a variety of sizes on hand. I keep my eyes open for catalog specials, and buy four or six clamps whenever I see a good deal. Plan to have a few light-duty bar clamps as well—they're available in lengths as short as 4" and have a deeper reach than typical bar clamps. Again, a variety of sizes will be useful.

Definitely have at least several C-clamps and a few deep-reach clamps in your shop. Some spring clamps are handy for light-duty work—since you can set them with one hand, they can make life a lot easier. Occasionally you need a strap to clamp around an object. For that I use web straps with ratcheting buckles sold as automotive tie-downs.

Workbenches

You may not think of workbenches as tools, but in reality they are perhaps the most important tools in the shop—without them we could achieve very little. If you have the room, I recommend more than one bench.

Your first purchase should probably be a traditional European-style bench. Equipped with thick tops, often of maple or beech, and a sturdy base, these hefty benches provide a solid foundation from which to work. Typically mounted with a different type of vise on each end, they offer a variety of ways to secure your work. You can purchase plans and build your own bench, or you can buy one ready-made.

Your second bench should be a large multipurpose table, where gluing, sanding, and other messy tasks can take place. An easy way to create such a table is to build a frame 48" wide and 96" long from $1^1/2$"-thick poplar, then glue and screw a sheet of $1/2$" plywood to both sides of the frame. To create a solid base for the tabletop and some additional storage space as well, construct three cabinets out of $3/4$" shop-grade plywood.

Let the top overhang the cabinets by about 3" all around so you can easily clamp things down to the edges. Bolt a vise or two to this bench, if you like.

A folding workbench with a built-in vise (readily available at hardware stores and home centers) is right there when you need it. These small but sturdy benches are easily moved about the shop or folded down for storage or transport. For more stability, I add a shelf down low to hold a toolbox filled with heavy, little-used tools.

Finally, consider having a bench that is low enough to sit on, thus utilizing body weight as yet another way to hold parts while working on them (see the Low Bench on p. 80).

A traditional European-style workbench will provide a hefty foundation from which to work. This bench is fitted out with a wooden-jaw front vise, a shoulder vise, a magnetic bar for storing tools at hand, a slot along the back edge for holding chisels, and tool storage beneath, protected by sliding doors.

A folding workbench with a built-in vise like this one often comes in handy. It can serve as an extra bench vise, an outfeed table, a sawhorse, and more.

Safety equipment

Safety may not be the most stimulating subject in woodworking, but given the somewhat hazardous nature of working with sharp tools and flying bits of wood, it's an integral part of learning how to be in a wood shop.

Protecting your eyes and ears is fairly simple. Safety glasses or goggles are readily available and inexpensive. What you end up with is largely a matter of personal preference. The trick is to make sure you wear the devices every time a hazard is present. Don't let yourself get away with inventing any excuse for why you don't need to bother this one time.

Even though you have a dust collector and air filters working for you, don't rule out wearing a dust protection mask, especially when you're using a router or other tools that defy dust collection. A dusk mask is not the same as a respirator. A dusk mask is a fairly simple item, which protects against particles in the air. A respirator is designed to filter harmful chemicals from the air. The two are not interchangeable.

Wearing eye-, ear-, and respiratory-protection gear all at the same time can be problematic, especially if you wear eyeglasses. Many respirators fog up your glasses, and earmuff-type hearing protectors squeeze your glasses tightly against the temples. I've had a lot of success with an air helmet.

Safety gear only works when you use it.

Powered by a battery/filter pack worn at the waist, it pumps clean air into a face shield/helmet apparatus, thus protecting lungs and eyes at the same time.

Gloves can spare you from the most common woodworking injuries—splinters. I've come to prefer rubber-coated gardening gloves for milling tasks. Since gloves can make some tasks difficult (I won't wear them when using the drill press, for example), keep some tweezers, a needle, and a magnifying glass at the ready.

Keep a first-aid kit in the shop, and make sure it includes eyewash. Have an emergency plan ready in case of a more serious injury.

Have a couple of fire extinguishers (more if your shop is large). Locate them near the exits, and keep one in the middle of the room as well. Use those rated ABC, and get the rechargeable type with the metal head. Check them regularly to make sure they're fully charged and ready to go. Fire multiplies in intensity very quickly, extinguisher or not. Act fast, and don't hesitate to call the fire department sooner rather than later.

TECHNIQUES

Here's a short course in the fundamentals of woodworking.

This book's projects are designed to offer you an array of techniques and methods commonly used to build furniture—concepts that can be used repeatedly throughout your woodworking practice. Though there is often more than one way to accomplish the same task, I offer these particular techniques based upon ease, safety, and suitability for the novice to intermediate woodworker in a small shop situation. These are techniques I use on a frequent basis in my own shop as well. As you grow with your practice, you may wish to extrapolate from this information and try variations or entirely different methods. The woodworking book of rules is somewhat malleable, inviting change, experimentation, and adaptation.

This section covers the fundamental techniques required to build the projects. I have arranged the information based upon the techniques themselves rather than explaining them via each individual project. In woodworking, there are "ties that bind," whether you're building a box, cabinet, table, or chair. A groove is a groove, a dovetail a dovetail—the size or layout may vary, but the technique to produce it remains the same. In some instances, I offer both machine and hand-tool techniques.

Practice on scrap wood until you become comfortable with the various techniques. It's often easier to learn using softwoods, where resistance between tool and wood is lessened. Of all the techniques used in this book, dovetailing will probably require the most concentrated amount of effort and practice.

Moving your axis: woodworking and the body

While having a huge set of muscles may provide some advantages to a woodworker, it's certainly not a prerequisite for success. Enthusiasm, willingness, and curiosity are attributes that are more important. Woodworking is more about problem solving than anything else, and body strength is only part of the equation.

Keep in mind that when you first begin using many of the techniques here (hand planing is a good example), you'll discover your muscles are not up to the task. You might feel as if the wood is working you, not vice versa. Keep working, and your muscles will rapidly strengthen. Practice your skills, and before long, you'll reach what I call the fluidity stage, where your body, the wood, and the tools are all working in harmony.

Woodworking is a give and take activity. You can't force the tools or materials to do something just because you want it to happen. Nor can you force yourself to work beyond your (current) physical limitations or level of skill.

Mastering hand tools gives you the skills you need to fine-tune joints for a perfect fit.

When things don't work out the way you want, and your frustration level rises, take a step back. Reassess. Working wood is not about strength and control. It's about innovation and information.

Difficulties and mistakes are not things to be overcome and defeated. Most mistakes in the shop are merely the result of inadequate information or experience, and not an indication that the woodworker is inadequate to the job. Make this your mantra: "Mistakes are just information." Repeat it often.

Woodworking does involve a degree of hard work; much of the process is moving things around. If you decide to build a large, solid wood entertainment center, be prepared for hard physical labor from the get go. But information and innovation come into play here, too. You can design the center with your physical limitations in mind. Create the structure from three smaller units, each of which you can manage on your own. Once the units are on site, you can assemble them into the monolithic unit you had in mind from the start.

I suggest you work your way up to larger projects, building your physical and mental muscles in the process. Start with small, easily managed projects and build upon your mistakes (and success, though that's often more difficult). In time, you'll be able to handle the entertainment center in every sense of the word.

Milling lumber four-square

The journey from rough boards to refined parts is a logical sequence of steps, a well-worn path you must follow if you intend to mill parts that are flat and square. Parts that aren't flat and square cause problems at every step of your project—you can't make accurate measurements, machine identical cuts, or assemble close fitting joints. It's vital that you start your projects with every board milled four-square, even those that will be sawn or shaped into curves.

When a board is four-square, every surface is flat and every corner is square. It's flat along both its length and width. The two faces are parallel, and the edges are perpendicular to the faces. The ends are parallel to one another and perpendicular to both the sides and the faces (see fig. 1).

Exposing fresh surfaces by milling can cause a board to shrink or swell, depending on its moisture content and the ambient humidity. Ripping can release tensions developed as the tree grew toward the sun, possibly causing the boards to twist or bow. If you don't consider these things and plan your milling accordingly, your four-square lumber can twist out of shape in a matter of hours.

The key to preventing such a disaster is to run through the milling process twice. The first time, make the pieces larger in all dimensions than you need. Then let them sit in your shop for a least a few days. The oversize boards will acclimate to the humidity in your shop, moving and changing as they must (see p. 12). Then mill them again, going through each step, assuming the lumber is no longer four-square.

WHAT IS FOUR-SQUARE?

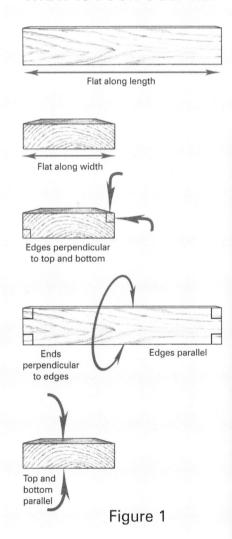

Flat along length

Flat along width

Edges perpendicular to top and bottom

Ends perpendicular to edges

Edges parallel

Top and bottom parallel

Figure 1

PRELIMINARY DIMENSIONING

The first step in milling is conceptual—deciding what parts of the project each board will yield. Take a close look at all the boards and note any problems, such as troublesome knots, hairline cracks, end checks, wild grain, and severe cup or twist. It takes practice to develop a sense about wood—there's a fine line between "defects" that might be called character and ones that mean trouble. Think about the visually important areas of the project and lay out those parts on the best-looking boards.

As you lay out all the pieces, leave plenty of room all around—at least an inch if possible. I use a grease pencil to mark out the pieces (dark pencils for light-colored woods, light ones for dark woods). Their bold lines are much easier to see.

Cut to Rough Length

Short boards are easier to deal with, so cut them down early in the process. In fact, I sometimes crosscut long boards outside, before I even get them into the shop. I use a circular saw, but you can also use a hand saw. Either way, support the wood in a few places so it won't buckle and bind the saw. If I need to rough cut the wood to shorter lengths once it's indoors, I use a radial arm saw.

Cut your boards at least 1" longer than you need, and 2" if you're going to laminate them or glue them into a wider panel.

Straighten One Edge

The simplest way to get a straight edge is to run it over the jointer. Make as many passes as necessary.

If the board is too crooked to joint, draw the line first and then

Run the workpiece through the jointer facedown to establish an initial flat, straight surface. To get a straight edge, run the piece through the jointer again, this time with the face side against the fence.

use the band saw to cut to the line (don't use a fence; cut freehand). Then use the jointer to get the edge truly straight.

Don't be tempted to use the table saw for this. Safe operation of that tool requires a straight edge to run against the fence, and you don't yet have one.

The first step in any project is deciding how to lay out the pieces on your lumber. Mark rough lengths and widths with a grease pencil. Use a dark color for light woods and a light pencil for dark ones.

Break down your lumber into manageable lengths with a circular saw. The author often does this outdoors, before the lumber even goes into the shop.

Rip to Rough Width

Ripping can release pent-up energy within the wood, sometimes causing it to bow and twist immediately after sawing. If you're using a table saw, this can result in a dangerous kickback. That's why I prefer to use the band saw (with fence this time) for rough ripping. Make your wood about 1/4" wider than your final dimension.

Resaw to Rough Thickness

If your project calls for boards that are significantly thinner than what you can get at the lumberyard, you can slice it up by resawing. Generally, if you need to plane off more than 3/8" to arrive at the desired thickness, consider resawing. If I need 5/8" lumber from 4/4 stock, I'd plane it down. If I needed 1/2" or less, I'd resaw. It takes less time than planing, and it would reduce the wear and tear on the planer knives (always a consideration because changing the knives is an involved process).

1. Resaw the stock on the band saw to about 1/8" thicker than the desired rough thickness.

2. Run the boards through the planer, taking them down to the desired rough thickness.

Though it's possible to resaw on the table saw, I prefer the band saw. With its thinner blade, you waste less material cutting the kerf. Table saws make a smoother cut (you may be able to forego the planer), but they make a much wider kerf, and the maximum blade height limits you to narrow boards (typically about 3 1/2" wide). You can resaw

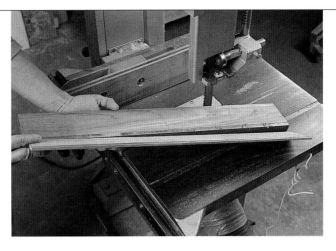

Resawing divides one thick piece of wood into two or more thinner pieces. The best way to achieve this is with a well-tuned band saw, with a coarse, wide blade.

wider boards on the table saw, but you still need to use a band saw. The usual process is to run a groove down both edges of the workpiece on the table saw, and then use the kerfs to guide your resawing on the band saw. You'll still have to run the pieces through the planer to remove the saw marks.

In any event, you can't use the table saw on rough lumber. The surface that goes against the fence on a table saw must always be jointed flat and straight, or you run a considerable risk of kickback.

FINAL DIMENSIONING

Woodworking mistakes are cumulative, so any errors you make during milling will lay the foundation for further complications later on. Monitor the process, checking for square at each step, and making corrections before it's too late.

Joint Face and Edge

1. Run one face of the board over the jointer as many times as necessary until the tool takes a full-length, full-width cut.

2. Put that face against the fence and flatten the adjacent edge.

Plane to Thickness

When milling parts to thickness, the actual final thickness is not as important as consistency. All the boards need to be exactly the same thickness, and it usually doesn't matter if it's a tiny bit more or less than specified.

It's hard to get the exact same thickness setting in a planer twice in a row, so run all the parts through the planer at a given setting, then lower the head and run them all through again. Continue until you reach the desired thickness.

1. Lay the jointed face down on the planer table, set the planer, and take a fine cut off the top. The first couple of cuts will only remove the high spots.

2. Plane the top surface until you get a full-width cut on the top. Then plane the faces alternately as you work toward the desired thickness. This equalizes tension in the wood.

Rip to Width

1. Set the table saw fence for the final width.

2. Run the jointed edge against the fence and rip to final width.

Crosscut to Final Length

1. Square up one end by crosscutting on a miter saw.

2. Use this square end as the origin, and carefully mark the final length.

3. Cut to final length.

When cutting multiple parts, assure consistency by clamping a block of wood to the fence (usually to the left of the saw), positioning it so that when the squared end is pushed against it, the saw automatically cuts the correct length.

Biscuit joinery

A biscuit is nothing more than a football-shaped wafer of pressed wood set into semicircular slots on either side of a joint (see fig. 2). When saturated with glue, the wafer expands, locking the wood in a joint that's easy to make and incredibly strong.

Biscuit joinery can solve any number of woodworking problems, but in this book, we mainly use these joints for alignment when gluing up wide panels from two or more narrower boards, for attaching solid wood edging or frames to exposed plywood edges, and for corner joints in frame and panel construction. While the football wafers come in several sizes, all of this book's biscuit joinery uses moderately sized #20 biscuits.

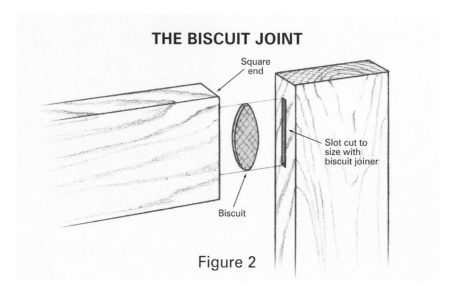

THE BISCUIT JOINT

Square end

Slot cut to size with biscuit joiner

Biscuit

Figure 2

LAYING OUT AND CUTTING THE SLOTS

1. Position the pieces on the bench in their final configuration.

2. Draw a pencil line across the joint at a 90° angle. This line represents the centerline of the biscuit slot. If you're working on a corner joint, the centerline of the biscuit slot should be in the middle of the end grain piece. When joining edges, it doesn't matter where the slots go. Just make sure you locate them so a later step won't expose the pressed wood biscuit.

3. Label each piece so you know exactly what it is because once you cut the slots, the pieces will only go together the way they were when you first marked the slots.

4. Adjust the biscuit fence to position the slot relative to the workpiece's face. The slots should be in the approximate middle of the material. Move the fence up or down, testing the cut in a piece of scrap until the slot is in the correct location.

5. Line up the reference mark on the biscuit joiner's fence with the mark on your workpiece. Then just press the trigger and push the cutter into the work. Small side-to-side misalignments don't matter since the biscuit is a little smaller than the slots. You can adjust the alignment a bit during glue-up, at least until the glue causes the biscuits to swell and lock the joint closed.

6. While position is not crucial, the orientation of the slot is. It's essential to hold the machine steady so the slot is parallel to the top of the workpiece. Otherwise, the biscuits won't slip into their slots when the pieces are joined. This is much easier when the workpiece doesn't move around. Clamp the piece to the bench or make a simple fixture such as the one shown in the photo at the right.

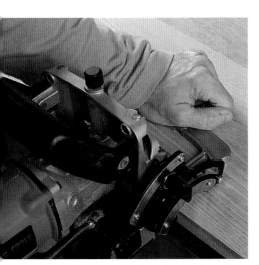

To cut a slot, just align the mark on the indexing fence with the mark on the workpiece. Press the fence firmly downward to cut the biscuit slot parallel to the face.

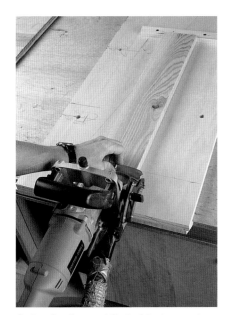

A simple plywood jig holds the work steady, even under the inward pressure of the cut.

BISCUITS AND EDGE-GLUING WIDE PANELS

Most lumber from commercial suppliers ranges in width from about 5" to 12". Occasionally you can find wider boards, but these days it's difficult to find boards even 12" wide. When your plans call for a wide surface such as a tabletop (or even a shelf), you'll have to create it by edge joining two or more pieces of lumber to create a panel. There are two keys to success in this operation: Mating edges that are perfectly straight and square, and keeping the panel flat during clamp-up.

A long edge-to-edge glue joint is quite strong but is also slippery and prone to shifting under clamping pressure. Biscuits are an excellent way to keep the boards properly aligned and under control while applying clamps and cauls. Here's how to put together a strong, flat panel with the aid of biscuits.

1. Start the process with your boards milled to the desired thickness. Lay them out as a panel, and arrange them so the grain patterns seem to flow across the joints. If adjoining boards have very different color or grain patterns, the eye is drawn to the joint (see photo above right).

2. Draw a large triangle across the surface so you can reposition the boards in correct order during the glue-up (see the photo at right). Additionally, mark the face of each board with "in" and the back with "out" for quick, positive identification later.

Position the boards in a panel to minimize the glue line. Try to match the color tone of adjoining boards, and do your best to align the boards so the grain appears to swirl across the joint.

Preserve your layout by drawing a large triangle across the panel. Reassemble the boards incorrectly, and the triangle won't come out right.

Square edges are the foundations of successful joinery. When milling lumber four-square, assume nothing—frequently check that your jointer continues to cut square.

3. To get good joints, it's important that the edges be straight and square to the face. Make sure your jointer fence sits at 90° (see the photo above). Get into the habit of periodically checking it, and calibrate it as necessary.

4. Having good joints on the edges of the boards is so important that even after setting the fence, you should work as though the fence is not perfect. Account for any minor discrepancies by running each edge over the jointer, alternating the face in or out to the fence, so mating edges will end up with complementary angles.

5. Once you've achieved straight edges, lay the boards back in order. Mark for biscuits and cut the slots as described above.

6. Make a test run of your glue-up, without setting any biscuits or applying glue. This alerts you to any problems and ensures that all the necessary materials are at hand. Follow steps 10 to 13 below, omitting the glue and biscuits. Then repeat from step 7, as written.

7. While applying glue, it is helpful to hold the first board in a bench vise. Use a roller to apply glue to the edges, and a bottle with a special biscuit tip for getting glue into the slots. Similarly, apply glue to the mating edge of the next board.

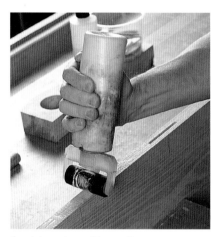

Applying glue with a roller assures even coverage. It's also neater.

Biscuits swell quickly; add them just before closing the joint.

8. Tap biscuits into the slots on the board in the vise only.

9. Assemble the joint, tapping it closed with a wooden mallet.

10. Lift the entire piece onto awaiting clamps. Draw the boards

A special biscuiting glue tip spreads glue down in the slots. A glue-starved biscuit joint isn't very strong.

Lightly tap the joint to close it. Don't clean up the squeezed-out glue—you'll only spread it around. Wait until it's dry.

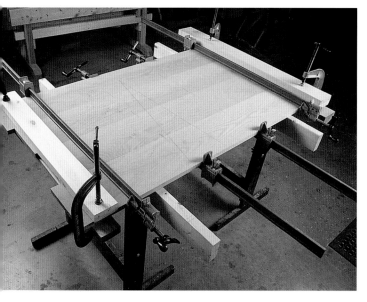

Good clamping technique helps keep wide panels flat. Position the long bar clamps so at least two span the top surface of the panel, and clamp stiff cauls on the end.

DOUBLE BISCUIT JOINTS

For additional strength, you can cut two biscuit slots per joint (see the photo below). Proper procedure is important here. Test your setup on scrap wood exactly the same thickness as your workpiece. It may take a few cycles of trial and error to get the right setup.

together with light clamping pressure, then clamp 2 x 4s (or any wood of similar dimensions) across the ends of the panel to hold the surface flat, as shown in the photo above. Known as cauls, these boards distribute the clamping pressure as well as protect the surface of the panel from being damaged by the clamps. A little paste wax on the cauls keeps them from sticking to the panel.

11. Crank each panel clamp tight, and then tighten down the C-clamps on the cauls.

12. Check for flatness and adjust the clamps as necessary.

13. Don't clean up any glue squeeze-out—it only smears the adhesive into the grain. Wait until the glue is dry, and then remove it with a scraper.

14. Leave the panel under pressure for at least an hour.

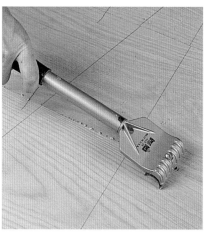

After the glue cures (about an hour at room temperature), remove it with a paint scraper.

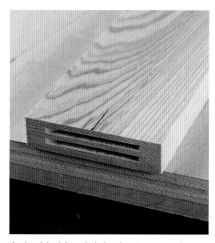

A double biscuit joint is stronger than one joined with a single biscuit.

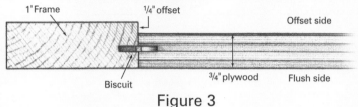

OFFSETS IN FRAME AND PANEL

1" Frame   ¼" offset   Offset side

Biscuit   ¾" plywood   Flush side

Figure 3

1. Always work from the same side of the material (top or bottom). From the start, label everything clearly to avoid confusion.

2. Cut the first slot in the lower third of the thickness, about ⁷⁄₁₆" down from the top for ³⁄₄" material. The exact position is not crucial—but don't cut the slots too close together or too close to the edge.

3. Slip a spacer under the fence (on top of the workpiece) for the second cut). For ³⁄₄" material, a ³⁄₁₆" spacer works well.

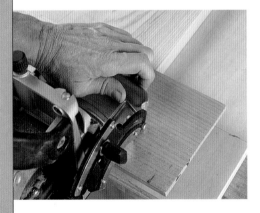

When you're cutting double slots in ³⁄₄" material, place a ³⁄₁₆" spacer under the fence for the second cut.

BISCUITS FOR FRAME AND PANEL

Traditional frame and panel is an attractive method of construction, and it's also an excellent system for dealing with wood movement. The narrow frames bear the structural load, while a thin, lightweight panel keeps the dust out. The panel floats in a groove cut in the edges of the frame, allowing it to shrink and swell with changes in humidity.

These days, panels are often made of plywood, which doesn't have much seasonal movement. Rather than dealing with those grooves, we can simplify the construction by simply biscuiting the panel to the frame.

Most of the time, the joints are made with the face of the panel set back about ¼" from the edge of the frame (see fig. 3). Occasionally a design calls for the face of the frame and the panel to be flush, with no setback. Getting the desired outcome depends on the thicknesses of the materials used, as well as following the proper sequence when cutting biscuits.

Let's say your frame is 1"-thick solid wood fitted with a ³⁄₄" plywood panel. If you lay out the assembly face up on the bench, you'll be able to see the offset on the top. The natural tendency is to mark for the slots on the top surface, then use that top surface as a reference for the biscuit joiner fence. If you do it this way, when you assemble the panel the frame and panel will be flush on the top surface, with the offset in the back—exactly what you don't want.

Following is the proper sequence for building biscuited frames and panels:

1. Cut the panels to final length and rough width, do all surface prep, and apply the final finish.

2. Leave the rails and stiles a little long, and put some finish on what will be the offset. It's easier to do now rather than later, especially if the frames and panels have different finishes. It's important to keep finish off any gluing surfaces.

3. Lay out the rails and panels and mark the biscuit locations. Remember, the offset surface goes face down on the bench. Typically, this is the outside or front face of the frame and panel.

4. Cut the slots with the biscuit cutter fence on the surface that's supposed to be flush (that is, the non-offset surface—typically the back).

5. Apply glue to the rails, the mating edge of the panel, and the biscuit slots.

6. Tap the biscuits into the rails, and attach the panel. Do both rails on each panel, and clamp in place. You may need cauls across the ends to keep the assembly flat. Let dry for an hour.

7. When the glue is dry, remove the panel from the clamps, and clean off any excess glue from the setback with a sharp chisel.

8. Use a Japanese saw or miter saw to cut off most but not all of the rail overhangs on one side. Don't bother to get them flush—that comes later.

9. Run that side against the table saw fence, and cut the rails flush with the plywood of the other edge.

10. Run this edge against the fence, and cut the panel to final width.

11. Lay the panel on the bench with the rough length stiles in position.

12. Mark the locations of the biscuits that will attach the stiles to both the panel and the rails.

13. Apply glue and biscuits and clamp the assembly together. Use cauls as necessary to keep the assembly flat.

14. Remove the assembly from the clamps, cut off the overhangs, and sand flush with a stationary belt sander or a random orbit sander.

Keep the panel flat with sturdy cauls clamped from rail to rail.

Cut one edge of the overhanging rails so they are almost (but not quite) flush with one edge of the panel. Use a handsaw or miter saw so they end up like the top edge here.

Place the cut edge against the fence and rip a small amount off the panel, leaving a flush edge. Then place that edge against the fence and rip to final width.

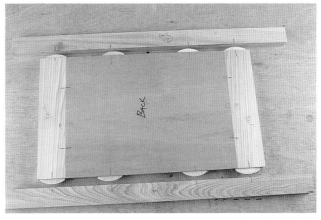

With the panel at final width, biscuit the rough length stiles in place. Trim the excess flush after the glue dries.

Using hand planes

Efficient hand planing is not something most people can do without practice. It takes a while to get used to the movement and find your rhythm. It's a little like learning how to ride a bicycle—it's hard to do until you've done it.Then you never forget.

The biggest problem with learning how to use hand planes is that no amount of practice or technique can overcome a dull or poorly adjusted hand plane. I remember struggling with hand planes until a knowledgeable woodworker friend led me through the process. With an experienced guide, it took less than an hour for me to make the breakthrough. A sharp blade is half the battle. If you're just learning how to hand plane, I suggest you start with sharpening (see p. 35). Next, learn to adjust the blade for a good, clean cut.

1. Hold the plane close to your chest, with its front handle up, and sight down the sole.

2. Extend the blade by turning the depth-adjustment screw counterclockwise until you can see it above the sole.

3. Adjust the skew with the lever located just behind the blade assembly. Turn it side to side until the blade is parallel to the sole, with no skew at all.

4. Retract the blade until it's just barely visible above the sole. At some point, you may realize it's skewed again. Adjust as necessary.

5. Make a test cut. If the blade is retracted too far to make shavings, lower it with less than a quarter turn of the depth-adjustment screw.

6. Keep your cuts light and your shavings thin. Light cuts create a smoother surface with less effort.

Before starting any planing operation, sight down the bottom of the plane and adjust the blade parallel with the sole. Then retract the blade until it appears as a barely visible line.

Thin shavings equal light cuts. And light cuts mean a smoother surface with less effort.

Hold the work at waist height and you can get your whole body behind the plane. The vise in a traditional European bench is just the right height for most situations.

A low bench supports wide boards at the right height. Here, the low workbench is angled slightly downward for planing with a traditional Japanese plane, which cuts on the pull.

Another key factor in planing success is holding your work. Proper planing uses your whole upper body, not just your arms. If the workpiece is too high, it's impossible to get your strength behind the plane. I like to work with the piece at waist height. When I'm working with small pieces, it's usually easiest to lock them in the bench vise of my traditional European workbench. This method puts wider pieces well above my waist, so I clamp them to my low workbench.

Using Japanese saws

Japanese saws are thin and delicate. They cut on the pull stroke and are sensitive to your alignment. If you're perfectly positioned, with saw, hand, wrist, and arm in one straight line, sawing is effortless. If you're not aligned, the saw will bend, bind, and drift off the mark. Hand sawing to a line is a skill that requires practice to get and keep. I suggest making many practice cuts in softwoods as a way of gaining intrinsic knowledge of the tool (and yourself).

CUTTING JOINTS

1. Use a square to mark your cut lines on both sides of the material.

2. Stand directly in front of the material and grip the saw with your dominant hand. Make sure your hand, wrist, and arm are aligned with the handle.

3. Angle the saw slightly, rather than cutting parallel to the surface. Check your cut lines on both sides of the board frequently as you saw.

CROSSCUTTING

1. Lay out cut lines with a square on the face of the material.

2. Place the workpiece on a low surface and kneel on it to hold it down.

3. Keep your alignment and hold the saw at a slight angle.

Keep the work low when crosscutting, and use your knee as a hold down.

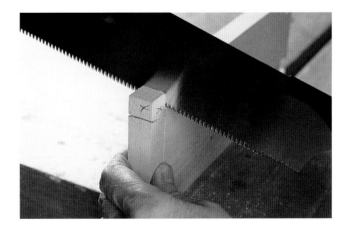

Japanese saws cut well when the handle is tilted downward slightly, rather than with the edge parallel to the floor.

RIPPING

1. Lay out your cut lines with a square or marking gauge. Lightly pencil in the knife cut so you can see it.

2. Angle the workpiece in a vise or on the low workbench. Alternatively, put the work on the bench and climb on top to hold it.

3. Keep your alignment and hold the saw at a slight angle to the work.

Ripping requires less effort when the work is held at an angle (here on the tilted top of the low workbench), and the saw is held approximately parallel to the floor.

A light shaving planed off the corner of an edge softens the arris.

Successful hand sawing is all about positioning your body so the blade tracks straight and true.

Edge treatments

SOFTENING THE ARRIS

Though it's a perfectly modern word, most people don't know what an arris is until they take up wood-working. It's the sharp edge or ridge at the point where two surfaces meet—the edge of the tabletop or the cutting edge of a chisel. In furniture making, we treat every arris to make the piece softer to the touch (you can actually cut yourself on a crisp hardwood edge) and to give a more elegant, refined appearance.

1. Take a very light shaving right off the arris with a block plane.

2. To prevent tear-out at the corners, change the planing direction at each end so you're always planing into the long grain from the end grain.

3. Light softening can also be done with sandpaper, but be sure to use a block or pad with a flat surface. The arris is very sharp, and sanding without a block is a splinter hazard.

To avoid tear-out at the ends, plane inward from each corner.

When softening an arris by hand sanding, always use a block or pad so the sanding surface is flat.

Layout lines make it easier to hand plane consistent chamfers. The angle on the side gives a visual clue for how to tilt the plane when starting.

CHAMFERS

A strongly beveled arris is called a chamfer. While you can cut chamfers by eye, they'll be more consistent and look better if you take the time to lay them out and plane to a line.

1. Rest the combination square with its base on the edge to be chamfered. Draw lines on either side of this edge to set the limits of the chamfer. It's helpful to connect the lines on the side. This gives you a visual clue for the angle at which you should hold the plane.

2. Plane the end grain with a block plane. If you're chamfering long grain, use a bench plane. Depending on the species of wood, you may need to plane towards the middle from each end to prevent tear-out.

On big projects, I sometimes use a handheld router with a 45° or 30° chamfer bit (see p. 25). It's faster and makes chamfers that are more consistent.

Use a block plane for chamfers on end grain and a bench plane on long or side grain.

EDGE PROFILES WITH THE ROUTER

While chamfers are simple and elegant, some projects want a more complex edge treatment. In the old days, every woodworker had a collection of specialized planes to do this, but we have routers. Any woodworking catalog lists an inspiring collection of edge profile bits that can be use singly or in combinations.

One combination I like to use on a table or cabinet top is a 3/8" roundover bit on the top edge, and a 30° chamfer on the bottom edge. Whenever possible, I use a hand-held router and profile the edge after assembly.

Narrower pieces (2" wide or less) make it hard to stabilize the router for handheld operations. Think ahead—it may be easier to profile the parts on the router table before assembly.

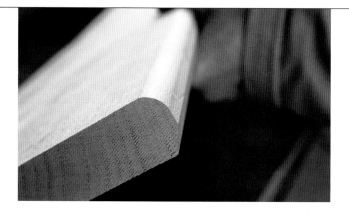

The router-made combination of 3/8" roundover on the top edge and a 30° chamfer on the bottom is an easy and attractive edge treatment.

Whenever possible, profile the edges after assembly with a hand-held router and your choice of bearing bit.

MAKING AN EDGE APPEAR THINNER

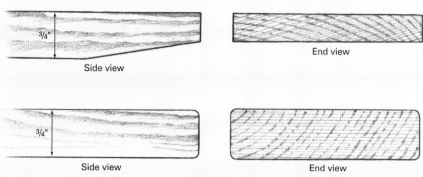

Side view

End view

Side view

End view

Figure 4

MAKING AN EDGE APPEAR THINNER

Rather than calling attention to an edge, you sometimes want to minimize it. This is common on tables, where a long chamfer on the underside makes the edge appear thinner and more elegant (see fig. 4).

Use a hand plane to cut the long, wide chamfer on straight edges (see p. 33). For curves, you'll need to use a spokeshave (see p. 78).

MORTISE & TENON JOINT

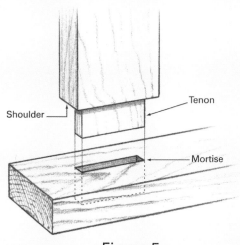

Shoulder

Tenon

Mortise

Figure 5

Mortise and tenon joints

The mortise and tenon joint is one of the strongest joints in woodworking. It's best for connecting things at right angles, such as aprons to table legs or door rails to door stiles. Sturdy, stable, and good looking, the joint has a number of variations to its credit.

The basic joint consists of a square or rectangular socket cut into one piece of wood—the mortise. The end of the mating piece is trimmed into a tenon with a close fit for the socket (see fig. 5). The shoulders on the tenon prevent the joint from racking into a parallelogram, and cover any of the mortise's imperfections.

Long the gold standard for strength and beauty, mortise and tenon joints can be time-consuming to construct. Careful layout and fitting is crucial—a sloppy mortise and tenon is simply not a strong joint.

THE OPEN MORTISE

Over the years, woodworkers have devised a variety of ways to make square holes. I typically use a plunge router or a drill press, but the easiest way to make mortises is to plan ahead and use the sandwich method for open mortises.

Create an open mortise by laminating two grooved pieces. In this case, two halves make a hole.

In this case, two halves make a hole. Rather than trying to cut a square hole in the middle of a board, glue up the necessary thickness from two narrower boards and cut half of the mortise out of each board before assembly. These cuts can be accomplished with a number of methods, using both hand and power tools.

1. Clamp the laminates in position and clearly mark the mortises on each piece. Careful layout is important here, and so is labeling the parts so you can keep track of mating pieces.

2. Using the drill press, bore 1/4" alignment holes near the ends of the piece. Later, you'll insert dowels into these holes to keep the mortises aligned during glue-up.

3. Remove the clamps and cut the half mortises using either a table saw, a band saw, or by hand.

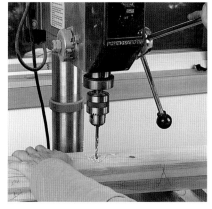

Alignment is crucial when creating open mortises. Clamp the pieces together in perfect alignment, and then bore two holes near the ends of the pieces. To return to this perfection during glue-up, slip wooden pins into the holes. Trim them flush after the glue dries.

Table saw method

A good dado blade capable of cutting a clean, flat bottom makes short work of open mortises. It's essentially the same process as cutting a dado (see p. 63).

If you don't have the right dado blade, you can use a regular blade. Use your miter gauge to make the shoulder cuts, and then make a number of passes between the shoulder and the ends. With the intermediate cuts, it's easy to pop out the waste with a sharp chisel. A router with a 1/2"-wide straight bit quickly removes final waste from the bottom while leaving it perfectly flat. Keep the router about 1/16" away from the sides and clean up the corners with a chisel.

After cutting the groove on the table saw, clean up the bottom of the cut with a router and a wide straight bit, keeping the bit away from the shoulders. Clean up the corners with a chisel.

Band saw method

You can also remove most of the wood with a band saw. It'll take a couple of cuts to get close to the line. Cut just shy of the bottom and use a router with a straight bit to get it just right.

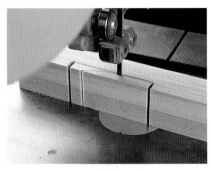

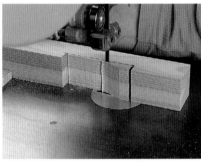

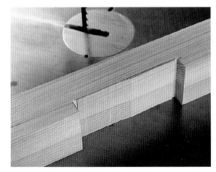

Cutting an open mortise with a band saw is a multistep process. Cut the shoulder lines first, then cut from near the left edge toward the right, angling down to the depth line gradually. Saw along the line right up to the right shoulder line. Flip the piece over and saw from roughly the middle back to the other shoulder, right on the line. You'll need to clean up the bottom of the open mortise with a shoulder plane or router.

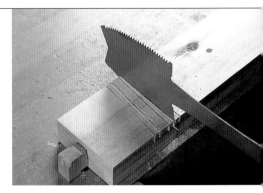

Lay out the shoulders and cut to the line with a Japanese azebiki saw. Cut a few lines between the shoulders, taking care not to cut too deep.

The waste pops out with a light blow to the chisel. (This is an angled mortise.)

Hand tool method

Cut the shoulders with a Japanese azebiki saw. Make a number of intermediate cuts between the shoulders and pop out the waste with a chisel. Clean up the bottom of the cut with a router and a straight bit, or a shoulder plane if there's room. Check that the mortise halves align before glue-up.

4. Once the mortises are cut, apply the glue, and sandwich the pieces together. Put the $1/4"$ dowels in each alignment hole to keep the pieces from sliding around.

5. Clamp up the pieces.

6. When the glue is dry, use a sharp chisel to flush-up any minor misalignment. You'll cut the tenon to fit, so this is not a problem.

STANDARD MORTISES

Drill Press Method

When half mortises are not possible or desirable, you can use a drill press and chisel to make a mortise. The drill press removes most of the waste, and then you use the chisel to square up the ends and clean up the sides.

1. Lay out the mortise with a wheel-type marking gauge. Mark the centerline and determine the depth of cut.

2. Use a drill bit with a diameter about $1/8"$ less than the width of the mortise.

3. Drill a series of holes along the centerline. If this is a through mortise, drill down from both sides of the piece to prevent tear-out.

4. Use a sharp chisel to finalize the mortise borders. Orient it with the bevel side to the mortise.

5. Chop out the waste to the line, using a mortising chisel.

Remove the waste on the drill press, using a bit that is smaller than the finished mortise.

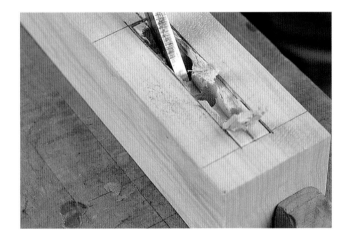

Use a mortise chisel to chop out the waste.

PLUNGE ROUTER MORTISING JIG, SIDE VIEW
Figure 6

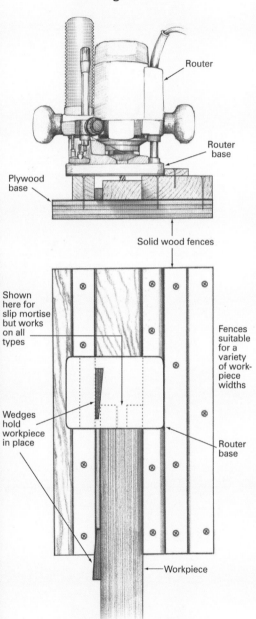

Router

Router base

Plywood base

Solid wood fences

Shown here for slip mortise but works on all types

Fences suitable for a variety of workpiece widths

Wedges hold workpiece in place

Router base

Workpiece

PLUNGE ROUTER MORTISING JIG, TOP VIEW
Figure 7

Plunge Router Method

A plunge router and the right jig make mortising almost easy. The jig defines the sides of the cut; gradually plunging the router more deeply handles the depth (see figs. 6 and 7). The jig takes a little time to make, but it's readily adaptable to other projects, so you'll use it again and again.

If you want to forego the jig-making for now, a portable workbench with a vise works well. Clamp the fence into the vise as shown in the photo below.

Because of the bit radius, the corners of a router-made mortise are always rounded; you'll need to square up the mortise corners with a chisel.

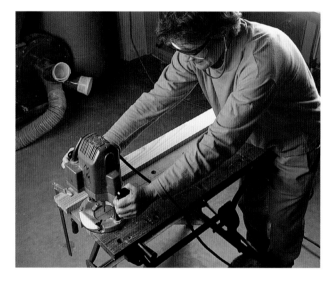

A portable workbench with a vise makes a good "jig" for plunge routing mortises. Hold the workpiece in the vise, and clamp a straight-edged board to the bench top as a fence.

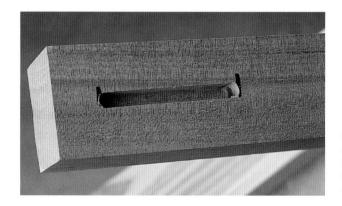

Router bits always leave rounded corners. Square them up with a chisel.

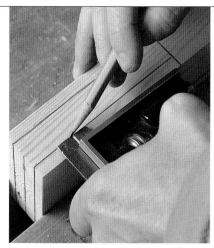

Lay out the tenon on all sides of the workpiece.

Saw the tenons on the band saw (use the fence), and clean up and fit the tenon with a block plane and a shoulder plane.

THE TENON

Always cut the tenon to fit the mortise. It should just slide in with a bit of friction. You need to leave room for the glue. The ideal fit requires no force to put together but is not loose.

1. Use a combination square to find the centerline on the tenon piece, and mark it.

2. Hold the tenon over the mortise, with its centerline aligned with the centerline of the mortise.

3. Mark the sides of the mortise on the tenon piece.

4. Using a sliding square, lay out all the sides of the tenon.

5. Set the height of your table saw blade to match the width of the tenon shoulders, and use a miter gauge and stop block to cut the

shoulders all around. If the shoulder is not long, you can use a dado blade to cut the shoulders and length in one step.

6. Move to the band saw to cut the tenon thickness. Use a fence to keep the sides parallel. Err on the side of too thick; you can easily trim the tenon with a block plane and/or a shoulder plane.

7. Check the fit. A good fit is snug but doesn't require excessive force to drive home. If the tenon is too tight, use a shoulder plane to take a thin shaving from each side of the tenon. If it's too loose, glue a shim of paper (business cards work well) or veneer to the tenon.

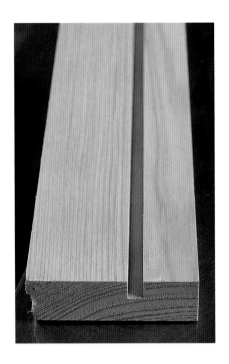

Dadoes, rabbets, and grooves

Though many people use the words interchangeably, properly speaking, a groove runs in the same direction as the grain, while a dado goes across the grain. You'll find dadoes and grooves in a variety of woodworking situations. They're often cut as part of a joint but can also be used for decorative purposes. Simple though they may seem, careful cutting and fitting is crucial for both appearance and structural integrity.

You can think of a rabbet as a groove right on an edge, or to put it another way, it's a shoulder. Rabbets are typically used at corner joints for simple boxes and drawers (see fig. 8). While not as strong as a dovetail, the joint is adequate when reinforced with dowels or screws. Rabbets are often cut around the back edge of a cabinet to hide the end grain on the back panel.

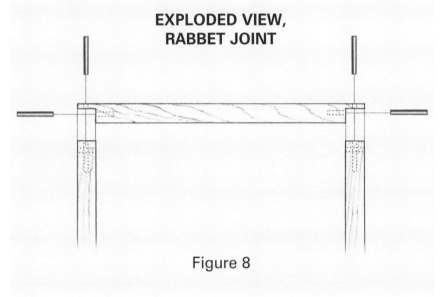

EXPLODED VIEW, RABBET JOINT

Figure 8

A groove runs the length of a workpiece; a dado runs across the width.

A rabbet is a shoulder along an edge. It can be cut lengthwise or across the end of a board.

A rabbeted corner joint is not as strong as a dovetail, but it's much easier to make. When reinforced with dowels or screws, it's adequate for light- to medium-duty applications.

FULL-LENGTH DADOES AND GROOVES

The table saw is the easiest and fastest method to cut dadoes and grooves, and is best used for cuts that go from one edge of the material to the other. If you need a stopped cut, use a router or router table instead.

When cutting grooves, set things up so the part you're removing is closest to the fence. If you're removing much material, you'll get better results with less effort and more safety if you take two or more passes to do it.

Always use a miter gauge when cutting dadoes, using the fence as a stop or point of reference. It's perfectly safe to use the fence as a stop when cutting in this manner, but never use the table saw fence as a stop when you're crosscutting all the way through a piece of material.

You can cut narrow grooves and dadoes with a standard table saw blade, but for anything wider, you'll want to use a dado blade.

To cut a full-length groove or dado on the router table, you use essentially the same method as you do on the table saw. Set up so the material to be cut is nearest the fence, and use hold downs.

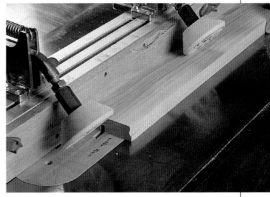

When cutting a groove, set up the table saw so the material you're removing is near the fence.

Although it doesn't show clearly in this photo, always use a miter gauge when cutting dadoes on the table saw.

A stopped groove doesn't extend all the way to the edge of the material.

STOPPED DADOES AND GROOVES

A cut that doesn't go full length and that starts or ends away from an edge is called a stopped cut. A quick way to make small stopped cuts (less than $1/4$" deep) is with the router table and fence.

1. Mark the workpiece with the location of the stopped cut.

2. Put the workpiece on the table and determine where the cut will begin and end. Make marks on the fence to indicate where to start and stop feeding the material.

3. Set the blade height to match the desired depth of cut.

4. With the blade turning, just lower the material onto the blade while holding it firmly against the fence.

5. Run it against the fence for the middle portion of the cut.

6. Lift the workpiece up and off the bit when reaching the marks that indicate the end of the cut.

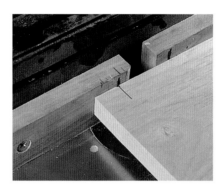

Start a stopped groove on the router table by lowering the work onto the bit.

Run the workpiece over the router bit, making the middle portion of the groove.

Lift the work up and off the bit at the stopped end of the groove.

It's best to make deeper stopped cuts with a plunge router guided by a fence clamped to the workpiece.

1. Lay out the dado (or groove), clearly marking the stopped ends.

2. With the router unplugged, locate the router bit directly over the dado, and make a mark at the outside of the base.

3. Use a square to extend this line the full length of the stopped cut. This is where you should clamp the fence.

4. Holding the router firmly against the fence, make the plunge, and rout until you get to the stopped end. Then raise the router.

5. Make the cut in two or more passes, lowering the bit about $1/8$" with each pass.

After laying out the stopped cut, position the plunge router with the bit centered over the dado.

Mark the outside edge of the router base to locate the fence.

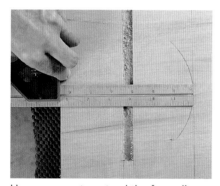

Use a square to extend the fence line parallel to the edge.

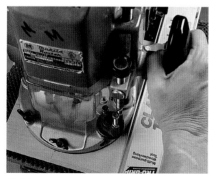

Hold the router against the fence, and plunge to start the cut. Raise the router when you reach the stopped end.

GROOVES AND SPLINES ON MITERS

A groove and spline joint is similar to a biscuit joint, except it spans the joint with one long solid wood spline rather than several small biscuits. It was a common joint before biscuits became popular. These days, I use it mostly for strengthening big mitered joints.

1. Tilt the table saw blade to 45° to cut a bevel along one edge of the workpiece. This is a table saw situation that produces a lot of heat and friction during the cut. You can make things a lot easier by making the cut in two passes.

2. Raise the blade only enough to cut about halfway through the material, and run the workpiece through the saw.

3. Raise the blade to cut all the way through and complete the angle on the second pass.

4. Install a 1/4" dado blade in the table saw. Set it at 90° and raise the blade to cut a 1/4"-deep groove.

5. Put the miter face down on the table and guide the material along the fence for the cut. This is a safe and easy operation. You may need to attach an auxiliary fence to the table saw to facilitate a smooth operation.

A rectangular hardwood spline slips in the grooves on the two angled faces of the splined miter. The spline spans the joint, significantly strengthening it.

Though the face is angled, cut the groove with the dado blade at 90°.

RABBETS

You can make rabbets in any number of ways, but the easiest is with a router and a rabbeting bit (see p. 25). Since the bit has a bearing, there's no need for a fence or any complicated setup.

For long rabbets in four-square milled wood, nothing beats the efficiency of the table saw and a dado blade. Always work so you're removing material from the side against the face—it's safer and gives you more control.

If you're cutting a narrow rabbet, attach a sacrificial wooden auxiliary fence to your existing table saw fence. Rather than trying to get the exact dado width, it's easier to just let the blade chew into the sacrificial fence.

DADOES, RABBETS, AND GROOVES BY HAND

Cutting dadoes and end rabbets by hand is amazingly simple and fun to do.

1. Lay out both sides of the cut with a marking gauge. If you're making dadoes and grooves, you'll lay out the two sides of the groove. If you're making a rabbet, mark the width on the face of the board and the depth on the side.

2. Use an azebiki saw, with a jig if desired, to cut on the lines.

3. If you're making a groove, remove the waste between the kerfs with an offset chisel. Check the depth frequently.

4. If you're making a rabbet, you can sometimes skip the sawing and just run your shoulder plane against the jig.

When cutting narrow rabbets on the table saw, save your fence by attaching a sacrificial wooden face.

Use an azebiki saw and a shop-made fence to guide it when cutting the shoulder line.

Remove the waste between the shoulders with an offset chisel. Check the depth often.

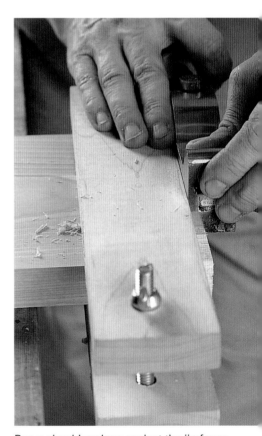

Run a shoulder plane against the jig fence and plane the rabbet. Alternatively, remove the bulk of the waste with the azebiki saw and clean up the cuts with the plane.

EXPLODED VIEW, HALF-LAP JOINT

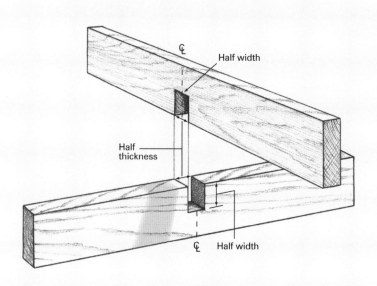

Half width

Half thickness

Half width

Figure 9

Half laps

When two pieces of wood form an X (or a +, or something similar), we join them at the intersection with a half-lap joint. As the name suggests, half of each part is removed at the overlap (see fig. 9). Though made of two pieces of wood, the resulting joint is the same thickness as a single piece.

1. Lay out and mark the intersection point (usually the centerline) on one edge of both pieces.

2. Determine the measurement of half the thickness of the pieces.

3. On each piece, measure half the thickness outward from the intersection point toward both ends. This establishes the shoulders.

4. Square this line downward from the edge.

5. Set a sliding square at half the width of the pieces and use it to mark the depth of cut on both pieces.

6. Set a dado blade in the table saw to equal the thickness of the material, or alternately make multiple cuts with a regular blade and remove the waste with a chisel.

7. Raise the saw blade to the depth of the cut mark. Use a miter gauge and make a few test cuts on scrap to get the setup perfect. The fit should be snug and the top and bottom surfaces flush.

8. Cut the shoulder lines.

9. I often reinforce half laps with a screw right in the middle of the joint.

Dovetails by hand

You don't need dozens of tools to cut successful dovetails, but you do need the right tools. Over the years, I've settled on these: A wheel-type marking gauge; a dovetail gauge (you could use a sliding bevel instead); a marking knife; a set of saddle squares that includes a dovetail saddle; sharp chisels; a mallet; and a general purpose ryoba saw. I don't recommend using saws with extremely fine teeth, even though they are sold as dovetail saws. The finer the teeth, the more strokes it takes to complete the cut. And more strokes means more opportunity to wander off the cut line. Since most of the saw cuts you make in dovetails are rip cuts, what you really want is a not-too-coarse rip blade, such as the blade on a ryoba saw.

VISUAL AIDS

The spatial relationships between the two boards that make up a dovetail joint can be confusing (see fig. 10). Don't worry if you don't get it—

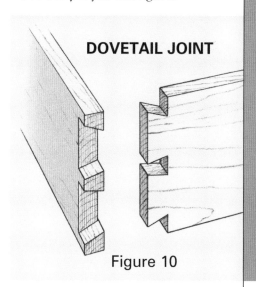

DOVETAIL JOINT

Figure 10

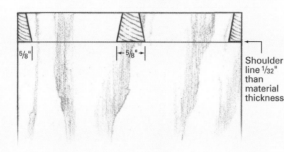

LAYOUT FOR VISUAL AID EXERCISE

5/8" 5/8"

Shoulder line 1/32" than material thickness

figure 11

Lay Out and Cut the Tails

Throughout any dovetail project, it is important to keep the parts oriented. Always mark what will be the inside of the box. Think of each tail/pin combination as a matched set, and keep these numbered.

1. Set your marking gauge for approximately 1/32" larger than the thickness of the boards. This will ensure that the completed joints stand proud of the surface. Later, you'll sand them flush.

2. Mark the shoulder lines all the way around both ends of all your pieces. From here on, you'll fit one set of pins and tails at a time.

most woodworkers struggle with the concept at first. It's helpful to make a full-size drawing on wood and boldly mark the material to be removed (see fig. 11 and the photos below). This gives you something to hold in your hands so you can get a better sense of what's going on in three dimensions. Keep this visual aid handy when you cut your first

joints—the most common dovetail mistake is to remove exactly the material you want to keep.

Follow steps 1 through 4 in the next section to lay out your sample board. When you cut the joint, you'll create the tails by removing the material around them. In this exercise, use a black marker and blot out the area to be removed.

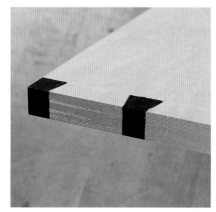

Use a black marker to color the negative space around the tails. This is what you'll remove when you cut the joint.

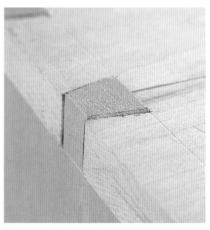

If the marking gauge is set for a little more than the thickness of the board, your dovetails will stand a little proud of the outside surface.

Mark the shoulder line on all four sides of the board. For the visual aid, you need to mark only one end of each board. When you're making dovetails, use the same setting to mark both ends of each board.

3. Draw the tails on the face of one board, using a sharp pencil and a dovetail gauge or a sliding bevel set at 12°.

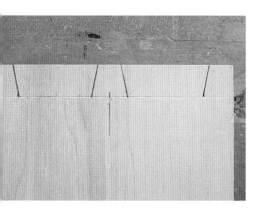

You can mark the tails with a dovetail gauge as shown, or use a sliding bevel set to 12°. Draw them from the end of the board down to the shoulder line.

4. To mark the saw cut, first cut a small kerf in the end grain of the board with a marking knife. Place the tip of your pencil in the kerf and slide the saddle square up to it. This positions the saddle square correctly for marking the end of the board.

Cut a small kerf at the top of the tail line with a marking knife.

Place your pencil in the kerf and slide a saddle square up to it. Draw the line across the end of the board.

5. Mark the waste with a bold X.

6. Hold the piece on the edge of a low workbench, with the tail end slightly overhanging.

7. Using the rip edge of a ryoba, begin cutting at the top corner, gradually working the saw across and down with each stroke. Strive to split the line—that is, cut away about half of its thickness, but do not obliterate the line. You need to leave the line as a point of reference. Later, you may need to trim down to the line with a chisel, but that usually does more harm than good. It's better to split the line with the saw rather than trying to refine it with a chisel.

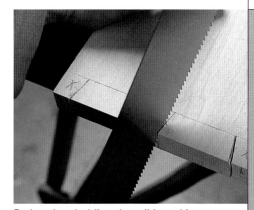

Rather than holding the tail board in a vise for sawing, let it hang over the edge of a low workbench. Cut the tails with the rip edge of a ryoba.

Chop the Waste

The tails are created by the negative space around them. You'll use a chisel and mallet to chop away the waste. A crisp shoulder line is critical to the final appearance of the joint, so take care. Make sure you're chopping against a solid surface.

1. Place the tip of the chisel in the shoulder line, with the bevel toward the end of the board. Angle the chisel backward slightly to undercut the line.

2. Chisel and mallet work in tandem; tap down from the top, then in from the end.

3. Don't try to remove too much material at once. Work down halfway through the material, then flip the piece over and work down from the other side. The undercutting will leave a slight hollow in the middle of the board.

4. Remove the waste at the outer corners by crosscutting with the ryoba.

Work slowly when chopping waste, down from the top and then in from the end. Cut halfway, then flip the board and work down from the other side.

To remove the waste, first place the tip of the chisel in the shoulder line. Use the mallet to make a light cut, then cut inward from the end, removing a small chip.

Remove the waste at the outermost corners by crosscutting, then ripping with the ryoba.

Mark the Pins

Use the completed tails as a template to mark the pin board.

1. Hold the pin board in a vise.

2. Position the tail board across the end of the pin board, taking care to align the edges.

3. Mark the pins from the tails.

4. Before you lose track of their positions, mark bold X's on the ends of the pin board, on the surface that was covered by the tails in step 3. This is the material that must be removed to accommodate the tails; it's the negative space that creates the pins. The X marks the waste.

5. Remove the pin board from the vise and use a saddle square to continue the marks around the face of the board. Mark both sides of the board.

Hold the pin board in a vise and position the tail board over it.

Mark the pins from the tails.

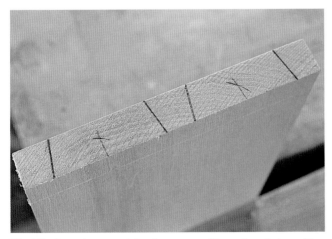

The X's show the material to be removed from the pin board to accommodate the tails.

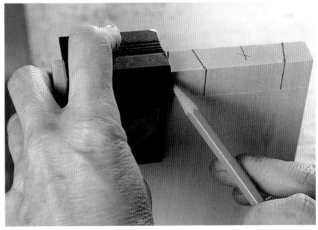

Use a saddle square to continue the pin lines down the face of the board. These lines are perpendicular to the end.

When cutting the pins, squat down to hold the saw at the correct angle.

Chop the pin waste down and then in, undercutting slightly to hold a crisp shoulder line.

Cut and Chop the Pins

Check the layout against your visual aid to make sure you've marked the waste correctly.

1. Split the line to cut the pins with the ryoba. Hold the piece on the edge of the bench and squat down to hold the saw at the correct angle.

2. Chop the pin waste using the same undercutting technique used for the tails.

Test the Fit

Dovetails go together in only one way. Don't worry if it takes you a while to figure out exactly how they mate. The joints should slide together with a little friction. You should have to push but not pound. Forcing the pins into the tails can split the board like a wedge. Ultimately, you'll glue the joints, so you need to leave a little room for the glue.

The joints will probably need a little fine-tuning. Remember that the pins were cut to match the tails—if you need to remove any material, it should be from the pin board, not the tail board.

Gluing Up a Dovetailed Box

You can't just clamp up the corners of a dovetailed box—because the joints stand a little proud of the surface, they can prevent the clamps from working. You'll need to make cauls with cutouts so the clamping pressure is properly applied.

1. Cut four cauls on the band saw from 3/4" scrap material.

2. Lay a sheet of plastic on the bench and lay out the parts in order. with the inside faces up. Sequence is important, so be sure to run through the assembly process once without glue. Orient the pieces so assembling the joint can be done with a light downward pressure.

3. Spread glue into the joints with a small acid brush.

4. Slide the pieces together, tapping lightly with a mallet to seat the joint.

5. When the box is assembled, position the cauls and clamps.

6. Before tightening the clamps fully, check for square.

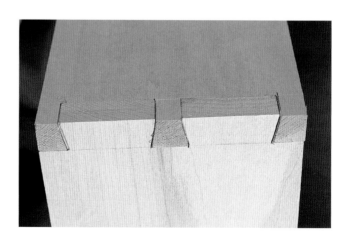

A finished set of dovetails goes together only one way. The joint should be tight enough to slip together with a light mallet tap. Forcing the joint closed can split the wood.

Use an acid brush to spread glue in the negative spaces of both the pin board and the tail board.

Slide the joints together, tapping with a mallet to seat the joint.

To clamp up a dovetail box, you'll need cauls that make way for the proud ends of the pins. Without them, you can't properly apply the clamping pressure to the tails.

Clamping a box requires two bar clamps and four cauls.

Check for square before tightening the clamps.

Final Smoothing

To get the protruding pins and tails flush with the surface of the box, use an orbital sander and 100-grit paper. If you have a stationary belt sander, use it instead.

Sand the protruding pins and tails flush. A stationary belt sander works best, but you can also use a random orbit sander and 100-grit paper.

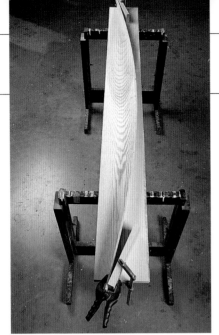

Clamp the batten at both ends of the curve, and spring a plywood batten up to the high point.

Dealing with curves

DRAWING CURVES

The hardest part of working with curves is drawing them. The first step is easy—lay out the beginning and end points, as well as one or two points in between. Then you bend a flexible batten through the points and draw the curve.

The key to this operation is a batten made of a material that's flexible enough to sweep through the curve yet stiff enough to prevent localized bumps or hollows. For smaller curves, a metal ruler fits the bill nicely. For longer curves, such as the top of the headboard or the stiles in the Freestanding Cabinet (see p. 150), use a 2"-wide strip of 1/4" plywood on edge. Hold the ends in place and bend the middle up to the intermediary points. This is at least a three-handed job, so if you're alone, use clamps or light weights to hold the batten in place while drawing.

TEMPLATE ROUTING CURVES

Whenever you need two or more parts with identical curves, the easiest and most accurate way to make them is to use a shop-made template with a router and a flush trim bearing bit. The template sits atop the workpiece, and the bearing runs against the template edge. Because the bearing diameter matches the bit diameter, the bit trims the workpiece beneath exactly flush with the template.

Use 1/2" or 3/4" plywood for your templates, and take special care to lay out and cut smooth curves. The flush trim bit cuts exact copies of the pattern, flaws and all. My preferred flush trim bit uses a shank mounted bearing on a 1/2" shank, with a 1/2" cutter diameter and a 2" cutting length.

1. Start by laying out your curve on the template material.

2. Cut the curve on the band saw, leaving the line as a reference point. Refine the template, but trim down to the line with files, a spokeshave, and/or any helpful sanding devices at your disposal.

3. Use the template to draw the outline of the curve on each workpiece.

4. Cut away most of the waste with the band saw or jig saw. There's no need to cut any closer to the line than about 1/8"; the router will take care of the rest.

As the bearing runs along the template, the bit reproduces the curve in the wood below.

Keep the bearing against the template, routing from left to right.

5. Use clamps, hot-melt glue, or double-sided carpet tape to secure the template to the workpiece.

6. Secure the workpiece/template to your bench and adjust the bit height so the bearing is against the template. Rout from left to right.

Circle inlays with a plunge router

Inlay is an easy way to embellish furniture. Though wood is the most common inlay material, you can use almost anything—stones, glass, metal, plastic, even jewels.

To do the inlay as described here, you need a router inlay kit consisting of a guide collar, a bushing that fits over the guide collar, and a 1/8" spiral down-cut carbide bit. There's a precise relationship between these pieces that makes it easy to use the same template to cut the recess for the inlay and the inlay itself without a lot of math. All you do is make the template larger than the finished inlay by a set amount, and cut the recess with the bushing in place. Remove the bushing and use the same setup to cut perfectly fitting inlay.

CREATE THE TEMPLATE

1. Draw a large + on the 1/4" plywood template. The center point marks the center of the circle, and you'll need those lines to position the template on the workpiece. Make sure your template is large enough so the clamps that hold it down are well out of the way when routing.

2. The circle in the template must be 3/8" larger than the inlay circle. This is to accommodate the guide collar and the bushing. When positioned against the oversize template, they'll cut in the correct location.

3. Set the cutting arm on a circle cutter to the template diameter and cut the circle with the drill press.

CUT THE RECESS

1. Clamp the template on the workpiece and set up the inlay kit in the router.

2. The guide collar and bushing run against the template, positioning the router before plunging. You'll have to run some tests on scrap to get the bit set at the right cutting depth (slightly less than 1/8").

3. Plunge the router and run it around inside the template, then move to the middle of the template and remove all the material in the recess.

A router inlay kit consists of a carbide spiral bit, a guide collar that screws into the router base plate, and a special bushing that fits over the guide collar. This setup lets you use the same template to cut both the recess and the inlay.

Cut the circle into the template with an adjustable circle cutter chucked in the drill press. Note the marked lines that extend beyond the circle. These help position the template on the work.

Rout the recess with the bushing in place.

Remove the bearing to cut the inlay. It will perfectly fit the recess.

CREATE THE INLAY

1. Resaw the inlay material to about 1/8" thick (see p. 45).

2. Stick the template to the inlay material with double-sided tape. Put the band-sawn side up, and be sure some tape is on the part you'll cut out so the inlay can't shift at the end of the cut.

3. Remove the bushing from the guide collar.

4. For this final cut, it's very important to keep the guide collar firmly against the template. Stick to the perimeter and don't wander into the middle. When the cut is complete, don't raise the bit. Just turn off the router and remain motionless until it stops.

5. The result should be a perfect circle 3/8" smaller in diameter than the template, but exactly the rise of the recess.

INSTALL THE INLAY

1. Glue the inlay to the recess, with the smooth side down. Use hand pressure, clamps, or a vise, if necessary.

2. Sand the top surface smooth.

Installing butt hinges

Learning how to deal with hinges is an integral part of woodworking. Over the years, I've used many types of hinges, but for fine cabinetry, my favorite is the old-fashioned butt hinge. Typically, butt hinges are used for inset door applications, where the door hangs within the frame, as contrasted to the overlay door frames commonly used on kitchen cabinets.

When it comes to hardware, especially hinges, adhere to one important rule: Don't buy cheap products! Poor-quality hinges are more difficult to install because the manufacturing isn't precise or consistent, and in the long run, they simply don't hold up under use. Don't expect to find furniture-quality butt hinges in home centers, and be wary of woodworking supply catalogs that sell, but don't specialize in, hardware.

Butt hinges are sized according to their fully opened width and length. The projects in this book use 1 3/8" x 2 1/2" brass hinges. These come in bright brass or with an antiqued patina, which I prefer. You have a choice of loose pins or fixed. Loose pins slip out of the hinge barrel, allowing the two halves to separate, which makes them much easier to install.

Whether used on a jewelry box or a heavy front door, a properly installed butt hinge is mortised into the door and the frame, flush with the surrounding surfaces. Both small and large mortises require the use of a few hand tools and a router or laminate trimmer and a 1/8" bit. Careful layout and correct orientation of the hinge to both frame and door are necessary for successful results.

Hold the hinge in place and trace its outline on the workpiece.

Bore the hinge screw holes with a self-centering bit.

Mark the edges of the mortise with a knife. The tip of the chisel will slip into the kerf, making it easy to cut clean edges.

1. Locate the hinges. Hold each hinge in place and carefully mark its perimeter.

2. With a knife and sliding square, carefully mark the edges of the mortise.

3. Remove the waste with a router or laminate trimmer, staying away from the lines you have marked. Fine-tune the shoulders with a sharp $1/2''$ chisel. Work incrementally, taking out only small pieces at a time. Use a light touch—chisels can easily cause wood to split. Check the mortise for fit often, and sneak up on it.

4. Once the mortise is cut, position the hinge in the mortise and use the proper diameter self-centering bit to bore the screw holes.

5. Fasten the hinges after the final finish is applied to the project. Use a small amount of paste wax to lubricate the screws and the pins.

With a bit of wax on their tips, screws are easier to drive. While you're at it, put a little wax on the hinge pins to keep them swinging freely.

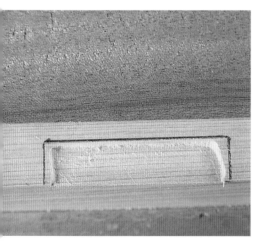

Remove the waste with a router or laminate trimmer, keeping well away from the shoulders. Trim back to the line with a sharp chisel.

Low relief
with a spokeshave

Low relief may sound like a gastric remedy—something we might need by chapter's end. Humor aside (but never far away), let me tell you how I spell relief: s-p-o-k-e s-h-a-v-e.

I first learned about this amazing (and inexpensive) tool early on in my career, at a chair-making class. Ironically, I have made very few chairs since then, but the spokeshave has become a favorite tool of mine. I often use it for light shaping tasks and creating subtle contours.

The spokeshave is a free-form tool guided by eye, hand, and intuition. Learning to use it is a process of unfolding, deciding where to begin and end each cut as things take shape. The workpiece must be firmly held by clamps or a vise, and the blade must be very sharp and adjusted for light cuts. Set correctly, the blade should sweep over the material as it cuts—not grab.

The spokeshave can be used by pulling or pushing. For working across the grain, you'll have more control when you push. Working long grain usually goes better when pulling, but it can go either way.

When using the spokeshave, push down on your index fingers, applying pressure to the front area just over the blade. This gives you a good sense of contact with the material so you can make small adjustments in the pressure and angle to make clean shavings.

Creating the low-relief contour requires only a couple of marks to show how far from the end the relief extends, and how deep to cut. There's no need to draw the curves.

Work from both edges toward the center of the relief to avoid tearing out an edge. Work your way down to the lines, using your hands and eyes to blend the cuts. Light sanding is acceptable to finish, but I don't fuss much over the tool marks—they're part of the character.

Hold the spokeshave so you can push down with your index fingers and feel the cut.

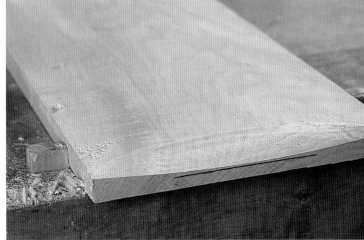

Irregular tool marks are part of the character of handmade furniture.

Surface prep for finishing

A fine smooth finish adds beauty and value to a piece, but that shining surface can also magnify its flaws. Undulating surfaces, scratch marks, and dust can make an otherwise fine piece of work look less than ordinary. It's been said that 90 percent of achieving a fine finish is in the surface prep. If you prepare the surface properly, even a thick coat of paint looks good.

Good surface prep involves a lot of steps, and if you want the best results, you must complete each one in order. It's not a difficult process, but it is time-consuming and often rather dull. Your goal is to create surfaces that are flat (or sweetly curved), smooth, and clean.

SAND FOR FLATNESS

1. Remove machine marks and other high spots, using 100-grit sandpaper. If hand sanding, use a block or pad to create a truly flat sanding surface and sand with the grain.

2. If you're using a random orbital sander, keep the machine moving randomly over the surface. Staying in one place too long creates a low spot.

3. Take care not to round the edges.

4. Be careful when sanding end grain. It scratches very easily, and those scratches are hard to see. But once the finish goes on, they'll be all too visible.

STEP THROUGH THE GRITS FOR SMOOTHNESS

Smoothing any surface is a matter of replacing coarse scratches with finer ones. This is most easily done by increasing the grit in small steps. It doesn't take long for 150-grit sandpaper to remove enough wood to get below the depth of 120-grit scratches. It takes considerably longer to sand away 120-grit marks with 220-grit paper.

1. Clean the surface with a brush, compressed air, or a vacuum cleaner to remove dust and grit.

2. Sand with 120-grit paper until the surface is smooth. Typically, this takes about half the time it took to flatten. Take care with the edges.

3. Clean the surface again. Leaving any 120-grit dust or abrasive will nullify the effects of finer grit.

4. Sand with 150-grit paper, and clean the surface. Repeat with 180 and then 220 grit.

5. Clean the surface with a vacuum or compressed air.

RAISE THE GRAIN

These next steps are very important, albeit a little strange. If you omit them before applying finish, the wood soaks up the first coat and raises the grain. It ends up needlessly rough, requiring you to sand it smooth, thus removing most of the finish you just applied. Raise the grain before applying any finish and save time.

1. Take a fairly damp cloth and wipe down the entire surface.

2. Allow it to dry (this usually takes only a few minutes).

3. Sand with 220-grit paper.

4. Wipe down the surface once more, allow it to dry, and sand it again with 220-grit.

5. If you wish to do some final sanding by hand, use 400-grit black wet/dry paper to leave a nice surface.

FINAL CLEANING

Thoroughly vacuum the piece to remove all dust. While you're at it, vacuum the bench top and as much of the surrounding area as you care to clean. If the area is dusty, your every movement during finishing can churn up dust. Dust in the air can settle on the finish, making it appear as rough as if it hadn't been cleaned.

LOW BENCH

Hone your skills on a bench that makes woodworking easier.

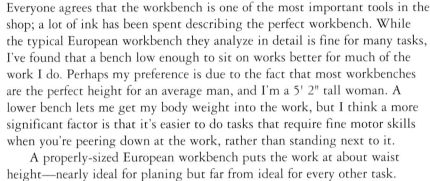

Everyone agrees that the workbench is one of the most important tools in the shop; a lot of ink has been spent describing the perfect workbench. While the typical European workbench they analyze in detail is fine for many tasks, I've found that a bench low enough to sit on works better for much of the work I do. Perhaps my preference is due to the fact that most workbenches are the perfect height for an average man, and I'm a 5' 2" tall woman. A lower bench lets me get my body weight into the work, but I think a more significant factor is that it's easier to do tasks that require fine motor skills when you're peering down at the work, rather than standing next to it.

A properly-sized European workbench puts the work at about waist height—nearly ideal for planing but far from ideal for every other task. Sawing requires some kind of vise or clamping arrangement to hold your work, and getting that organized for every cut takes time and energy. A bench that's low enough to sit upon allows you to use your body weight for some of the holding operations. Rather than downing tools to crank the vise or wield the clamps, just shift your foot, knee, or butt.

Sitting on the workpiece is the perfect position for chopping dovetails. Not only can you see better, but your hand/arm/shoulder position is ideal for straight, clean mallet blows. When you're assembling furniture, you'll still be over your work and not trying to operate tools at eye level.

This low workbench is different from most bench projects out there. It doesn't try to be the ideal traditional bench scaled down for women. It's something completely different. It may work better for women simply because the average woman isn't tall enough to work comfortably on a typical bench, but every woodworker can benefit from the biomechanical advantages of a seat-height bench.

Using two sets of rails rather than a solid top, this bench gives you more options for holding your work. You can sit, kneel, step, or climb all over it as needed. If you do use clamps, you can crank them down just about anywhere. The rails attach to the posts with big removable pins, which allows you to pivot the top to make some operations easier.

This is not a fancy workbench to fuss over and perfect; it's meant to be built quickly and then used. I suggest you build it from construction-grade softwood lumber. Find some good, dry spruce 2 x 4s. They're easy to machine and cut with hand tools. Working with inexpensive softwood will

Instead of a solid top, this bench uses two sets of rails that pivot on 3/4" dowels. The open arrangement offers a range of convenient clamping options.

A workbench low enough to sit on is preferable to a traditional bench for many hand-tool operations. Built of inexpensive softwood, this bench will hone your skills and add a very useful tool to your shop.

help you relax into this first project without worrying about mistakes. If something goes wrong, just grab another 2 x 4 and start over.

Because most of the components in this project are created by laminating together two thinner boards, it's important to do your milling in the proper sequence. Start by milling the pieces to the dimensions in the Materials chart, which will yield laminations significantly larger than the finished dimensions of the parts. After glue-up, mill them down to the finished dimensions given in the Comments column.

Cut List & Supplies

NUMBER OF PARTS	DESCRIPTION	DIMENSIONS IN INCHES			COMMENTS
		Thickness	Width	Length	
No. 2 construction-grade spruce					
4	Feet	$1^{3/8}$	$3^{3/8}$	25	*Yields two feet—two laminates per foot. Run though jointer and planer after lamination to yield 2³/4" x 3¹/4", then cut to final length of 24¹/2"*
8	Posts	$1^{3/8}$	$2^{3/4}$	23	*Yields four posts—two laminates per post. Joint and plane 2¹/2" x 2¹/2". Then cut to final length of 22"*
4	Trestles	$1^{3/8}$	$3^{3/8}$	58	*Yields two trestles—two laminates per trestle. Joint and plane to yield 2¹/2" x 3¹/4".*
4	Top rails	$1^{1/4}$	$5^{3/8}$	60	
2	End rails	$1^{1/4}$	$2^{1/2}$	12	
6	Rail blocks	$1^{1/4}$	$2^{1/2}$	36	*Cut six blocks, each about 5¹/4" long.*
Other materials & supplies					
1	Wedge tenon stock (use a contrasting wood, such as walnut)	$3/8$	$1^{1/2}$	30	*Cut five wedges from this, each 6" long. This makes one extra, just in case.*
1	3/4" dowel rod (36" long)				*Cut four pivot pins, each about 9" long.*
	2" drywall screws				

How to Build the Low Bench

Feet first

All the mortises in this project are what I call open mortises. In this case, two halves make a hole, and it saves a lot of trouble. Rather than chopping out big holes in the thick feet, we simply laminate the feet from two thinner boards, first cutting half the mortise in each.

Mortise & tenon the posts; glue on the feet

Laminate the posts similarly to make the open mortises to accept the trestles. Once the posts are glued up, cut tenons in the bottoms to fit the mortises in the feet. Use the band saw or table saw, and trim the tenons to final fit with a hand plane. Glue the posts into the feet.

Mortise & tenon the trestles

The ends of the trestle are held in place with wedges lightly pounded into wedge-shaped mortises. Though they sound difficult, wedge tenons are easily laminated using the open mortise technique. Lay out the mortises and glue up the trestles. Clean up the trestles and then cut tenons in each end to match the mortises in the posts. Cut the wedges and trim the joints to fit. Cut and install the end rails.

Mount the top rails & posts

Assemble the two top rails and mount them to the posts. Kit out your bench with various accessories to make it even more useful. (See Using Your Bench on p. 89.)

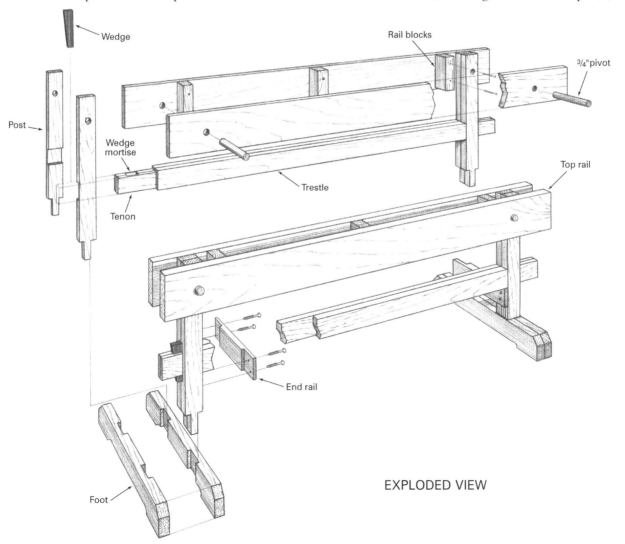

EXPLODED VIEW

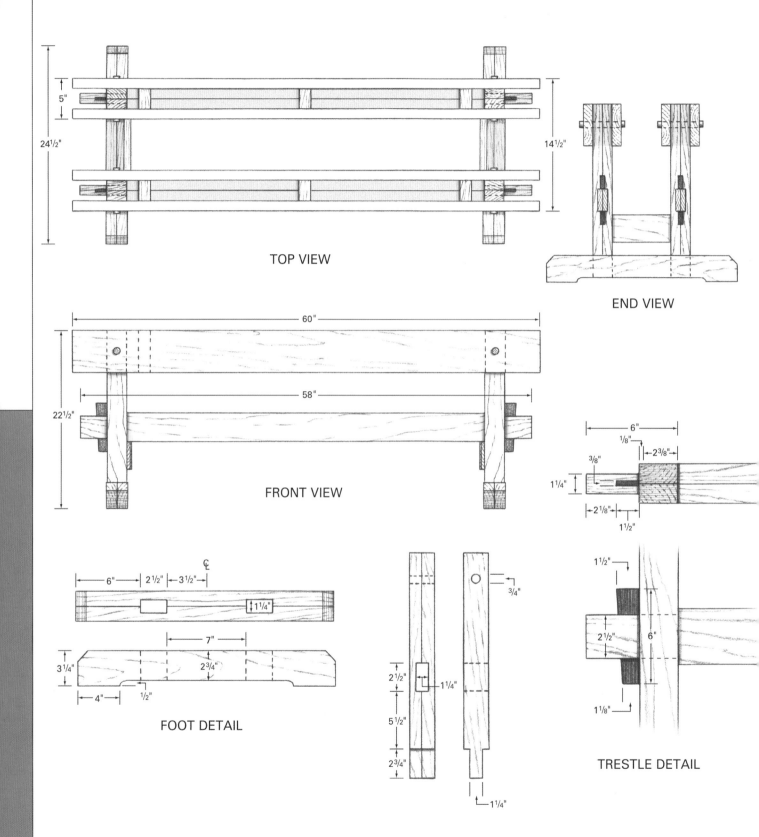

TOP VIEW

END VIEW

FRONT VIEW

FOOT DETAIL

POST DETAIL

TRESTLE DETAIL

Building the Low Bench

Two halves make a hole. Make mortises by removing material from the insides of the laminates and then gluing them together to form the square mortises.

Feet first

To create the mortises that lock the posts in the feet, we'll use the sandwich method to create open mortises. The big issue here is alignment. If the halves don't match during the glue-up, you'll have a fair bit of chisel work to tidy things up.

1. Lay out the mortises on the laminates and cut them as described on page 57. Work outward from the centerline.

2. Glue up and clamp the foot laminates. Remove the excess glue with a scraper after the glue dries.

3. Pass one edge of each foot over the jointer a couple of times until the surface is smooth. Then mill the feet four-square (see p. 43), removing the minimum amount of material.

4. Measure outward from the mortises to establish the ends, and cut to final length.

5. Use a band saw to cut the curve at the bottom of the feet. The curve not only gives the feet a nicer appearance but also allows them to sit better on uneven floors. Clean up and smooth the cut with a file and coarse sandpaper.

6. Lighten up the look of the feet and get rid of the tripping hazard by sawing the top corner off each end. Make the cuts at a 45° angle with a miter saw or by hand with a Japanese saw.

7. Chamfer the edges all around with a block plane (see p. 55).

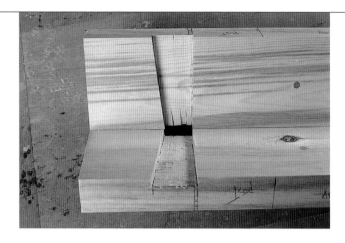

Wedge tenons sound difficult to make, but they're not if you use the two-halves-make-a-hole method.

Mortise and tenon the posts; glue on the feet

1. Lay out the mortises (see the Post Detail) and laminate the posts, using the same method used on the feet.

2. After the glue is dry, clean off the excess and run the posts over the jointer. Mill four-square and cut to final dimensions.

3. It's easy to cut the tenons on the wrong end or side of a board, so check and label the parts with all the information you'll need to avoid confusion.

4. Rather than measure the tenons, lay them out from the mortises and cut them as described on page 57. Refer to the Post Detail for the length.

5. Check the fit.

6. Use the drill press to bore a 3/4"-diameter hole near the top of each post for the pins that secure the rails to the posts.

7. Use a block plane to chamfer all the edges except for the edges of the tenons.

GLUE THE POSTS TO THE FEET

With our feet back on the ground, it's time to mesh the negative with the positive.

8. Apply glue to one mortise and tenon at a time, then drive them together with a mallet.

9. If the glue makes for a tighter fit, don't pound away at it. Use a bar clamp to pull the joint together. If the fit is good and the tenon snug and firmly seated, it's not necessary to keep the joint clamped while the glue dries.

Mortise and tenon the trestles

The trestles tie the two foot/post assemblies together. A main tenon on each end goes through the post and is locked in place by a wedge pounded into a smaller mortise cut in the tenon. This joint is pleasing to look at and incredibly strong. It's also fun to make.

CUT THE OPEN WEDGE MORTISES

The small mortises in the ends of the trestles are made exactly the same way you made the previous open mortises, except that they're not parallel sided.

1. Clamp the two boards that make up each trestle and lay out the main tenon shoulders (see the Trestle Detail) and the location of the mortise for the wedged tenon. Note that the inner 1/8" of the wedge mortise extends with the post. This ensures that the wedge draws the trestle tight.

2. Remove the boards from the clamps and lay both parts on the bench with the insides facing up.

3. To lay out the sides of the angled mortises, use a protractor to draw a line 97° to the edge of a piece of scrap wood. Set a bevel gauge against the edge and line it up with the line, locking it in position. Use the bevel gauge to draw the 97° mortise sides on the workpieces.

4. Set a combination square to half the width of the mortise (3/16") and mark the sides of the mortise on the edges of each board.

5. Cut the shoulders as described on page 61.

6. Glue up the trestles. When the glue is dry, remove the clamps, clean off the glue, and do the final dimensioning.

Marking out tenons by measurement rarely results in a tight joint. Mark the centerlines and use the mortise to lay out a perfect-fitting tenon.

TENON THE TRESTLES

7. Let the mortises in the posts tell you how big to make the tenons. Mark them as you did the post tenons, and complete the layout (see the Trestle Detail).

8. Cut the tenons.

9. Test fit each trestle tenon to its post mortise. Trim if necessary. Clean any glue beads out of angled mortises and flush any misaligned edges.

10. Chamfer all the edges with a block plane.

ASSEMBLE THE BASE

11. Begin by inserting both trestles into mortises of one foot/post assembly.

12. Work the other post mortises onto the trestles, firmly seating all the tenon shoulders. Once the parts are together, the piece takes form. A sense of accomplishment and joy elevates my mood, and I feel like singing. That's when I know woodworking is part of my being!

CUT AND FIT THE WEDGES

13. Mill the wedge material to final thickness. The angled mortises should be about $3/8$" wide, and the stock you've milled for the wedges is more like $1/2$" thick. By now you know there's no point in measuring; just run the walnut through the planer until it fits. Use a caliper to determine the final thickness, or just take light cuts and keep trying to fit the corner of your stock into the mortise.

14. Draw the wedges on the stock. First, use a protractor to draw a line 97° to a point on the edge of a piece of scrap. Then set your bevel gauge against the edge and lock it along the line. Use the bevel gauge thus set to draw the correct angle on the wedges.

15. Cut the wedges on the band saw and smooth them up with a block plane. See p. 177 for a useful jig.

16. Fit a wedge into each mortise and drive it home with a mallet. Amazingly, these small wedges create enough force to pull the trestles up tight to the posts and make for a sturdy, wobble-free base.

ADD THE END RAILS

For added stability, end rails bridge the space between the posts. Rather than troubling with mortise and tenon joinery, the end rails are simply screwed to the posts. For a more elegant appearance, remove about half the thickness of the material where it overlaps the posts. I call this rabbeting the end of each piece, but you might also call it half tenon, or even half of an open mortise.

17. Cut the end rails to length, and cut the rabbets in each end, using a band saw, table saw, router, or hand saw.

18. Chamfer all the edges, including the ends.

19. Bore two $1/8$" pilot holes for the screws in both ends of each end rail.

20. Position the end rails on the insides of the posts, right below the trestles. Clamp them in place and fasten with 2" drywall screws.

Mount the top rails & posts

The rails attach to the posts with 3/4" dowels, providing pivot points. You've already bored the holes in the posts on the drill press; also use the drill press to bore the same size holes in the rails to assure that these holes are also perpendicular.

1. Cut the rails to length and clamp each pair together with the ends and edges flush.

2. Mark the locations of the holes and bore them on the drill press.

3. Label the pieces and remove the clamps.

4. Chamfer the edges of each rail with a block plane, including the ends.

5. Cut the dowels to length and chamfer both ends. A stationary belt sander works well for this, or you can simply sand them by hand.

6. Apply a little paste wax to a dowel, and insert it into the post. Use a mallet if necessary. Mount the inside rail first, then the outer one.

7. Sandwich the rail blocks between the rails and attach them with 2" drywall screws. You'll have to use the pivot function of the rails to get enough room to drive the screws on the inside rails.

The wedged tenons lock the trestles in place for a sturdy wobble-free base. Removable pins in the fronts of the rail increase your holding and clamping options.

Here are a few accessories that can make your low bench more useful from the get-go. Later, as you acquire more skills (and learn more about hand-tool techniques), you'll start to customize your bench to better meet your needs. Remember, woodworking is all about innovation!

MAKE YOURSELF A SEAT

Use 3/4" plywood to fashion a seat or a small work surface. To keep it from moving, cut some scrap to fit closely between the rails and screw them to the underside of the plywood.

A piece of 3/4" plywood makes an easily replaceable seat and/or cutting surface that's ideal for chopping dovetails.

PIVOT SUPPORT BLOCKS

To pivot a rail, remove one end pin and lift the rail to the desired angle. Slip a block of wood between the rail and the trestle. The weight of the rail is usually adequate to hold it in place, though clamping may be in order on occasion.

An appropriate length block set atop the trestle rail supports the rail when it's pivoted.

HAND PLANING

Hand planing is hard work and an activity that can often lead to frustration, for a number of reasons. Aside from tools that aren't tuned or sharpened properly, a workbench that is too high doesn't maximize upper body strength. You want the work to be low enough for you to push down on the plane easily, but not so low that you stoop.

You'll probably want to clamp your workpiece to the bench when planing a long piece. I often pivot the rail slightly to plane with greater ease.

Planing works best when the work is low enough to lean into it without stooping. You can clamp just about anywhere on the low bench, which makes it easy to position any workpiece at the optimal height.

USING HANDSAWS

Ripping with a handsaw is not something you can easily do on a European bench. It's easy on this one. Just lay the piece so you'll be sawing between the rails and climb onto the bench. The work is supported on both sides of the cut, and it won't move. In some cases, it's easier to use clamps and pivot the rail. Crosscut off the end of bench, holding the work with your knee or clamps.

Crosscut off the end of the bench, holding the work down with a knee or some clamps.

The low bench is ideal for ripping. Support the work with the kerf positioned between rails, and do whatever you need to do to hold it in place.

TABLE FOR TWO

Engaging curves and profiles create romance.

What could be more romantic than tea and biscuits at a one-of-a-kind table for two? With its elegant tapered legs and gracefully curved top, this table looks great in any room. The base is simple to build—four legs attached to two rails that cross in the center with half-lap joints.

On this table, the base is oriented on the diagonals, making for an interesting play of shadows on the profiles of the tapered legs. But you could also orient the base more conventionally along the axis. And this design, with its four legs and two half-lapped rails, readily adapts to a wide variety of sizes and types of tables; I've used it to build a dining table for six, a round table, a desk, and an oval coffee table with a lower shelf. For larger tables, just increase the leg and rail dimensions.

The most difficult part of building any table is the top. In most cases, you'll need to glue up a wide panel from several narrow boards, and building that top panel so it's flat requires some care. You must start out with boards that are milled four-square. If the edges aren't flat and square, you'll never get a tight joint. Clamping technique is important. If the clamps put any twisting pressure on the boards, they'll cause the top to bow up and rise up off the bars. If your boards are twisted, the joints won't be flush even if clamped properly. If something goes wrong and your joints don't come out right, run the top through the table saw, making a couple of rip cuts to remove the offending joint. Your top will get narrower, but you can try again.

A table for two with a subtly curved top and boldly profiled tapered legs. The top is hickory, the base walnut. This table design scales up or down and works just as well for side tables, dining tables, and desks.

Cut List & Supplies

NUMBER OF PARTS	DESCRIPTION	DIMENSIONS IN INCHES			COMMENTS
		Thickness	Width	Length	
Solid wood (hickory or another wood similar in hue)					
5	Top	$7/8$	$5 1/2$	40	*Edge-glue boards into wide panel and then cut to final length and width— 27 1/4" w x 36" l*
Solid wood (walnut)					
4	Legs	$1 3/4$	$2 1/2$	$28 1/4$	*Cut taper and profile on band saw*
2	Rails	$1 1/2$	$2 3/4$	$31 1/4$	
Other materials & supplies					
4	$3/8$" washers				*For attaching top*
4	$3/16$" washers				*For attaching top*
	2" drywall screws				*For attaching top*
	Nylon gliders (optional)				*Protects floor from scratching and makes table easy to slide.*

How to Build the Table for Two

Top first

Build the top to get the most out of your best-looking wood, and then build the base to fit the top. Choose the grain pattern for the top, then glue up the large panel. Cut it to width, and then cut the curves on the ends. Plane a long chamfer on the bottom edge to make it appear thinner. Sand smooth and brush on a couple of coats of durable finish.

Cut & shape the legs

Mortise the legs first, while the edges are square and they're easy to clamp and hold. Then you can taper the legs and cut the beveled profiles on the outside edges.

Cut the rail joinery

Fit the rail tenons to the leg mortises, and then cut the half laps in the middle of each rail. Bore the holes for attaching the top, and chamfer all the edges before assembly.

Assemble the base & attach the top

It's much easier to sand and finish the legs and rails before they're assembled onto the base. Sand them smooth and put on a couple of coats of finish (but not on the places that will be glued). Glue the legs to the rails, and when the glue is dry, join the laps and attach the top.

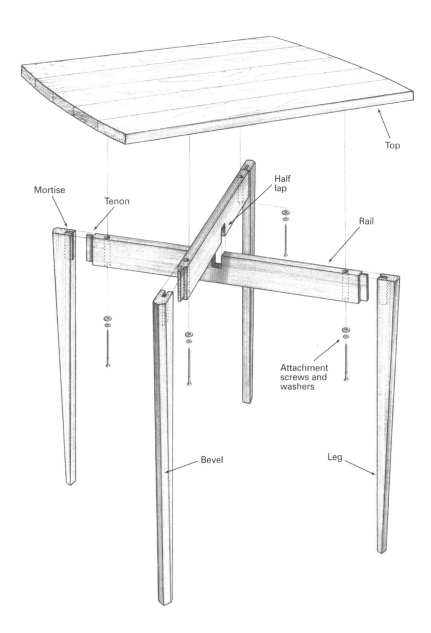

EXPLODED VIEW

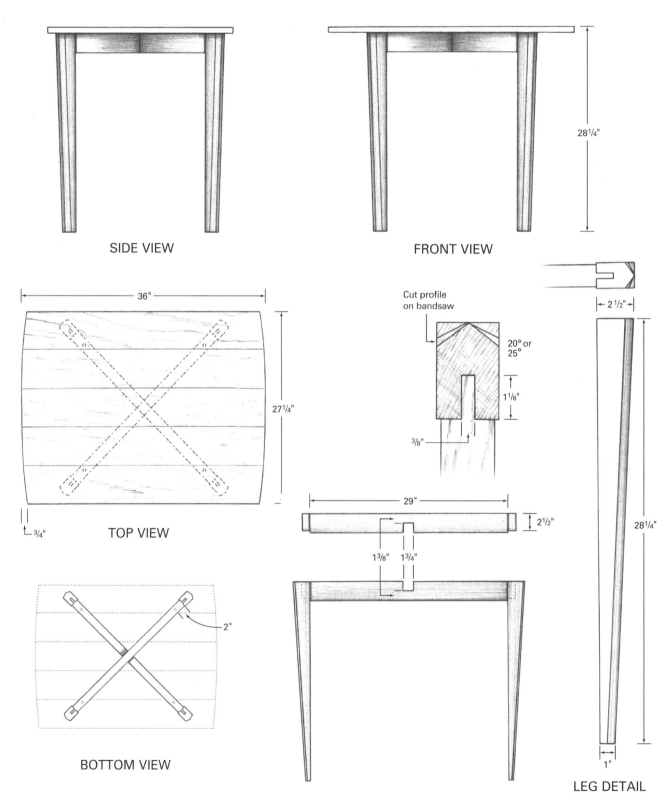

SIDE VIEW

FRONT VIEW

28¹⁄₄"

36"

27¹⁄₄"

³⁄₄"

TOP VIEW

BOTTOM VIEW

2"

Cut profile
on bandsaw

20° or
25°

1¹⁄₈"

³⁄₈"

2¹⁄₂"

29"

2¹⁄₂"

1³⁄₈"   1³⁄₄"

28¹⁄₄"

1"

LEG DETAIL

LEG/RAIL SUBASSEMBLY DETAIL

Building the Table for Two

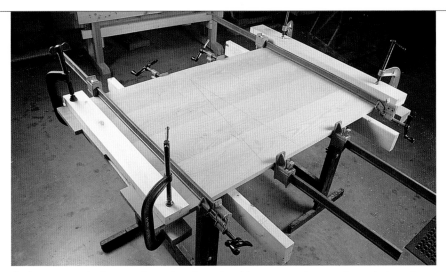

Gluing up a truly flat panel requires boards with square edges and good clamping technique. Pipe clamps hold the panels together, while C-clamps and cauls keep the ends flat.

Top first

LAY OUT THE TOP

1. Go through your boards and pick the best ones for the top. Select boards with similar grain pattern and color.

2. Cut the boards to rough length—about 4" longer than the final length.

3. Mill the boards four-square (see p. 43), to their final width and thickness.

4. Lay the boards out on sawhorses or on the bench, and arrange them for the best match of grain and color at the joints.

5. Draw orientation marks so you can reassemble them correctly.

GLUE UP THE TOP

Glue up and clamp the top as described on page 47, but don't try to glue the entire top at once. The wider the panel, the more difficult it is to achieve flatness. Glue it up in stages.

6. Glue up two boards and clamp them with care so they're flat.

7. Glue up and clamp the remaining three boards in the same way.

8. After the glue has fully cured, glue these two sections together. Be very aware of flatness, and clamp as needed to achieve it.

CUT THE TOP TO FINAL WIDTH

9. The top is $27\,1/2$" wide at this point; the finished width is $27\,1/4$". If you simply saw the excess off one edge, you'll lose symmetry. Instead, rip half the excess off each edge; this way, the boards on both edges will end up the same width. Use a plane to remove the saw marks from the edges.

LAY OUT AND CUT THE CURVES

10. Draw the curve on one end of the top (see p. 74).

11. Draw the second curve so its widest point is 36" from the widest point of the first curve.

12. Cut both end curves on the band saw.

PROFILE THE EDGES

If the edges of a tabletop are too severe, it can be uncomfortable to rest your arms upon the top. A simple rounded edge solves this problem, and the easiest way to achieve this profile is with a router and a roundover bit. It's fast, but the results are so perfect that I think it leaves the table looking too generic. To give this table more charm and character, I suggest you cut the profile by hand.

13. Using hand planes on the straight sides and a spokeshave on the curved ends, lightly round the top edge. Then flip the top and cut a long, wide chamfer around the underside to make the edge appear thinner (see p. 56).

Draw the layout lines boldly—they'll be your guides when you cut the bevels on the band saw.

FINISHING THE TOP

14. Lay the top face down on the bench with a clean nonslip pad beneath it.

15. Use an orbital sander and sand with 100-grit paper. Remove any dried glue and surface irregularities. Don't obsess too much over the bottom (it won't show), but it's important that the edge profiles are clean and have been sanded smoothly.

16. Now's the time to be obsessive: Flip the top and start sanding the good side. If your glue-up went well, the joints between the boards are reasonably flush. If they aren't, well, you have a lot of sanding to do (see p. 79). Sand up to 220 grit.

17. For tabletops, it's very important to have a substantial protective surface finish. Choose your finish (see p. 19) and apply several coats.

Cut & shape the legs

MORTISE AND TAPER THE LEGS

1. Lay out the mortise on each leg. These are slip mortises, where the mortise extends to the top of the leg. The rail is not socketed into the leg; it just slips in place.

2. Cut the slip mortises with the plunge router (see p. 60).

3. Lay out the taper on each leg. Note that the outside edge tapers, while the inside edge (with the mortise) remains straight.

4. Cut the taper on the band saw.

5. Clean up the saw marks and smooth out any wobbles in the taper with a hand plane.

CUT THE LEG PROFILES

6. Set your sliding square to 7/8" and mark the centerline full-length of each taper.

7. Change the sliding square to 7/16" (see the photo above). Place the base of the square on the taper and draw the kerf line on both sides of each leg.

8. On each end of the piece, draw a line connecting the centerline with the kerf line.

9. Set the band saw table at 25°, sloping down toward the right as you face the saw (see the lefthand photo on the next page).

10. Before you cut, place the leg on the saw table and make sure that the cut you're about to make is correct relative to the line. The cut needn't line up perfectly. Being off a degree or two isn't significant, but you can adjust the table to match the line if you like. Note that you'll have to turn the leg end-for-end for the second cut.

11. Start this cut standing in front of the saw, but soon you'll find it easier to cut if you move to the side of the saw. Remove the bulk of the material, cutting just wide of the centerline.

12. Smooth the surface with a hand plane and/or a spokeshave.

Cut the rail joinery

LAY OUT AND CUT THE HALF LAPS

1. Lay out the half laps (see Leg/Rail Subassembly Detail).

2. Cut the half laps as described on page 67.

TENON THE RAILS

3. Lay out the tenons (see the Leg/Rail Subassembly Detail).

4. Cut the shoulders on the table saw and the cheeks on the band saw (see p. 61).

5. Check the tenons for fit in the leg mortises; trim them as needed.

BORE HOLES
FOR TOP ATTACHMENT

To allow for seasonal movement, this table uses a simple system of washers, 2" drywall screws, and oversized holes to attach the top to the base (see p. 13).

6. Lay out the attachment hole locations.

7. Bore a $3/4$"-diameter (O. D.) hole to a depth of about $1/4$" in each location.

8. Using the center point of those holes, bore a $5/16$" hole all the way through each of the rails.

CHAMFER THE EDGES

9. Chamfer all the edges of each rail with a hand plane.

Use the band saw to cut the profile on the legs. Lay out the lines first, and set the band saw table to cut the bevels.

Though you'll start your beveled cut facing the blade in the usual band-saw stance, move around to the side to finish the cut. This keeps your fingers well away from the blade.

Cut the rail tenons to fit the stopped mortises in the legs.

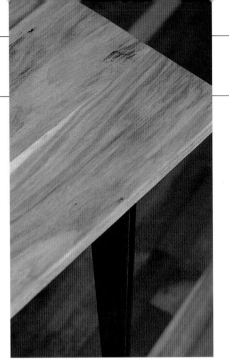

Prefinish all the parts of the table before assembly. Attaching the top is the final step.

Assemble the base & attach the top

PREFINISH THE LEGS AND RAILS

It's difficult to apply the finish after the base is assembled, but easy to do in pieces on the bench. Just make sure you don't apply any finish to the areas that will be glued.

1. Use tape to mask off the laps, the tenons, and the area around each mortise where the tenon shoulder meets the leg.

2. Apply three coats of finish to the rails and legs.

GLUE THE LEGS TO THE RAILS

3. Apply glue to the mortises and tenons, and glue the legs to the rails.

4. Since the legs are tapered, you'll need a piece of leather under each clamp head to prevent slipping.

5. Use two clamps for each rail to distribute the pressure evenly.

6. Check for any glue squeeze-out. Remove it at the rubbery stage of cure—after it's cured enough not to smear but before it's rock hard.

JOIN THE LAPS

7. Slip the two subassemblies together. It's not necessary to apply glue to the half-lap joint, though you can if you like. Sometimes I reinforce the half lap with a screw.

ATTACH THE TOP

8. Lay the top face down on clean nonslip pads atop your bench.

9. Put the base on the top, with the legs up. You'll have to do some trial and error to get the correct position. Move it around until it's centered along both the length and the width—the overhangs should be the same on the two sides and on both ends (see the Bottom View for details).

10. Mark the position when you get it right, in case you bump the base during the next steps.

11. Chuck a $1/8"$ drill bit into a portable drill for boring pilot holes in the top. You'll use the holes previously bored in the rails as guides.

12. Check to make sure the base hasn't moved from the original position, and drill one pilot hole. Be careful not to drill through the top.

13. Make sure the base is still in position. Then slip the $3/8''$ and $3/16''$ washers onto a drywall screw and drive the screw home.

14. Move to the opposite attachment hole. Check that the base is still in position, and drill another pilot hole. Drive another screw with washers. Repeat these steps for the remaining attachment holes.

15. Before turning your table upright, attach nylon gliders to the bottoms of the legs to protect your floors from scratches.

DOVETAIL BOX

Tease the mind and tame the saw.

Woodworkers love the virtuous dovetail— it is a wonder to behold. The joint is both an eye pleaser and brain teaser. Mastering it adds visual interest and strength to your work and challenges your brain to think along a different path (see p. 67).

(see p. 67)

Some people are so apprehensive about this ingenious joint that they head right out and buy the latest router jig for making dovetails. There are a number of arguments against this approach. Using a dovetail jig is no walk in the park. It creates an enormous amount of dust and noise, and setting up the jig for the first time is not easy. Plus, with their seamless perfection and symmetry, router-jig dovetails lack character. I think hand-cut dovetails add intrinsic value to a piece—imperfections and all.

With a little practice, hand-cut dovetails don't take that long to make. At first, your mind will want to play tricks—so make several practice joints before you start this project. Once you've made a set, you'll understand why woodworkers hold it in such esteem.

With a couple of well-fitting practice joints under your belt, you'll be ready to build this small basswood toolbox. Granted, basswood isn't the most exciting-looking wood, but its demure character seems to help you relax and not worry about mistakes. It is an excellent wood for learning handwork, and is slightly aromatic—a pleasant surprise when you remove the lid.

This box is designed for carrying tools. The inner tray keeps delicate tools out of the bottom of the box and provides a resting place for the lid. Simple leather handles make it easy to grasp the box, as well as to remove the lid and tray. I have a number of these boxes in a variety of sizes. I use them for transporting my tools when I teach or take a woodworking class. I always experience a sense of joy when my tools arrive safely, and these boxes provide a welcome sense of organization and familiarity when I'm in a strange land.

Handle your box with care, but don't pamper it. This is a working box, made all the more interesting by the marks of time.

Cut List & Supplies

NUMBER OF PARTS	DESCRIPTION	DIMENSIONS IN INCHES			COMMENTS
		Thickness	Width	Length	
Solid wood (basswood or other softwood)					
2	Sides	$5/8$	5	15	
2	Ends	$5/8$	5	8	
2	Tray sides	$1/2$	$2\,3/8$	$13\,1/2$	
2	Tray ends	$1/2$	$2\,3/8$	$6\,1/2$	
2	Lid	$1/2$	$6\,5/8$	$13\,3/4$	*Glue up from narrower pieces if necessary*
Plywood					
1	Box bottom	$1/4$	$7\,1/8$	$14\,1/4$	
1	Tray bottom	$1/8$	$5\,3/4$	13	*Use plywood or hardboard, and cover with decorative paper if desired*
4	Tray posts	$1/4$	$1/4$	$2\,1/4$	
Other materials & supplies					
	Leather	$1/16$	1		*Cut to length as needed for handles*
	Brass screws				*For attaching handles, use #4 or #5, $3/8$" long*

How to Build the Dovetail Box

Build the main box

Build the main box using simple hand-cut dovetails and a plywood bottom set in stopped grooves.

Fit the tray and top it off

The tray is simply a smaller, lower box that fits neatly inside the main box. It's built in the same way as the main box, but of lighter, more delicate materials.

Details, details

There are no fancy latches or hinges on this box. The chamfered lid simply slips inside the box and sits atop the tray. Finish with shellac and wax.

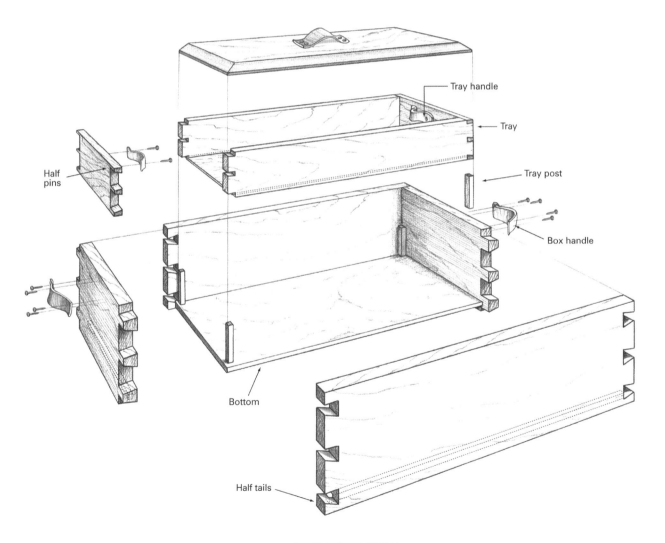

Tray handle

Tray

Tray post

Box handle

Half pins

Bottom

Half tails

EXPLODED VIEW

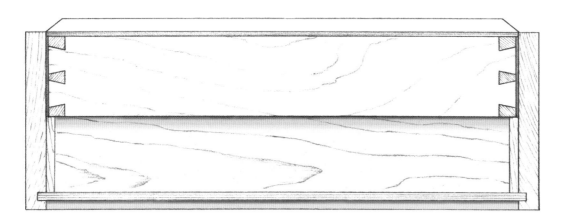

CUTAWAY FRONT VIEW

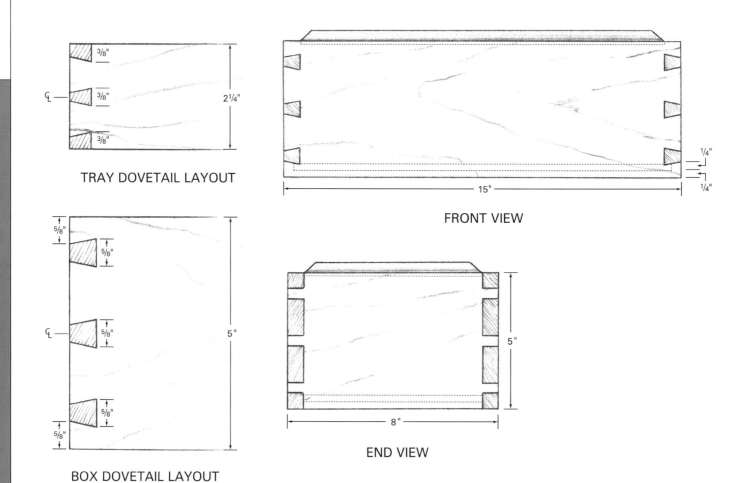

TRAY DOVETAIL LAYOUT

3/8"
3/8"
3/8"
2¼"

FRONT VIEW

15"
1/4"
1/4"

BOX DOVETAIL LAYOUT

5/8"
5/8"
5/8"
5/8"
5/8"
5"

END VIEW

8"
5"

Building the Dovetail Box

Proper dovetails fit so well you'll need a few taps with a light mallet to close the joint.

Build the main box

CUT THE DOVETAILS

1. Start by making the dovetails following the steps outlined on page 67.

2. Note that the dovetail layout for the main box uses half tails on the side pieces, while the layout of the tray uses half pins on the end pieces (see the Dovetail Layouts).

3. Since you're building a box rather than sample joints, be careful about labeling all your parts. Cut all the joints and refine the fit, but don't glue it up. Once the joints mate, you can proceed.

LAY OUT AND CUT THE BOTTOM GROOVE

4. Lay out the groove for the plywood bottom on the inside face of the sides and ends. Note that the groove is full length on the sides, but stopped on the ends. If the groove extended the length of the end pieces, it would show as a notch in the lower pin.

5. Rout $^1/4$" x $^1/4$" grooves (full length and stopped) using a router mounted in a table (see p. 64).

FIT THE PLYWOOD BOTTOM

6. Dry fit the box and bottom to check the fit of the bottom. Make sure there's plenty of room for the glue. It's common to misjudge this fit, only to find during the clamping that the joints won't draw closed because the bottom is too big.

FINISH THE INSIDE

7. I like to use clear shellac on the insides of the box. Because it dries quickly, you can apply three coats in an hour. Shellac looks nice, but it also makes cleaning up the glue eas-

ier. If any glue seeps out during assembly, just let it dry. The glue won't stick to the shellac, and it pops off easily with a chisel. If you prefer not use any finish, I suggest you wipe a thin coat of paste wax along the shoulder line. Whether you use shellac or wax, keep it off the pins and tails so it doesn't interfere with the bond.

GLUE UP AND SMOOTH THE BOX

8. Remember to make a test run with the clamps before applying glue; make sure the bottom fits properly.

9. Apply the glue. After it has dried, clean off the excess and sand down the protruding tails and pins with an orbital sander and 100-grit paper (or a stationary belt sander if you have one).

The tray is simply a more delicate box that fits inside the main box.

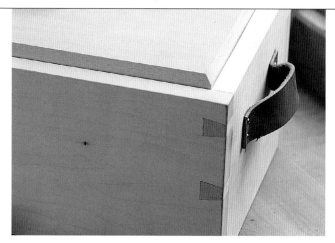

The chamfered lid merely sits on top of the tray.

Fit the tray and top it off

1. The tray is just another, smaller box. Size it for an easy fit inside. Dovetail the corners and cut the grooves for the bottom. It's easier to cut these smaller grooves with a plunge router and fence (see p. 64). For an even nicer appearance, you can add decorative paper to the bottom (see p. 171).

2. Sand, and if you're finishing the inside of the tray, do so before assembly. The tray doesn't require much clamping pressure, so you don't need bar clamps or cauls.

MAKE WAY FOR THE TRAY

3. A fast and simple way to create a tray support is to glue four small posts ($1/4$" x $1/4$") into each corner of the box. Cut the posts to length with a handsaw. Apply the glue and simply press the posts into place. You don't need clamps; the suction from the glue is strong enough to hold them.

TRAY HANDLES

4. Without handles, the only way to remove the tray is to tip the box upside down. Attach the handles to the inside upper edge. I use leather, tacked or screwed in place, but you could make wooden pulls instead.

5. If you have material that's wide enough, the lid can be one piece, but you can also edge-glue two pieces together. There are no fancy latches or hinges; the lid simply rests on top of the tray. Don't get too fussy with the fit—you want easy access to your tools.

6. Once the lid fits, plane a 45° chamfer around it (see p. 55). Take care to avoid tear-out during this process.

Enhance the simplicity by attending to the details—crisply chamfered edges, rustic handles, and the soft sheen of a waxed finish.

Details, details

1. Lightly soften all the edges with a plane or sandpaper.

2. Apply finish to the outsides of the box and tray, and to both sides of the lid. Apply a thin coat of paste wax over all.

3. Fasten a handle to the lid.

MANTEL

Create a warm space.

Years of building fires, hauling wood, and dealing with soot and ashes jaded me. I just couldn't warm up to the whole prospect of burning wood for warmth and ambience, so I installed a gas log stove. It's as practical as can be—flame and heat at the flip of a switch. Though warm, it's not cozy. Yet family and friends seem compelled to gather around it, as though it were some kind of primal fire pit. I decided that if the stove were going to act like a fireplace, I'd build it a mantel so it would look like one.

A mantel seems very complicated, but in essence, it's nothing more than a fancy shelf secured to the wall. This basic shelf is easy to build and readily customized. It can be longer or shorter, with a different shape to the top, or it can have deeper shelves. If you don't have a fireplace, you can even modify it into a one-of-a-kind bookcase or display area for your treasures.

The back piece practically calls out for some added visual elements. Circles work to good effect with the back's classical proportions. I inlaid a circle and line design in contrasting exotic woods—an easy process with a router and inlay bit. You could also check out a gem and mineral shop for accents such as interesting stones or orbs. Use the same inlay techniques and/or epoxy the stone in place. If you don't want to inlay, a 1 1/2" hole bored at the apex and softened with a 1/4" roundover router bit is simple and elegant.

Attaching the mantel to the wall is not a tough job. It requires little more than a level, a drill, and some long screws. Once in place, you've got a sturdy focal point that can really hang in there.

A mantel makes any type of fireplace a focal point of the room. This one is a simple shelf bracketed to the wall. The mantel is made of ash, with cherry and walnut inlay.

Cut List & Supplies

NUMBER OF PARTS	DESCRIPTION	DIMENSIONS IN INCHES			COMMENTS
		Thickness	Width	Length	
Solid wood					
1	Back	3/4	8 1/2	67	
1	Shelf	1 1/4	8 1/2	67	
2	Bracket verticals	3/4	6 1/2	10	
2	Bracket horizontals	3/4	4	4	
2	Bracket centers	3/4	4	11	*This is rough length. Cut to final length after bracket center is fitted to vertical*
Other materials & supplies					
	3/8" dowel caps				*For covering screw heads on bracket horizontals. Choose a matching or contrasting wood.*
	1 1/4" drywall screws				
	2 1/2" drywall screws				

How to Build the Mantel

Shape the parts

Shape all the pieces, transforming them from four-square parts into angled, rabbeted, inlaid mantel parts. Start with the back, and once it's shaped and smoothed, add your choice of embellishments. Get the shelf in shape, and then cut rabbets and grooves in the bracket parts.

Prefinish, and assemble the shelf and brackets

After prefinishing, glue up the two basic subassemblies—attach the shelf to the back, and create the two brackets (each from three parts).

Hang it level

Use a stud finder and a level to determine the locations and heights of the brackets. Screw the brackets to the studs, and then screw the shelf to the brackets to tie it all together.

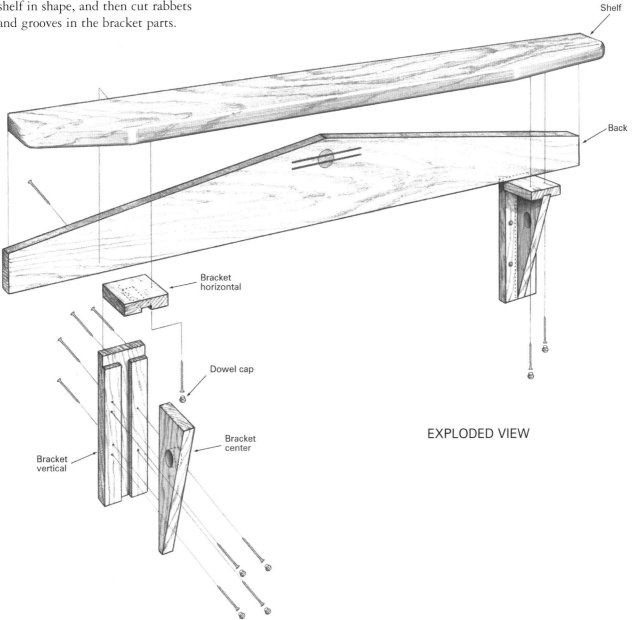

Shelf

Back

Bracket horizontal

Dowel cap

Bracket center

Bracket vertical

EXPLODED VIEW

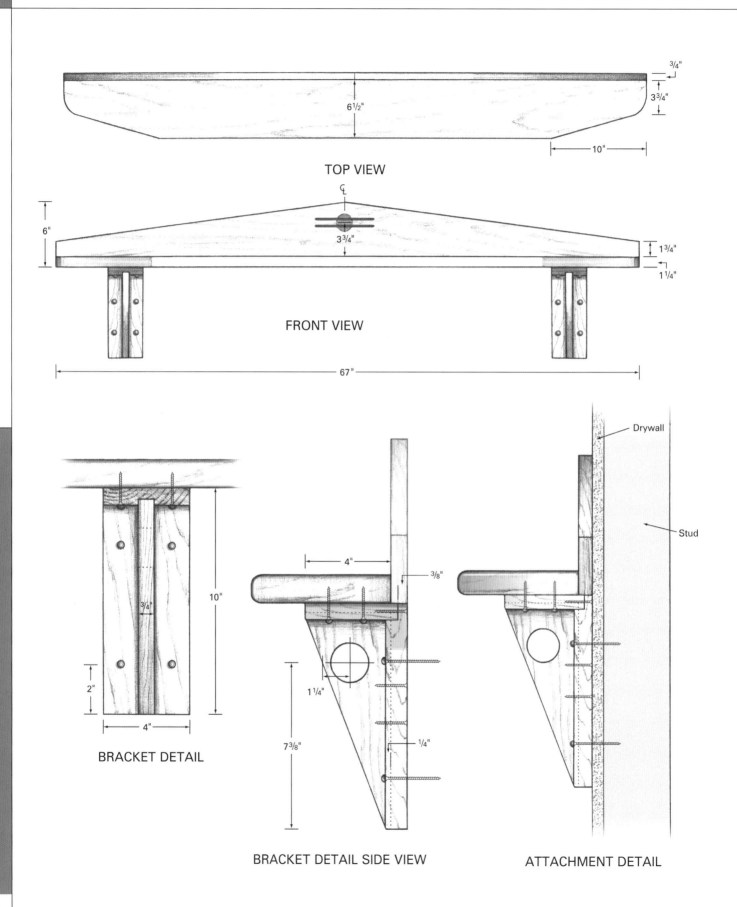

TOP VIEW

6"

3 3/4"

FRONT VIEW

67"

BRACKET DETAIL

BRACKET DETAIL SIDE VIEW

ATTACHMENT DETAIL

Drywall

Stud

Building the Mantel

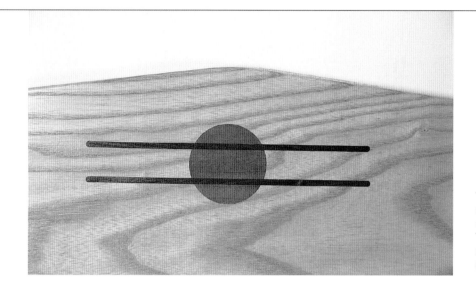

The back piece of the mantel practically calls out for embellishment. This inlay is easy to create with a router and template.

Shape the parts

SHAPE AND EMBELLISH THE BACK

1. Lay out the tapers on the back and cut them on the band saw.

2. Remove the saw marks with a hand plane or on the jointer.

3. On the back side of the piece, mark the locations of six or so evenly spaced screws. Don't put any screws within 2" of the ends.

4. Bore and countersink for the screws.

5. Embellish the back with inlay (see p. 75).

6. Round over the top front edge with a router fitted with a $1/4$" roundover bit.

SHAPE THE SHELF

7. Lay out the shelf from the drawings and cut it on the band saw.

8. Remove saw marks with a hand plane or jointer. Use a belt sander on curved areas and edges that need further smoothing.

9. Round over the front edges (top and bottom) with a router and a $1/4$" roundover bit.

BRACKET VERTICALS

10. Cut the $1/4$"-deep grooves on the bracket verticals with a dado blade mounted in the table saw. Set the cutting width at $3/4$".

11. Switch to using the miter gauge. Cut the end rabbets $3/8$" deep and $3/4$" wide.

BRACKET CENTERS

12. Check the fit of the centers in the grooves cut in the verticals. You may need to do a little orbital sanding to get a good fit. It should be snug, but the center should slip into place without much force.

13. Cut the center pieces to match the length of the verticals.

14. Mark the locations of the decorative holes and bore them on the drill press.

15. Use a $1/4$" roundover bit on both sides of the decorative hole.

16. Fit the centers in the brackets and lay out the hypotenuse of the bracket triangle. Cut it on the band saw.

17. Clean up the saw marks with a hand plane.

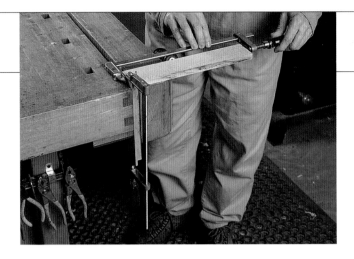

A couple of clamps help to hold the bracket parts together while driving the screws.

Prefinish, and assemble the shelf and brackets

Shelves are more architectural in nature, so I don't feel it's necessary to get obsessive with the sanding thing. Give the most attention to the back piece, and make sure the front edge of the shelf looks good.

PREFINISH

I suggest using a water-based poly finish for most shelving projects. It will look far better than an oil finish and be easier to maintain and keep clean.

1. Sand all the parts up to 180 grit.

2. Hand sand all the edges not yet rounded over to soften them.

3. Apply at least two coats of finish, keeping it off any areas that will later receive glue (notably the bottom edge of the back and the back edge of the shelf). Be sure to finish the back side of the back, as well.

ATTACH THE SHELF

4. Spread some glue on the back edge of the shelf.

5. Line up the edges and clamp the shelf in place. You can only use clamps on the straight middle portion.

6. Bore pilot holes in the shelf so driving the screws won't cause splitting.

7. Install 1 1/4" drywall screws.

FINAL FINISH THE SHELF

8. Removing any glue squeeze-out and general shop handling may have left some scratches on the shelf/back assembly. Lightly sand it with 220-grit paper and apply another coat of finish over the front and sides.

ASSEMBLE THE BRACKETS

9. Apply glue to the vertical end rabbets.

10. Clamp the horizontal to the vertical. Make sure it's fully seated at 90°.

11. Drive the screws.

12. Apply a small bead of glue to the back edge of the center piece. Fit it in the groove and drive the screws to fasten it to the vertical.

BORE THE BRACKETS FOR SCREWS

18. Bore two 1/8"-diameter holes in each vertical piece, right through the groove for attaching the center piece (from front to back).

19. Bore two more holes in the end rabbets, also from front to back. These are for attaching the bracket horizontals.

20. Flip the verticals over, and countersink the back so the heads of the screws will end up slightly below flush.

21. Bore four 1/8" holes in the bracket horizontals for attaching the shelf.

22. Using the center point of each of those holes, counterbore a 3/8"-diameter hole deep enough to accommodate the dowel caps (do a test run on scrap).

23. Bore similar holes in the front side of the verticals. These are for the screws that will attach the brackets to the wall studs.

Hang the brackets level with—not parallel to—the floor, then screw the shelf/back subassembly to the brackets.

Hang it level

1. Use a stud finder to locate the wall studs over your fireplace.

2. Determine how you want to space your brackets so each one falls on a stud. Also determine the shelf height.

3. At the desired height, lightly mark the wall at the top of the bracket horizontal.

4. Use a level to extend this mark across the wall to the other bracket location. If you measure up from the floor, the mantel will end up parallel to your floor, which isn't necessarily level.

5. Center the bracket screw holes over the stud and fasten it in place with 2 1/2" drywall screws. Cover the heads with dowel caps.

6. Set the shelf atop the brackets and clamp it in place. Double-check with the level.

7. Drill pilot holes in the shelf, up from the underside of the horizontal brackets.

8. Attach the shelf to the brackets with 1 1/4" drywall screws. Be very careful not to drive the screws too deeply. The last thing you want at this point is for a screw to penetrate all the way through the shelf.

FURNITURE FROM A BOX

Simple elements combine to make the whole.

When I was a child, I didn't play much with dolls, but building blocks captured my imagination. The fascination continued during my college years, and I was still at it—building furniture in my dorm room out of cinder blocks and cheap planks. The furniture was easy to reconfigure into a variety of coffee tables, seats, bookcases, and storage units, and quick to deconstruct when it was time to depart for life's next adventure.

Many moons later, as a woodworker, I updated the idea, using wooden boxes for blocks, nice hardwood planks, and few additional elements for stability and visual interest. I used different construction methods for the boxes, but finally settled on dovetail joinery. Taking the extra time to hand cut dovetails adds character and strength to a piece, and is an excellent way to increase its intrinsic value.

The linear design lends itself to experimentation, and it's fun to find ways to transform the boxy, basic look into something elegant. In this case, I used my trusty spokeshave to cut a gentle relief curve into the bottom of each end of the top. From a distance, the slight curve offers relief to the eye and adds an exotic Asian flavor. Laminated feet stabilize the piece and provide another opportunity to move away from straight lines.

Though this project makes an elegant bench or table, you can reconfigure the dimensions and stack the elements to make a bookcase. Simply build a few more boxes, and bolt them together with carriage bolts for strength and easy disassembly.

It takes me back to the simplicity of my first furniture creations. Life changes, but some things never do.

As simple as cinder blocks and planks, but far more elegant, this bench features a mahogany top, hard maple boxes, and ebonized poplar feet.

Cut List & Supplies

NUMBER OF PARTS	DESCRIPTION	DIMENSIONS IN INCHES			COMMENTS
		Thickness	Width	Length	
Solid wood					
2	Top (mahogany)	1 1/2	6	52	*Glue up into one 12"-wide panel; cut to finished length of 48". Some species of wood are easy to find in 12"+ widths; use them if available and skip the glue-up.*
4	Box sides (maple)	3/4	4 1/2	12	
4	Box ends (maple)	3/4	4 1/2	8 3/4	
2	Cross piece (mahogany)	3/4	3 3/8	9 3/4	
6	Foot laminates (poplar)	1 5/8	2 3/4	12	*Laminate and mill to make two feet, each 2 5/8" x 5" x 11 3/8"*
Other materials & supplies					
	2" drywall screws				*For attaching top and feet*
16	3/8" washers				*Under the heads of the drywall screws*

How to Build Furniture from a Box

Build the top

The top is just a 12"-wide panel—use a single plank if you can get one wide enough, or glue up a panel from narrower boards. Cut a low relief curve in the underside of the ends, using a spokeshave.

Build the boxes

Two boxes hold up the top. Hand-cut dovetails look great for the box joinery, but a rabbeted joint works as well. Before assembling the box, cut and fit the crosspiece. It's mortised into the sides of the box. Shape the curve on the lower edge of the crosspiece. Once all the joinery fits, glue up the boxes with the crosspieces in place.

Build the feet

Laminate the foot blanks from three layers of 1 3/4" wood. Square up the blanks and then cut the curves on the band saw. Refine and smooth the curves and countersink and bore the screw holes for fastening to the boxes. Stain or ebonize the feet at this point if so desired.

Stack 'em up

Attach the feet to the boxes, then attach the boxes to the top.

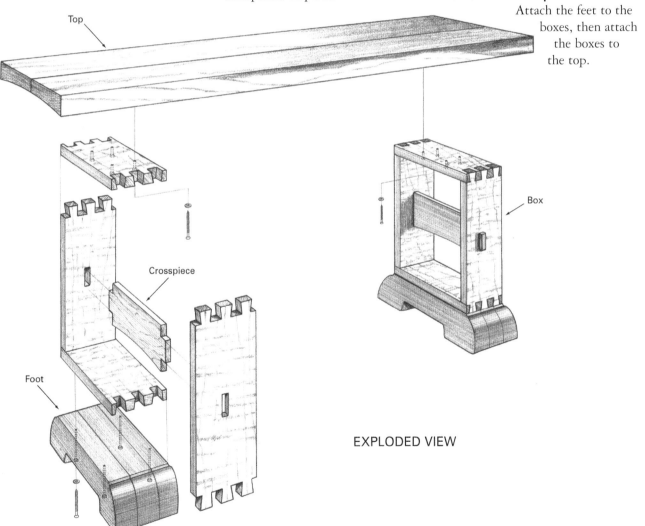

Top

Crosspiece

Foot

Box

EXPLODED VIEW

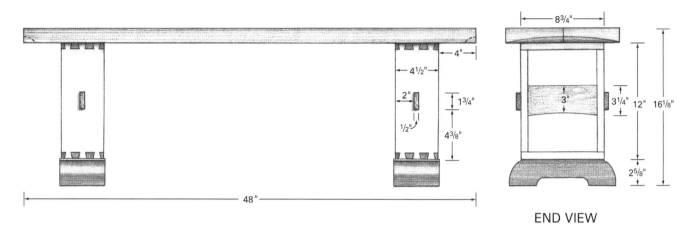

FRONT VIEW

END VIEW

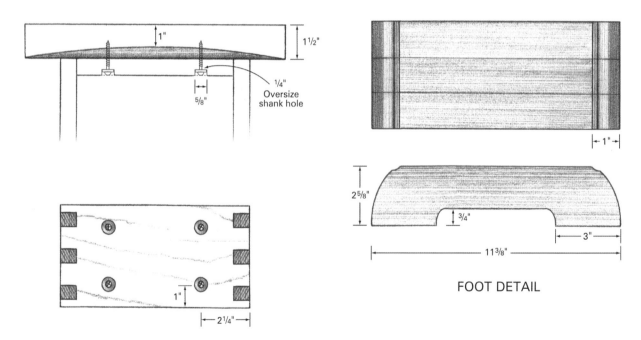

TOP FASTENING DETAIL

FOOT DETAIL

Building Furniture from a Box

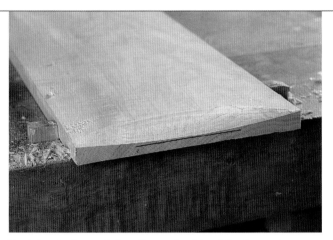

Sculpt out a low relief on the underside of the top, using a spokeshave. This adds visual interest and lightens the appearance of the top.

Strong as well as beautiful, hand-cut dovetails increase the intrinsic value of this or any other piece.

Build the top

GLUE UP THE PANEL

1. If you're not using a single wide board for the top, glue up a 12"-wide panel from narrower boards. Use biscuits, as described on page 47.

2. Cut the top to final length and width.

SHAPE THE TOP

3. Cut a small relief area on the underside of each end of the top, as shown in the illustrations. See page 78 for details on using a spokeshave.

4. Refine the surfaces with hand and orbital sanding. Since these areas are below eye level, you needn't go crazy with the sanding.

SURFACE PREP

5. Spend some time sanding the visible surface of the top.

6. Pay careful attention to the end grain and edges.

7. Work your way up to 220 grit.

Build the boxes

CUT THE BOX JOINERY

1. Cut the box joinery. Dovetailed boxes look impressive (see p. 67). However, if you want to paint or stain the boxes, I suggest building them with no visible joinery. Painted dovetails just don't look good.

MORTISE THE BOX SIDES

2. Once the structural joinery on the boxes is complete, you need to cut mortises in the box sides to accept the crosspiece. Lay out the mortises as shown in the illustrations.

3. Cut the mortises with a drill press or plunger router and jig (see p. 57).

COUNTERSINK THE BOX TOPS

4. Bore and countersink screw holes on the underside of the box tops. Make the shank holes oversize to allow for seasonal movement.

TENON THE CROSSPIECE

5. Temporarily assemble the box, clamping it so the corners are tight and square.

6. Measure the inside dimensions of the box to determine the location of the tenon shoulders. Note that the ends of the crosspiece protrude beyond the box sides by 1/2".

7. Cut the tenons as described on page 61.

8. Test fit the crosspieces.

9. Remove the crosspieces, and use sandpaper on a block to hand sand a bevel on the protruding ends of the tenon. Keep these edges crisp—no rounding over.

SHAPE THE CROSSPIECE

10. Lay out the curve on each crosspiece (see p. 74).

11. Cut the curve on the band saw.

12. Smooth the curve with a 3"-diameter sanding drum mounted in the drill press. Alternatively, smooth it by hand with a spokeshave, files, scrapers, and sandpaper.

SURFACE PREP

13. Final sand the crosspieces and the inside surfaces of the boxes up to 220 grit.

ASSEMBLE THE BOXES

14. Glue up and clamp the boxes.

15. Sand the outside of the box so the joints are flush and smooth (see p. 73).

16. Finish sand up to 220 grit, softening all the edges.

The thick poplar foot blanks are easily shaped on the band saw. Refine the curves by hand and random orbit sanding.

After sawing the curves on the feet, make a crisp shoulder line with the table saw and refine it with a shoulder plane.

Build the feet

GLUE UP THE LAMINATES

1. Each foot is built up from three thinner laminates. You can glue up and clamp both feet (two sets of three laminates each) at the same time.

2. Apply enough clamps to provide even pressure all around the block.

3. Allow at least two hours for the glue to dry.

SHAPE THE FEET

4. Remove all the dried glue with a paint scraper.

5. Run one face of each lamination through the jointer to establish a flat reference surface.

6. Mill the feet four-square to their final dimensions.

7. Lay out the curves on the foot blocks.

8. To cut the outside curves, start on the band saw and saw up to where the profile terminates, then slowly back out of the curve. To complete the cut, use a miter gauge on the table saw to create a crisp shoulder line.

9. To cut the curve on the bottom of the foot, make one continuous cut on the band saw.

10. Refine and smooth the curves by hand and orbital sanding. For the radius on the bottom of the feet, wrap sandpaper around a 1" dowel.

11. Sand up to 220 grit.

12. Countersink and counterbore as you did to attach the top.

STAIN THE FEET

13. If you want to stain or ebonize the feet, do so now (see p. 19).

PREFINISH

14. Flood the top and boxes with oil and let them dry thoroughly before handling.

Feet, boxes, and top are simply stacked up and screwed together.

Stack 'em up

1. Drive 2" drywall screws with washers up from below to attach the feet to the boxes.

2. Lay the top face down on some soft padding and position the boxes.

3. Make a couple of marks to check that the boxes don't shift during fastening.

4. Drive 2" drywall screws with washers through the boxes and into the underside of the top.

5. Because the top gets hard use, it needs extra protection. Lightly sand it and apply a couple of coats of poly.

PLATFORM BED

Rest easy with color, curves, and inlay.

Beds are big, but they're not complicated. The rails simply bolt to the feet with decorative carriage bolts. The headboard is an independent construction and isn't fastened to the frame at all; it hangs on the wall. The platform frame and headboard posts are ebonized poplar. The feet and headboard panels are made of mahogany, with a zebrawood inlay.

When the futon craze hit in the early '80s, I was living in Tucson, Arizona. Chic futon stores were rolling into town like tumbleweeds on a windy day. Retailers were desperate for bed furniture, and small woodworking shops couldn't produce fast enough. Thus began my bed phase, which kept me afloat for almost a decade. Then I moved back to North Carolina, where the futon craze was just hitting.

Over the years, I've built hundreds of beds. I've looked at them from every possible angle and tried every piece of bed hardware known to humankind. Beds are big, but they aren't complicated to build. While bed design fashions might change, two things never do. First, every bed must come apart for easy transport. Second, it's much easier to build a bed when the frame and headboard are independent pieces of furniture. This project features a headboard that's essentially nothing more than a large biscuited frame and panel hung on the wall.

The queen-size platform bed frame is designed for a futon, 4" to 8" of foam, or a standard mattress sans box spring. If you want a king, double, or twin size, adapt this design by cutting the frame rails and headboard panels to the appropriate lengths.

This bed features a lot of miters in the frame construction. Miters have a reputation for being difficult, but you can rest easy. We're making a bed frame, not a picture frame where even the slightest gap is noticeable. If your miters aren't perfect, just remember that the mattress will cover most of the frame, and ebonizing the inside of the miter cuts as well makes them almost invisible.

Beds are one of the types of furniture that look good when you use dramatic contrasting tones. My favorite color combo is a mahogany headboard with an ebonized black poplar frame, both made more lustrous with a couple of coats of gel poly. Zebrawood inlay looks great with this scheme.

There's something very satisfying about making your own bed. You'll spend more than a third of your life there, tucked away from the world. You can rest easy, and sleep with the satisfaction of a job well done.

Cut List & Supplies

NUMBER OF PARTS	DESCRIPTION	DIMENSIONS IN INCHES			COMMENTS
		Thickness	Width	Length	
BED FRAME					
Solid wood					
2	Side rails (poplar)	1 3/4	4 1/2	83	*Cut to final length of 81", measured from the long end of the first miter*
2	End rails (poplar)	1 3/4	4 1/2	63	*Cut to final length of 61", measured from the long end of the first miter*
2	Mitered feet pieces (mahogany)	1 3/4	6	48	*Can be one long or two shorter boards. Keep workpiece as long as possible for cutting the splined miter, and then cut into eight pieces, each 11" long. After rabbeting one end, cut each of the pieces to a final length of 10".*
2	Spline material	1/4	1/2	48	*Locate the spline closer to the inside of the miter so it doesn't show.*
1	Center beam (poplar)	1 1/2	3 1/2	77 1/4	*Use a 2 x 4 if desired.*
2	Center posts (poplar)	1 1/2	3 1/2	7 3/4	*Use a 2 x 4 if desired. Fasten posts to beam with biscuits.*
Plywood (shop birch)					
2	Side cleats	3/4	1 1/2	74	
4	End cleats	3/4	1 1/2	25	
3	Platform leaves	3/4	25 5/8	57 1/8	
Other materials & supplies					
8	5/16" x 3" carriage bolts				*With nuts and washers*

Cut List & Supplies

NUMBER OF PARTS	DESCRIPTION	DIMENSIONS IN INCHES			COMMENTS
		Thickness	Width	Length	
HEADBOARD					
Solid wood					
2	Posts (poplar)	1 3/4	3 3/4	29	
2	Top panel (mahogany)	3/4	6	57	*Glue into wide panel and cut to final dimensions of 14 1/2" x 55 1/2"*
3	Bottom panel (mahogany)	3/4	5	57	*Glue into wide panel and cut to final dimensions of 14 1/2" x 55 1/2"*
1	Hanging cleat material (any wood)	3/4	4	50	
Other materials					
2	1 1/4" drywall screws				
4	2 1/2" drywall screws				*For attaching cleat to wall*
	#20 biscuits				

How to Build the Platform Bed

Build the rails

Cut the rails to length and miter the ends. Plane a chamfer on the top edge of each rail, taking care not to damage the fragile miter ends in the process. Finish sand the rails, stain them, and apply two coats of gel poly.

Build the feet

Cut the miters on the table saw before the foot material is sawn to final length. Tilt the blade to 45° and rip one edge. Retract the blade and change the fence setting to cut a groove in the beveled edge. Cut the leg pieces to rough length before rabbeting one end of each piece. Using a template, mark and cut the curved edge of the feet on the band saw, saving the offcuts for clamping cauls. Clean up all the edges, cut the feet pieces to final length, sand the inside surfaces, and glue the miters together with a spline in the groove. Clean up the feet, final sand, and apply stain followed by two coats of gel poly.

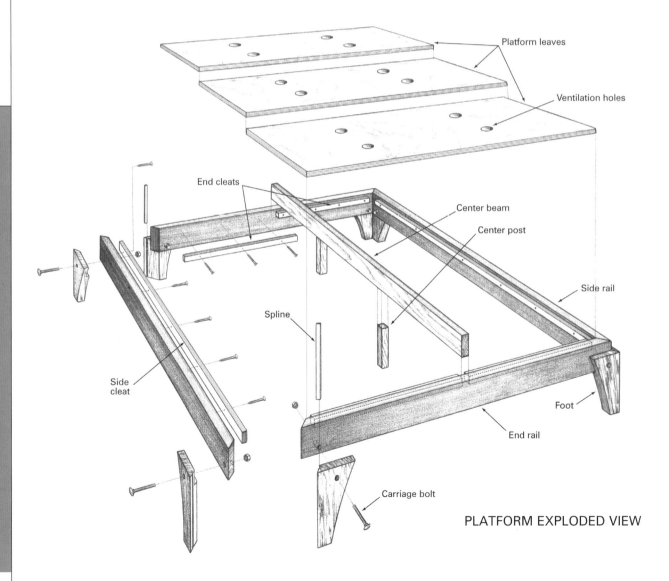

PLATFORM EXPLODED VIEW

Assemble the platform

Screw the cleats that support the plywood to the rails. Cut the plywood and bore ventilation holes. Bolt the rails to the feet.

Shape the headboard posts and build the panels

Inlay contrasting wood to the tops of the posts, using a router and template (see p. 75). Cut the curves in the tops of the posts on the band saw. Glue up the two headboard panels, and cut them to finished length and width. Cut biscuit slots that match the post slots. Cut the curve on the top edge. Final sand the headboard parts, and apply two coast of gel poly.

Assemble and hang the headboard

Glue and biscuit the panels to the posts. Cut beveled cleats for hanging the headboard on the wall. Attach the upper cleat to the back of the headboard and the other cleat to the wall.

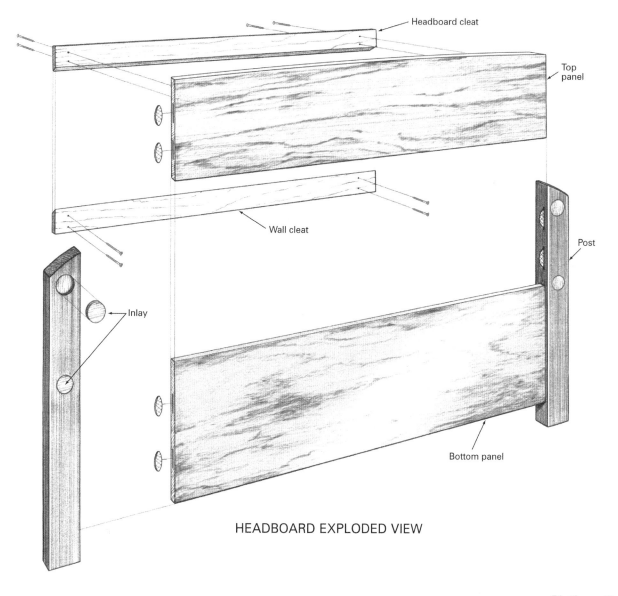

Headboard cleat

Top panel

Wall cleat

Post

Inlay

Bottom panel

HEADBOARD EXPLODED VIEW

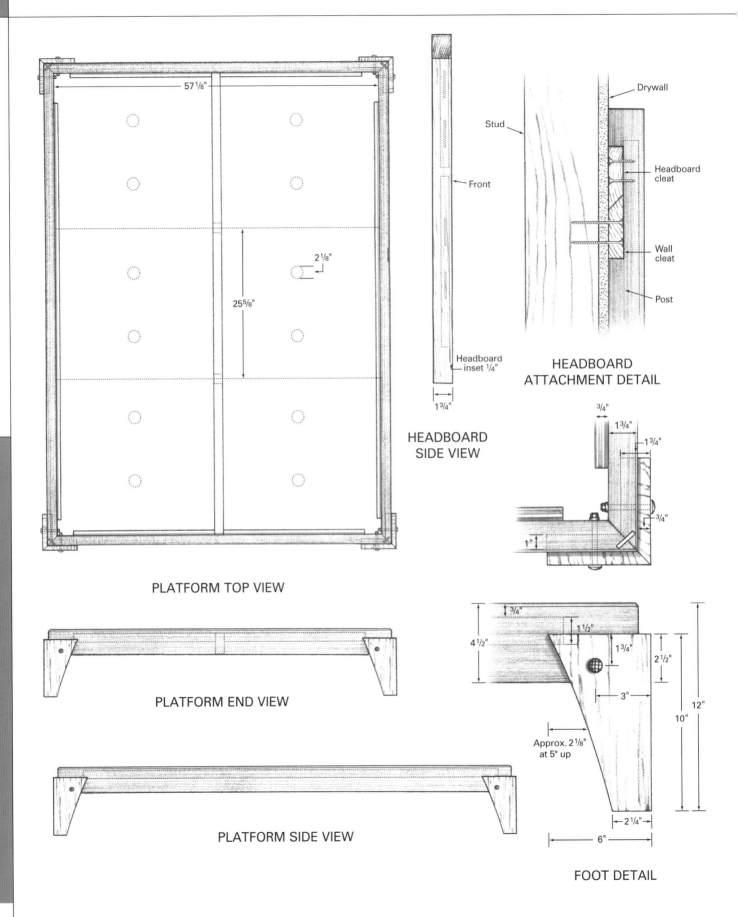

HEADBOARD ATTACHMENT DETAIL

Drywall

Stud

Front

Headboard cleat

Wall cleat

Post

Headboard inset 1/4"

1 3/4"

HEADBOARD SIDE VIEW

57 1/8"

2 1/8"

25 5/8"

PLATFORM TOP VIEW

PLATFORM END VIEW

PLATFORM SIDE VIEW

3/4"

1 3/4"

1 3/4"

3/4"

1"

3/4"

1 1/2"

1 3/4"

2 1/2"

3"

12"

10"

Approx. 2 1/8" at 5" up

2 1/4"

4 1/2"

6"

FOOT DETAIL

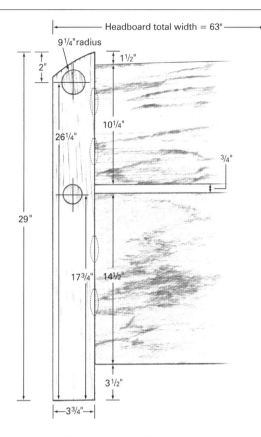

Headboard total width = 63"

9¼"radius

2"

1½"

10¼"

26¼"

¾"

29"

17¾" 14½"

3½"

3¾"

HEADBOARD FRONT VIEW DETAIL

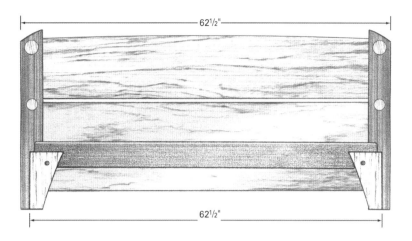

62½"

62½"

END VIEW, PLATFORM BED AND HEADBOARD

JAZZ UP THOSE CARRIAGE BOLTS

Transform off-the-shelf carriage bolts into designer carriage bolts by etching lines in the head with a triangular file.

This is a nifty way to turn ordinary carriage bolts into designer bolts. You'll need a metal-working vise and a triangular file.

While the bolt is firmly held in the vise, use the file to etch the bolt head. This is a freehand activity, and in fact looks better if the etchings aren't symmetrical.

Complete the look with a couple of coats of metallic spray paint.

Once you've completed your design, use emery paper (sandpaper formulated for metal) to remove any burrs and rough up the surface a bit to help paint adhere. I like to use black or metallic spray paint to complete the look. When it's time to install the designer bolts, be sure to drive them with a non-marring wooden or rubber mallet.

Building the Platform Bed

Build the rails

MITER THE RAILS

Handle mitered workpieces with care. Miters are not only sharp but are also easily damaged.

1. Cut a 45° miter on one end of each rail. You'll need a 12" miter saw to handle the 4 1/2" width. Or cut them by hand with a Japanese saw and guide, as described in the method for hand cutting dadoes on p. 66. It's entirely possible to cut these without a guide, but easy to fashion a guide if need be. The table saw isn't your best bet here because of the difficulty of supporting the length.

2. Measure the final length from the long end of the miter.

3. Make a mitered cut on the other end of the rail at the final length.

4. Cut a 45° chamfer on the top edge of each rail with a router or hand plane.

PREFINISH THE RAILS

5. Final sand up to 220 grit.

6. Ebonize the rails (see p. 21).

7. Apply two coats of gel poly for added luster.

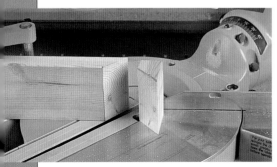

The rails join with miters. Cut them on the miter saw and take care when handling the mitered rails. The miters are not only sharp, but also easily damaged.

Build the feet

CUT THE SPLINED MITERS AND RABBET THE TOPS

1. Cut the miter and the groove for the spline in the leg material (see p. 65).

2. Square up one end of the mitered, grooved workpiece.

3. Measuring from the squared end, cut into eight pieces, each 11" long.

4. Set up a dado blade and use a miter gauge (and a stop) to cut the rabbet in one end of each of the eight pieces. The rabbet is 1" wide and 2 1/2" deep when the foot is in the upright position.

5. Cut each piece to a final length of 10".

BORE FOR THE BOLTS

6. Lay out the bolt-hole locations on each of the eight pieces.

7. Bore 5/16"-diameter bolt holes on the drill press.

SHAPE THE FEET

8. Make a foot template by drawing the Foot Detail full size on a piece of 1/4" plywood. This is your template. (See p. 74 for details on drawing curves.)

9. Cut the foot template on the band saw.

10. Smooth and refine the curve with a sanding drum mounted in a drill press.

11. Use the template to lay out the shape on each foot piece.

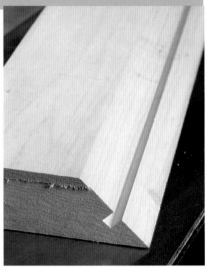

Locate the spline closer to the inside of the miter so it doesn't show.

12. Cut the curve on the band saw, saving the waste for use as clamping cauls.

13. Refine the curve with the drill press sanding drum, and smooth it by hand sanding.

SAND THE INNER SURFACES

14. Final sand all inside surfaces up to 220 grit.

15. Apply a small amount of paste wax along the inside edges where the miters meet. This makes it easy to scrape off any glue squeeze-out.

MILL THE SPLINES

16. Use the band saw to cut thin spline material. It takes a little trial and error to find the proper fence setting. You should end up with splines that fit in the groove snugly.

GLUE UP THE FEET

With the miters and splines, this is a moderately complicated glue-up. Do a dry run without glue to see what's in store.

17. Cut the spline to length.

18. Apply glue to each mitered surface and a small bead in the grooves.

19. Push in the spline.

20. Press the two parts together, sliding them back and forth to spread the glue and create suction.

21. Tape the curve offcuts back in place with masking tape to provide a flat clamping surface.

22. Make sure the rabbets are aligned, and clamp in three places, using $1/4"$ plywood pads between the clamps and the feet to prevent marring.

23. Double-check that the shoulders are aligned.

PREFINISH THE FEET
24. Remove dried glue and finish sand the outsides of the feet up to 220 grit.

25. Stain the feet.

26. Apply two coats of gel poly for added luster.

Cutting the spline looks hard, but it's a simple and safe table-saw procedure.

Assemble the platform

PLYWOOD
1. Mark the ventilation hole locations on each platform leaf.

2. Bore a $1/16"$-diameter hole with a portable drill in the center of the hole.

3. Using the previous hole as a center point, bore a 2"-diameter hole in the drill press. Drill halfway down from each side to avoid tearing out the plywood veneer.

4. Soften the edges of each hole with a router fitted with a $1/4"$ roundover bit.

5. Soften the edges of the plywood with an orbital sander and 120-grit paper.

FASTEN THE CLEATS
The plywood panels rest on a ledge created by fastening plywood cleats to the inside of the solid wood rails.

6. Bore and countersink the cleats for screws. Place them at about 16" intervals.

7. Mark a line on the inside edge of each rail, 3/4" down from the top.

8. Mark the location of the center beam.

9. Use $1\,1/4"$ drywall screws to attach the top edge of the cleat along the line marked in step 7.

FASTEN THE FEET TO THE END RAILS
10. Clamp a foot on each end of an end rail. Make sure the rail is tight in the corner and fully seated on the rabbet. Work carefully and make sure everything fits together correctly. Label all the parts for reassembly.

Decorative carriage bolts fasten the feet to the rails. The attachment is simple, elegant, and strong.

11. The existing hole in the foot is your guide. Use a portable drill to bore a $5/16"$ hole in the rail. Don't go all the way through the rail; just make a dimple in the surface.

12. Unclamp the feet and complete the holes in the drill press.

13. Bolt the feet to the end rails (see p. 131).

FASTEN THE SIDE RAILS
14. Clamp the rails to the end/foot assembly. Make sure everything's properly seated and positioned.

15. As with the end rails, use a portable drill to dimple the rail and then bore the bolt holes in the drill press.

16. Bolt the rails to the feet.

INSTALL THE CENTER BEAM AND POSTS
17. Attach the center posts to the center beam with biscuits.

18. Slip the center beam into position, and fit to the correct height.

Shape the headboard posts and build the panels

INLAY THE POSTS

1. Mark the locations of the inlay circles on the posts.

2. Inlay the circles using a router and inlay bit (see p. 75).

3. Cut your inlay pieces thick enough so they stand slightly proud above the post surface. Don't glue the inlays in place until after staining and applying finish.

SHAPE THE POSTS

4. Lay out the top curve on each post.

5. Cut the curve on the band saw.

The inlay makes a bold statement, but is easy to fashion with a router and the right setups.

6. Refine the curve with files, a belt sander, or a spokeshave.

7. Smooth the curve with an orbital sander and 150- or 120-grit paper.

8. Soften all edges with a hand plane or by hand sanding.

CUT THE BISCUIT SLOTS

9. Lay out the locations of the biscuits that attach the panels to the post.

10. Cut the biscuit slots (see p. 46).

PREFINISH

11. Final sand the posts down to 220 grit.

12. Ebonize or stain the posts.

13. Apply two or three coats of finish, always being careful to keep finish out of inlay areas or biscuit slots.

14. Use the drill press chuck or a bench vise to press the inlay material into the holes on the posts. Make sure the outer surface is smooth before it's pressed into place. Apply a few coats of poly gel to the inlay.

GLUE UP THE PANELS

15. Edge glue the two top boards into a panel (see p. 47).

16. Edge glue the three bottom boards into a panel in the same manner.

17. Cut the panels to final length and width.

18. Soften the bottom edge of the top panel and both edges of the bottom panel with a hand plane.

SLOT THE PANELS

19. Position the panels against the posts, and transfer the biscuit locations on the posts to the panels.

20. Cut the biscuit slots in the panels, locating them on the centerline of the panels' thickness.

CURVE THE TOP

21. Draw the curve on the top panel. Though it doesn't show clearly on the detail drawing, the center of the panel is 10 1/4" wide, and the ends are 9" wide. Sweep a gentle curve through the points.

22. Cut the curve on the band saw, or with a jigsaw.

23. Refine the curve with a belt sander, hand planes, a spokeshave, or any combination thereof.

24. Smooth the curve with an orbital sander.

25. Soften the edges of the curve by hand sanding.

PREFINISH

26. Final sand the panels to 220 grit.

27. Stain the panels if desired.

28. Apply two coats of gel poly to both sides of the panels.

Assemble and hang the headboard

ASSEMBLE THE POSTS AND PANEL

1. Make a dry test run of the clamp-up (without biscuits) before you apply glue.

2. Lay two pipe clamps on the floor.

3. Lay the headboard panels across the bench and put glue in each slot, followed by a biscuit.

4. Put some glue in the post biscuit slots.

5. Push the posts onto the panels, tapping with a rubber mallet if necessary. Remember that it needn't be a perfect joint at this point. The clamps will pull the assembly together.

6. Carefully lay the headboard on the clamps.

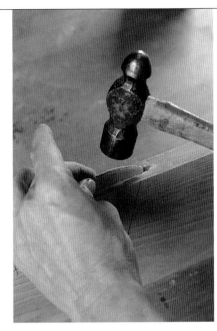

The headboard is nothing more than a slightly modified biscuited frame and panel.

7. Place protective pads between the posts and clamps.

8. Apply just enough pressure to pull the parts together.

9. Lay two more clamps across the top of the headboard and tighten them, thus creating even pressure across the top and bottom.

MAKE THE CLEATS

10. Tilt the table saw blade to 45° and cut the cleat material into equal halves. You now have two matching parts that will interlock to hang the headboard securely (see the Headboard Attachment Detail).

11. Countersink and bore screw holes in the headboard half of the cleat.

12. Fasten it to the headboard with 1 1/4" drywall screws.

INSTALL THE WALL CLEAT

13. Locate the wall studs. You should screw the cleat to at least three studs.

14. Mark the three studs at the height of the lower edge of the headboard cleat.

15. Hold the upper edge of the wall cleat along this line, and mark the centerline of the studs on the wall cleat.

16. Countersink and bore screw holes in the wall cleat.

17. Fasten the cleat to the wall with 2 1/2" drywall screws.

POSITION THE HEADBOARD

18. Place the headboard against the wall, slightly above the cleat.

19. Lower the headboard until the cleats interlock.

BEDSIDE CABINET

Open doors with this challenging project.

When I'm wallowing in the quagmire of my thoughts, I head to the closet to unleash…the vacuum cleaner. A brief cleaning never hurts. In fact, I find that chasing dust bunnies seems to loosen the cranial cobwebs. Ideas are set free. I call this "mind sweeping" and attribute many of my inspirations to sessions with my faithful clean machine.

Since at any given moment, women all over the planet are cleaning something, I like to think we are all engaged in a huge collective thought process, which, if harnessed—no, I'll stop and go back to the woodworking. But you can see where this cleaning thing can go.

Cleaning epiphanies are not always cosmic. Vacuuming is a great time to ponder furniture design. After all, the stuff is all around you, and it's not uncommon to crash into table legs, bump into sharp edges, and curse those corners where dust collects.

My latest revelation occurred while vacuuming the bedroom. After crashing into the bedside table legs for the umpteenth time, I suddenly realized there is no place for table legs next to the bed. This led to the notion of a pair of wall-mounted cabinets; it was clear they offered more storage space within and below. I designed the cabinets with sliding doors and an independent bank of drawers that are easy to position on the bed side of the cabinet, right or left as needed. You could have only doors, only drawers, none, or both, as you choose.

Rest assured, cleaning around the bed will take on a whole new meaning once the vacuum and your mind are free to roam.

Bedside cabinets make cleaning a lot easier—no legs to crash into with the vacuum cleaner. This cabinet is part of a matched pair, and is made of hickory with decorative paper door panels and wenge drawer pulls.

Cut List & Supplies

NUMBER OF PARTS	DESCRIPTION	DIMENSIONS IN INCHES			COMMENTS
		Thickness	Width	Length	
Solid wood					
Carcase (hickory)					
6	Top and bottom boards	3/4	4 1/2	24	*Glue into two panels, each with finished dimensions of 3/4" x 13" x 23 1/4"*
6	Side boards	3/4	4 1/2	17	*Glue into two panels, each with finished dimensions of 3/4" x 12 3/4" x 15 5/8"*
3	Shelf boards	3/4	4 1/2	22	*Cut to final width and length to fit after carcase assembly*
1	Cleat for hanging	3/4	5	20 1/2	*Rip into half with table saw blade set at 45°*
Drawers (soft maple)					
2	Upper drawer front and back	1/2	2	7 5/8	
2	Upper drawer sides	1/2	2	11 1/4	
2	Lower drawer front and back	1/2	2 1/2	7 5/8	
2	Lower drawer sides	1/2	2 1/2	11 1/4	
4	Drawer runners	1/2	1/2	11 3/4	*Final dimensions to fit drawer box*
1	Upper drawer face	5/16	2 5/8	8 1/2	*Final dimensions to fit drawer box*
1	Lower drawer face	5/16	3 5/8	8 1/2	*Final dimensions to fit drawer box*
Doors (hickory)					
1	Upper door track	5/16	2 1/8	20 1/2	*Final dimensions to fit cabinet*
4	Stiles	3/4	1 3/4	8	*Final dimensions to fit cabinet*
4	Rails	3/4	2 3/4	6 5/8	*Final dimensions to fit cabinet*

Cut List & Supplies

NUMBER OF PARTS	DESCRIPTION	DIMENSIONS IN INCHES			COMMENTS
		Thickness	Width	Length	
Plywood (Baltic birch)					
Drawer box					
2	Drawer box top and bottom	1/2	6	11 3/4	
2	Drawer box sides	1/2	6	11 3/4	
1	Box back	1/8	6	8 1/2	*Use hardboard rather than plywood*
Doors					
2	Panels	1/2	2 1/2	6 5/8	
Drawers					
2	Drawer bottom	1/4	7 1/8	11	
Other materials & supplies					
	1" screws				*For assembling box*
	1 1/2" screws				*For attaching cleat to cabinet*
	2 1/2" screws				*For attaching cleat to wall*
	Drywall inserts				*If only one stud is located correctly for fastening cabinet to wall, fasten to the drywall using inserts*
	Round toothpicks				*For reinforcing drawer corner rabbet joints*
	3/8" decorative plugs or dowels				*For plugging screw holes*

How to Build the Bedside Cabinet

Build the carcase

The solid wood carcase is an exercise in making stopped dadoes so the joinery doesn't show from the front. The sides slip into stopped dadoes cut in the top and bottom pieces, the shelf sits in stopped dadoes, and the bottom door track features them as well. Cut the deeper structural dadoes with a plunge router and fence; the shallow door track is done on the router table. Rabbet the sides and shelf where they slip into the stopped dadoes, and cut a small notch from the front corner with a handsaw.

Build the drawer box

The drawers sit in a self-contained plywood box that slips atop the shelf. Build it to fit the space, using rabbeted, screwed, and glued joints.

Build the drawers

Fit the drawers to the finished box, and join the corners with rabbeted joints reinforced with round tooth-picks. Dovetail them if you prefer. Once the drawers fit, glue the box into the cabinet. Then apply the drawer faces, using a credit card to set the gap between the faces and the cabinet.

Build the doors

Cut the grooves in the upper drawer track and fasten it to the cabinet. Build frame and panel doors and size them to fit the track and cabinet opening. You could also build solid panel doors if you prefer. Create and install door and drawer pulls.

Finish and hang

Rip the cleat material in half with the table saw blade tilted at 45°. Cut to length and install at the back of the cabinet, fastening from the sides. Sand everything smooth and apply an oil finish, with an optional two coats of clear poly for extra protection on the top. Rub a coat of paste wax over all. Install the cleat on the wall and hang the cabinet.

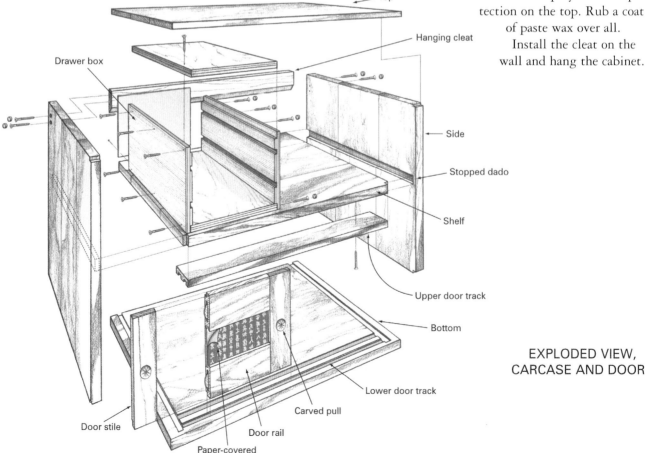

EXPLODED VIEW,
CARCASE AND DOORS

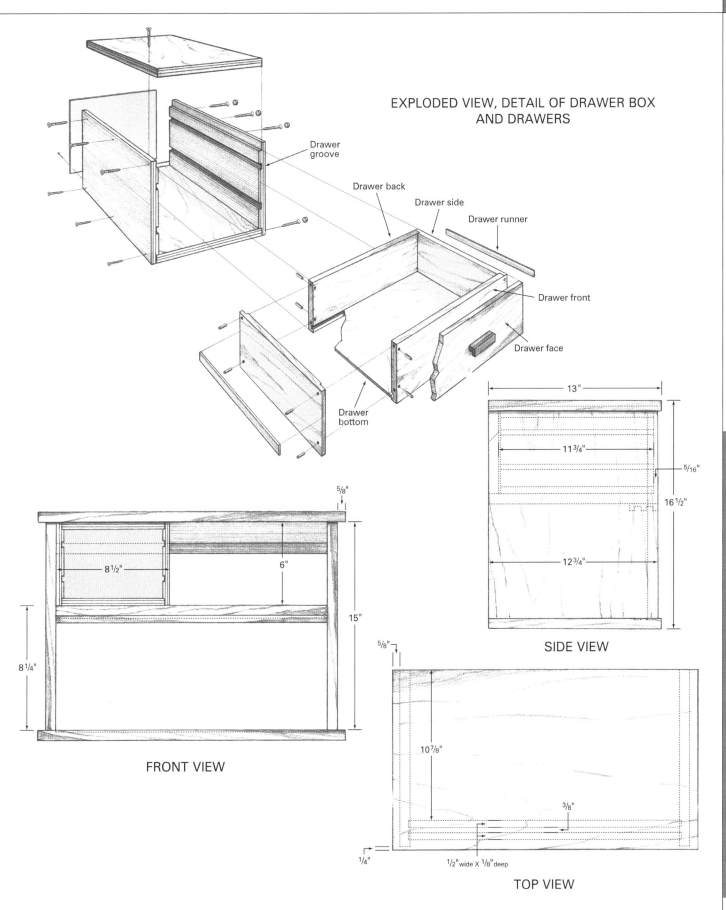

EXPLODED VIEW, DETAIL OF DRAWER BOX
AND DRAWERS

Drawer groove

Drawer back

Drawer side

Drawer runner

Drawer front

Drawer face

Drawer bottom

8¹/₂"

6"

15"

5/8"

8¹/₄"

FRONT VIEW

13"

11³/₄"

5/16"

16¹/₂"

12³/₄"

SIDE VIEW

5/8"

10⁷/₈"

3/8"

1/4"

1/2" wide X 1/8" deep

TOP VIEW

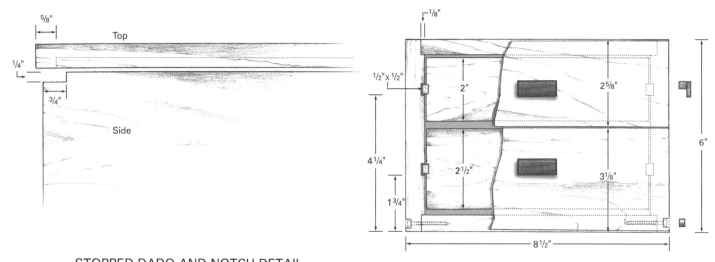

STOPPED DADO AND NOTCH DETAIL

BOX AND DRAWERS CUTAWAY VIEW

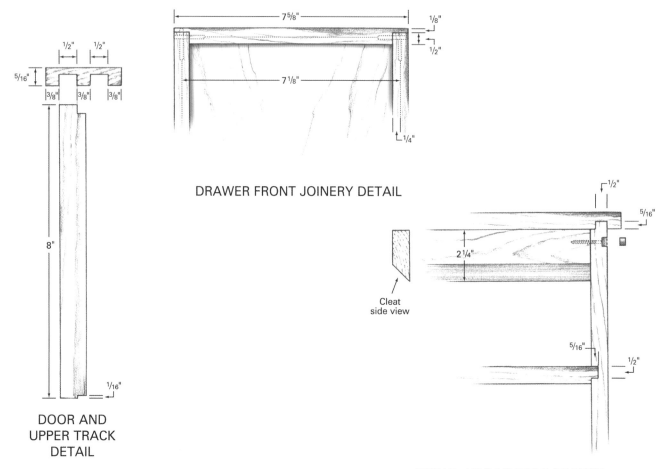

DRAWER FRONT JOINERY DETAIL

DOOR AND
UPPER TRACK
DETAIL

DETAIL AT BACK TOP CORNER

Building the Bedside Cabinet

The carcase joinery features stopped dadoes. Cut them with a plunge router or use a router table for those less than 1/4" deep.

Build the carcase

EDGE GLUE THE PANELS

1. Edge glue the boards to create the top, bottom, side, and shelf panels. Use the method described on page 47.

2. Sand both sides of each panel with a random orbit sander and 120-grit paper.

STOPPED DADOES

3. Lay out the stopped dadoes on the top and bottom panels (see the Top View). The dadoes are all 1/2" wide and 5/16" deep.

4. Cut the stopped dadoes, using the router method described on page 000. Start your cuts at the back of the cabinet, and cut to the stop.

5. Lay out the stopped dadoes on the side panels. They hold the shelf in place, and the dimensions are also 1/2" wide and 5/16" deep.

6. Cut the stopped dadoes in the side panel, using the same method.

GROOVE THE BOTTOM DRAWER TRACKS

7. Mark the outermost groove on the carcase bottom. The grooves show as dotted lines in the Top View. They're 1/8" deep x 1/2" wide. The top panel has stopped dadoes only. The bottom also has the grooves of the bottom door track.

8. Mount a 1/2"-diameter router bit in a router and set it up in the router table. Rout the stopped groove (see p. 64).

9. Mount a 3/8"-thick auxiliary fence and rout the second groove. Save the fence to use later, when you use the table saw to cut the deeper grooves in the upper door track.

RABBET AND NOTCH THE SIDES

10. Cut 5/16" x 1/2" rabbets on the top and bottom ends of each side piece. Use a router and rabbeting bit (see p. 66). Save the setup if you can—you'll use it later to rout the ends of the shelf.

11. To fit the stopped dadoes, the sides and shelf need a small notch cut in the front edge of both ends. Lay out the notches as shown in the Stopped Dado and Notch Detail, using a knife to scribe a line that can guide your Japanese saw.

12. Crosscut first, and then make the rip cut to form the notch.

13. Clean up the notch with a chisel.

TEST THE FIT

A dado/rabbet joint isn't the strongest joint in woodworking because you're gluing long grain to end gain. If the fit is loose, the joint is that much weaker. If the fit isn't all you could ask for, consider gluing paper or thin wood shims in the joint. You could also use epoxy glue, which is powerful enough to bridge small gaps with no loss in joint strength.

14. Clamp the carcase together, adjusting the fit of any joints as necessary.

SURFACE PREP

15. Final sand both the insides and outsides of the carcase sides, and the inside surfaces of the top and bottom pieces. Work up to 220 grit.

16. Apply a light coat of paste wax around the dado and rabbet joints to facilitate glue removal later. Avoid getting wax on the gluing surfaces.

ASSEMBLE THE CARCASE

17. Apply glue to all joint surfaces, and clamp in position using cauls to apply even pressure.

18. Check for square before fully tightening the clamps.

FIT THE SHELF

19. Square up one end of the shelf panel.

20. Rather than measuring the length, hold a piece of thin scrap up to the back of the carcase. Make sure one end of the scrap is squared.

21. Align the squared end with the outside of one of the stopped dadoes in the side.

22. Mark the scrap piece on the outside of the other dado.

23. Use this dimension to set up the saw to crosscut the shelf to finished length.

24. Using the same setup that you used to rabbet the sides, rabbet both ends of the shelf.

25. Cut the notches on the shelf, just as you did on the sides.

26. Slip the shelf into place. It should go in without much resistance. If it binds, slip it out and trim the rabbets with a shoulder plane. Make sure the front of the shelf is flush with the sides of the carcase.

27. When the shelf fits properly, put a small amount of glue in the dado and slide the shelf in place.

CLEAT FOR HANGING

28. Rip the cleat material in half on the table saw, with the blade tilted at 45°.

29. Cut the cleat length to fit the back of the cabinet, between the sides (see the Detail at Back Top Corner).

30. Drill and counterbore screw holes from the cabinet sides into the cleat end grain.

31. Soften the edges, especially the angled cuts.

32. Apply glue to the ends of the cleat, and a small bead on the mating surface of the cabinet.

33. Fasten the cleat in place and plug the holes with decorative plugs.

Build the drawer box

The primary objectives here are to make a box that is perfectly square and that fits the cabinet. Make sure the four pieces that make up the top, bottom, and sides are identical and that the crosscuts are truly at 90°.

1. Measure the distance from the front of the cabinet to the front side of the cleat. Subtract the thickness of your drawer faces ($^5/_{16}$"). This is the final length of the drawer box pieces.

2. Cut rabbets on the top and bottom edges of the side pieces, using a dado blade in the table saw (see p. 66).

3. Cut the $^1/_2$"-wide x $^1/_4$"-deep grooves in the interior side of the box side pieces.

4. Clamp the box and check it for square.

5. Bore pilot holes for screws in the corner joints (see the Box and Drawers Cutaway View and the photo to the right). The screws on one side of the box will be visible in the finished cabinet—which side

The drawers fit in a self-contained plywood box. This makes it easy to make mirror-image cabinets suitable for the right and left sides of the bed.

that is depends on whether you're building a right- or left-side cabinet. I countersink the heads of the visible screws and cover them with flush cut plugs. For fun, I then burned a design onto the plug with a wood burning tool.

6. Finish sand all the outside surfaces to 220 grit.

7. Attach the box back with a small amount of glue and some short screws.

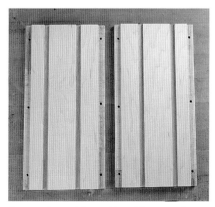

Drawer box sides with rabbets and grooves, ready for glue up

Countersink and bore the rabbet joints for fastening with screws.

Sometimes the author plugs screw heads with flush-cut dowels and then uses a wood burning tool to burn a decoration on the surface.

Build the drawers

PREPARE THE DRAWER PARTS

Fit the drawers to the box; don't rely on the dimensions in the Materials chart. Measure the interior width of the box, and make the drawers about 1/16" narrower for ease of operation.

1. Before cutting drawer components to their final lengths, cut the groove for the drawer bottom. You'll have to experiment with your dado blade to get the proper thickness for a good fit (1/4" plywood is less than 1/4" thick). If the groove is too wide, the drawer will rattle.

2. Cut the drawer components to fit the drawer box you built, using the dimensions in the Materials list as a rough guide. Since your box is likely different from the ones in the illustrations (this is hand woodworking after all!), it will be helpful to make a full-size drawing to determine the correct dimensions for your drawers (see the Drawer Joinery Detail.) When you're ready to glue up your drawer pieces, they should look like those shown in the photo above/below.

3. Cut the rabbets to join the corners (see p. 66).

4. Cut the drawer bottoms to finished dimensions and test fit them.

The sides and ends of a drawer, with their rabbets and the groove for the drawer bottom

5. Finish sand all drawer interior surfaces and apply two coats of clear shellac.

ASSEMBLE THE DRAWERS

6. Apply glue to the rabbets and clamp the drawers, checking them for square.

7. Reinforce the corner joints with round toothpicks. Drill appropriate holes in opposing corners, apply a small amount of glue, and tap the toothpicks in place.

8. Use a Japanese saw to cut the toothpicks flush after the glue dries.

SURFACE PREP

9. Sand the outer drawer surfaces flush.

10. Soften all the edges.

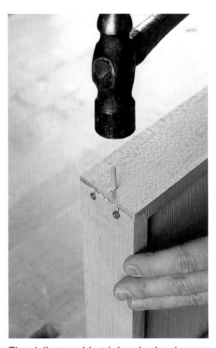
The delicate rabbet joints in the door are best reinforced with round wooden toothpicks or very narrow dowels set in a little glue. Cut them flush after the glue dries.

DRAWER RUNNERS

11. Cut 1/2"-wide x 1/4"-deep grooves in the sides of the drawer. Use a dado blade in the table saw, as shown in the photo below.

12. Cut the runners to length to fit the groove.

13. Apply a little glue to the groove and clamp the runners in place.

FIT THE DRAWERS

14. Slip the drawer runners into the grooves in the box.

15. If the runners are too tight and don't allow the drawers to move freely, use a hand plane to take off a shaving or two as needed. Later you'll apply oil and wax to the drawers and box, which will help to reduce friction and let the drawers slide more freely.

After the drawers are glued up, cut grooves in the sides for runners. Use a dado blade in the table saw.

INSTALL THE DRAWER BOX

Since the drawer box is plywood and the carcase is solid wood, wood movement is a consideration. While the plywood is dimensionally stable, the solid wood is not.

16. Position the box in the cabinet, $5/16$" back from the front edge so that when the drawer faces are installed, they'll be flush with the cabinet's side.

17. Apply a 1"-wide bead of glue down the center of the bottom of the box.

18. Slip the box in place. If the fit is good, you won't need clamps.

APPLY DRAWER FACES

19. Place an old credit card or thin magnetic material (such as that used for refrigerator magnets) as a shim between the bottom drawer face and the bottom of the drawer box. This gives the perfect visual gap between the two.

20. Check that the face ends are parallel to the box and cabinet sides, trimming the ends with a block plane or stationary belt sander if necessary.

21. Final sand the face to 220 grit.

22. Apply glue to the back of the drawer face and to the drawer front, and clamp in place.

23. Once the glue dries, use the lower face to position the upper face. Use the shim as before, and check the fit.

The drawer fronts are flush with the box. The drawer faces are flush with the cabinet sides.

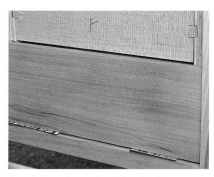

An old credit card or bit of refrigerator magnet makes a perfect shim for setting the gaps around the drawer faces.

24. When the upper face fits properly, pull out both drawers about 1" to allow room for the clamps needed to glue it in place.

25. Apply glue to the face and drawer front as above and clamp in place.

Clamp the drawer faces in place with spring clamps. To clamp the upper drawer, pull out both drawers and position it with the credit card shims.

Build the doors

CUT AND INSTALL
THE UPPER DOOR TRACK

1. Cut the door track to finished length. Rather than trying to get an inside dimension with a tape measure, first square one end of the track material, hold it up to the cabinet opening, and mark on the opposite end where to cut.

2. Lay out the groove locations on the track.

3. Cut the first groove using a dado blade in the table saw.

4. Retrieve the 3/8" auxiliary fence you used to cut the second groove on the carcase bottom. Attach it to the table saw fence.

5. Cut the second groove against this fence.

6. Countersink and bore the screw holes in the track, as shown in the photo below.

7. Fasten the upper drawer track to the underside of the shelf.

Cut the upper track grooves on the table saw, and then countersink and bore for the screws that attach it to the underside of the shelf.

DETERMINE DOOR HEIGHT

8. Temporarily place the upper drawer track in position.

9. The doors should be about 8" tall, but you can find the exact length with some scrap 1/4" plywood. Put the top end in the front track, and experiment with the length until you can easily slip the lower end into the track. That's the final dimension.

The proper door height lets you put the top in the upper track and just slip the door into the lower track.

FRAME AND PANEL DOORS

10. Build the frame and panel doors to fit the cabinet (see p. 50). Remember that both the frame and panel are flush at the back, and cut your biscuit slots accordingly.

11. Apply decorative paper to the plywood (see p. 171) before gluing up the doors.

12. When the glue is dry, cut the small rabbets on the top and bottom edges of the door backs. Note that they're different (see the Door and Upper Track Detail). Use the table saw and regular blade.

13. Plane a small chamfer on the inside shoulder of each rabbet.

14. Test fit and adjust as needed.

15. Finish sand up to 220 grit.

Let your imagination go wild on the door pulls. The author carved a design into the bottom of a hole drilled halfway through the door.

Make custom drawer pulls by gluing two strips of wood into an el with cyanoacrylate glue. Use the same glue to fasten them to the drawer front.

DOOR AND DRAWER PULLS

The doors need recessed pulls, but the drawers can have just about any type of pull. This is one place you can let your imagination run free. Just test out your ideas on some scrap first!

On my cabinet, I bored holes about halfway through the door and then used a carving tool to make a sunburst design in the recess. Sand by hand to soften the edges.

For drawers I made simple el-shaped pulls from two strips of wenge left over from another project. I simply used a cyanoacrylate glue to fashion them into an el, rounded the edges with a little hand sanding, and then glued the els to the drawer fronts.

Finish and hang

FINISH

1. Apply an oil finish to all surfaces, interior and exterior, including the box and drawers. Use a small brush to get into the door tracks. Oil helps the sliding parts to move more readily.

2. Wipe off all excess before the oil dries.

3. After at least 78 hours drying time, apply paste wax or an additional clear hard finish to the top for extra protection.

HANG THE CABINET

4. Remove the drawers and doors to eliminate any extra weight.

5. Determine the ideal height for your situation and mark the cleat location on the wall.

6. Use a stud finder to locate wall studs in the vicinity of the cleat.

7. Given the size of the cabinet, you'll likely have only one stud available for fastening, and the cleat should screw to the wall in at least two locations. If only one stud is available, you'll need to use one or more drywall inserts and fasten the cleat to the drywall.

8. Countersink and bore screw holes in the mounting cleat and screw it to the wall.

9. Cover the screw heads with 3/8" decorative plugs.

10. Hang the cabinet and replace the doors and drawers.

Finish with oil and rub down with paste wax for added luster.

FREESTANDING CABINET

Expand your horizons with plywood.

And now for something different—a curvy cabinet with a free-spirited attitude. The wide top, curved stiles, and funky pull radiate verve, but underneath it all, this is just a simple plywood cabinet.

Erase all those mental pictures you have of ugly plywood furniture. Used wisely and judiciously combined with solid wood, plywood is an ideal cabinet material. You can quickly cut up a sheet and make use of some quick and sturdy joinery—biscuits, screws, or dado/rabbet joints. Granted, there are those unsightly plywood edges to deal with, but the labor and material to hide them seems trivial compared with the hours you'd spend milling and cutting fancy joints to build the same cabinet from solid wood.

Then there's the dimensional stability angle. Since plywood doesn't shrink or swell with changes in humidity, you can just biscuit the solid wood frames to the plywood panels. Building this cabinet will give you a good grounding in the principles of working with plywood and combining it effectively with solid wood.

Solid wood stiles curved along their outside edges join the corners of the plywood. Incidentally, they also cover the unsightly plywood edges. Two internal frames (called web frames) tie the back and sides together structurally to compensate for the fact that the doors don't offer any strength. You can build this cabinet with the shelves as shown, or change the shelf spacing to suit your particular storage needs.

Building a freestanding cabinet may seem a little overwhelming at first, but like all woodworking projects, it's just a collection of simple steps. Each one is simple; the aggregate is wonderfully complex. Take it one simple step at a time, and you'll be fine.

The unusual design and simple construction of this freestanding cabinet make the most of plywood's virtues. The free-form curved pieces along the door rails are embellishments not shown in the illustrations.

Cut List & Supplies

NUMBER OF PARTS	DESCRIPTION	DIMENSIONS IN INCHES			COMMENTS
		Thickness	Width	Length	
Solid wood (cherry)					
4	Stiles	1	3 1/4	45 1/4	*Maximum width at top is 3"; tapers to 2" at bottom*
2	Upper rails	1	3	22 1/4	
2	Lower rails	1	4 1/2	22 1/4	
2	Top panel front/back	3/4	2 5/8	29 1/4	
2	Top panel ends	3/4	3	13 1/8	
2	Foot for side panel	1/2	3/4	18	
4	Door stiles	1	2	37 1/16	
4	Door rails	1	3	7	
1	Door stop	1	1	4	
1	Door pull	1	2	37 1/16	*After rabbeting, resaw to 3/8" thick*
4	Shelf support stock	1/2	1/2	48	*Cut to length as needed*
	Embellishments	1/4			*Various sizes to embellish the curves at the bottoms of the side panel or the fronts of the doors*
Plywood (birch)					
2	Side panels	3/4	16	44 3/4	
4	Web frame front/back, short	3/4	2 1/4	20	*Finished dimension will be close to 19 3/8", but cut final length to fit cabinet*
4	Web frame front/back, long	3/4	2 1/4	24	*Finished dimension will be close to 23 7/8", but cut final length to fit cabinet*
4	Web frame sides, short	3/4	2 1/4	12	*Finished dimension will be close to 11 1/2", but cut final length to fit cabinet*

Cut List & Supplies

NUMBER OF PARTS	DESCRIPTION	DIMENSIONS IN INCHES			COMMENTS
		Thickness	Width	Length	
Plywood (birch) continued					
4	Web frame sides, long	3/4	2 1/4	16 1/2	*Finished dimension will be close to 16", but cut final length to fit cabinet*
4	Shelves	3/4	15 7/8	23 3/4	
1	Top panel	3/4	13 1/8	23 1/8	
2	Door panels	3/4	7	31 5/8	
1	Dust panel	1/4	15 7/8	23 3/4	
1	Back	1/4	23	38	*Cut to fit rabbet in frame*
Other materials & supplies					
4	Butt hinges		1 3/8	2 1/2	*With removable pins*
28'	Veneer edge banding tape	7/8			*For shelf edges*
2	3/8"-diameter rare earth magnets				
2	1/4" flat washers				*For door catches*
	2" drywall screws				
	1 1/4" drywall screws				
	#20 biscuits				
	#6 x 5/8" pan head screws				*For fastening back*
	Toothpaste				*A small amount for locating the washers on the doors relative to the magnets in the doorstop*

How to Build the Freestanding Cabinet

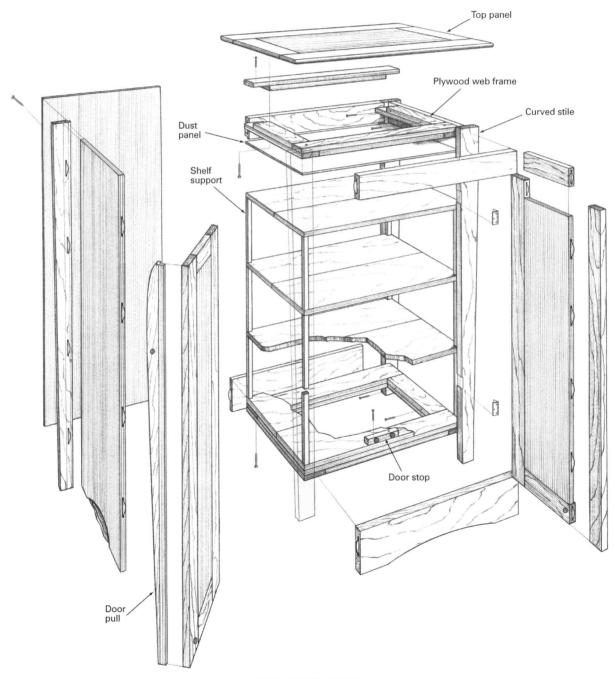

Top panel

Plywood web frame

Curved stile

Dust panel

Shelf support

Door stop

Door pull

EXPLODED VIEW

Build the front and back frames

The first thing to do is build the solid wood front and back frames, which are joined with biscuits. Then cut the side panels and biscuit them to the frames.

Fit the web frames, shelves, and back

Though the exterior dimensions are set, the cabinet isn't very sturdy. That will improve when you build the plywood web frames to fit inside the cabinet at the top and bottom. With easy access to the interior, now's the time to cut and fit the shelves and back; you'll install them later.

Top it off

Build a solid wood frame with a plywood panel for the top of the cabinet. Fasten it with screws driven through the web frames from the inside of the cabinet.

Build and fit the doors

The doors are also built with solid wood frames biscuited around plywood panels. Fit them with a uniform gap all around, and cut the mortises for the hinges.

Close it up

Once the doors fit properly, install the shelves. Then put an oil finish on the solid wood. When the finish is dry, install the doors, and fasten the back panel in place.

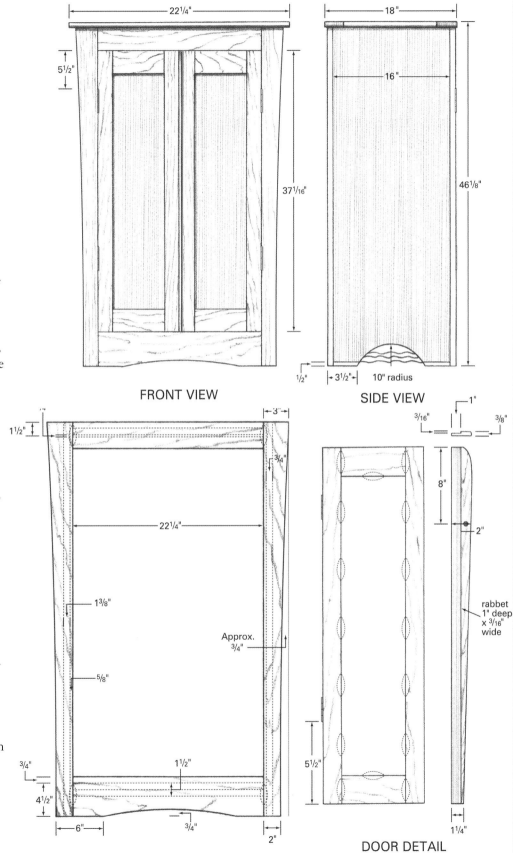

FRONT VIEW

SIDE VIEW

DOOR DETAIL

FRONT/BACK FRAME DETAIL

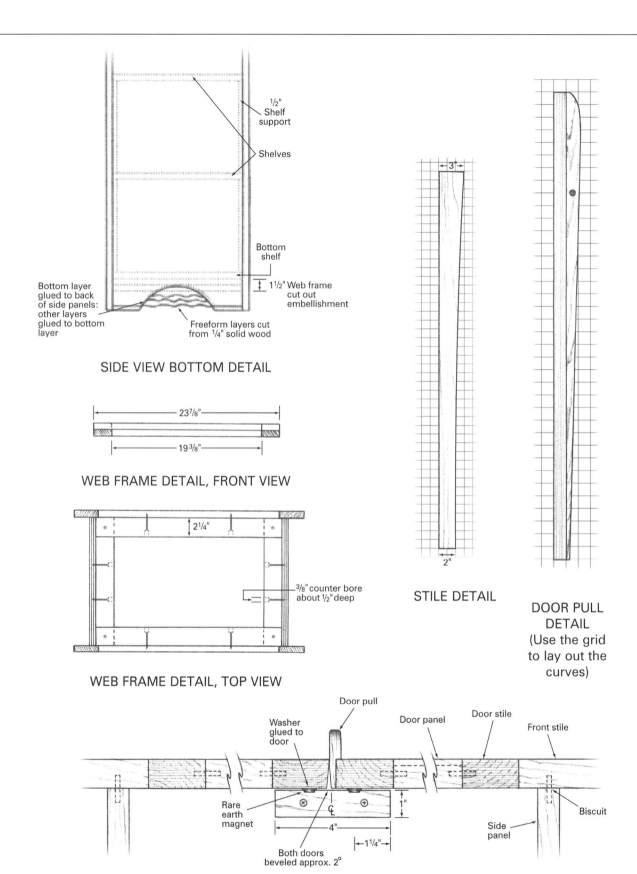

½"
Shelf
support

Shelves

Bottom
shelf

1½" Web frame
cut out
embellishment

Bottom layer
glued to back
of side panels:
other layers
glued to bottom
layer

Freeform layers cut
from ¼" solid wood

SIDE VIEW BOTTOM DETAIL

23⅞"

19⅜"

WEB FRAME DETAIL, FRONT VIEW

2¼"

⅜" counter bore
about ½" deep

WEB FRAME DETAIL, TOP VIEW

3"

2"

STILE DETAIL

**DOOR PULL
DETAIL**
(Use the grid
to lay out the
curves)

Door pull

Washer
glued to
door

Door panel

Door stile

Front stile

1"

Rare
earth
magnet

4"

1¼"

Side
panel

Biscuit

Both doors
beveled approx. 2°

DOOR STOP DETAIL

Building the Freestanding Cabinet

Build the front and back frames

1. Cut stiles and rails to final dimensions. Don't worry about the long curves on the stiles yet—we'll tackle them in a later step.

2. Lay out and mark each part for double biscuits in the corner joints (see p. 49).

3. The front and back rails extend down to the floor, but are arched so only their corners touch. This makes the cabinet more stable on uneven surfaces. Lay out the curves (see the Front View), and cut them on the band saw.

4. Smooth the curves with a sanding drum chucked into your drill press or portable drill. Alternatively, use files and sandpaper.

5. Lay out the biscuit locations on the inner edge of each stile where it joins the side panel.

6. Cut the biscuit slots (see p. 46).

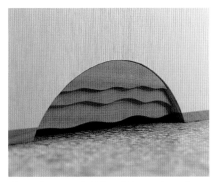

Three layers of 1/4″ solid wood cut in free-form curves add interest to the sides and hide the exposed plywood edges.

MAKE THE SIDE PANELS

7. Cut the plywood side panels to their final dimensions.

8. Lay out the curve on the bottom edges of both panels (see the Side View).

9. Before cutting the curves, apply the solid wood foot to the bottom edge. The easiest way is just to glue it on using a few finishing nails to hold it until the glue dries. Leave the foot a little long and cut it flush with a Japanese saw after the glue dries. Be sure to drill pilot holes for the nails so they don't split the thin strip, and set the heads so they're below the surface. Be careful not to put any nails where you'll be sawing.

10. Cut the curves.

11. Take care when smoothing out the curves after sawing. It's easy to tear out the veneers at the edges, so refine the curves carefully. The safest way is with a small sanding drum chucked into a drill press or portable drill. Finish by lightly hand sanding the edge with a downward stroke.

12. Use a Japanese saw to cut the solid wood feet nearly flush to the sides, then sand flush.

When you fasten the solid wood feet to the bottom of the side panel, leave them a little long. After you've cut the curve, you can saw the feet off nearly flush with the edge. Refine the edge by sanding until the foot is flush with the plywood.

EMBELLISH AND PREFINISH THE PANELS

Never one to pass up an opportunity to add something extra, I like to embellish the curve cutouts with a few layers of 1/4″-thick solid wood. It adds visual interest and covers most of the exposed plywood edges.

13. Start by gluing one layer onto the back of the side panel. Don't let it extend below the solid wood feet. The second and third layers go on top of the first, but are cut so they nestle in against the curve.

14. It'll never be easier to apply finish to the side panels, so do it now. Apply two coats to the insides, and then three coats to the outsides. While the finish is drying, you can go back to working on the solid wood frames.

COMPLETE THE STILES

15. The long curves on the front and back stiles give this project its distinctive look. Because all four need to be exactly alike, make a template and use a router fitted with a template cutting bit to cut four identical stiles (see p. 74).

16. Once the stiles are cut, round over the outer (curved) edges with a router and a $1/2$" roundover bit. Since the pieces are narrower at the bottom, it's hard to balance a hand-held router, so use a router table for this operation.

17. Smooth the profiles by hand sanding with 220-grit paper.

18. Mortise the stiles for the hinges. This may seem out of sequence, but woodworking is like playing chess—you'll do better if you keep ahead of the game by looking a few moves ahead. It's easy to do now, but once the frame is assembled it's much more difficult (see p. 76 for details).

ASSEMBLE THE FRAMES

19. Even though the curved stiles make the outside of the frame out-of-square, the frame is not as difficult to assemble as you might think. The secret is leather. Use small scraps of leather between the clamp and the frame to keep the clamps from slipping on the curves. For details on assembling a frame, see page 50.

20. Once the frames are dry, remove them from the clamps, and smooth and refine them by sanding up to 220 grit.

ATTACH THE SIDE PANELS TO THE FRAMES

21. Lay the back frame face down on a bench, with one stile near the front edge. Lightly hold it in place with a few small clamps.

22. Using a sliding square, make a mark 1 $3/8$" from the inside edge of the stiles. This mark locates the outside edge of the side panel.

23. Hold the panel in position with its outside edge along this line. Transfer the biscuit locations from the stile to the plywood.

24. Cut biscuit slots in the panel edges.

25. Start the glue-up with the back frame. Apply a thin coat of paste wax on the stiles—but only outside the line you marked. This keeps the glue from staining the stiles. It also makes it easier to clean up any glue that might seep out.

26. With a small glue brush, spread glue along the edge of the panel, put some glue in the slots, and insert biscuits. Apply a small bead of glue where the panel joins the stile.

27. Mate the biscuits with the slots in the panel, and clamp it down to the bench. Use at least six bar or pipe clamps. It's important to get even pressure and keep the panel square while clamping.

28. Once the glue is dry, you can repeat this process for the other side panel.

29. With the assembly still clamped to the bench, use the same method to glue the front frame onto the panels. Clamp the whole thing down to the bench.

Fit the web frames, shelves, and back

CUT AND FIT THE WEB FRAMES

The frames and panels are now one, but the cabinet is not very sturdy. A couple of internal web frames tie everything together. Rather than fuss with joinery at the corners, it's much easier to just glue them up from two layers of $3/4$" plywood. Stagger the corner joints for strength (see the Web Frame Details).

1. Cut the web frame parts to their final lengths.

2. It's a bit puzzling at first to see how the pieces go together, so lay them out on the bench and mark the proper arrangement.

3. Apply the glue, reassemble the web frame, and clamp it up.

Plywood web frames inside the cabinet give it strength and rigidity. The shelves are independent of the structure so you can reposition them in the future.

4. When the glue is dry, clean off the excess, and check the fit. If you need to remove any material, be sure to maintain the flatness of the edge. Use the jointer or a sharp hand plane.

5. Reinforce each corner with a 1 1/4" drywall screw. Figure out which side of the web frame is the best looking, and drive the screw into the other side.

6. Before you can secure the web frames to the cabinet, drill several 1/8"-diameter pilot holes right through the plywood (see the Web Frame Details). Use these holes as the center points for drilling another set of 3/8"-diameter holes. These are to let the screw heads sit below the surface. Make these counterbores about 1/2" deep.

INSTALL THE WEB FRAMES

7. Clamp the top web frame in place, with the reinforcing screw heads facing up. Take care to make the web frame's top surface flush with the top of the cabinet.

8. Screw the top web frame to the side panels through the counterbored pilot holes. Use 2" drywall screws.

9. Check the front and back of the web frame for position and fit relative to the frames. Adjust if necessary. Drive the remaining screws.

10. Mark the location of the bottom web frame and check its fit against the solid wood used to embellish the curve cuts at the bottom of the panel. Use the band saw to remove material from the edge of the web

frame to accommodate the first layer of the solid wood embellishment. Don't worry about weakening the web frame. It's plenty strong even when trimmed.

11. While you're still in the web frame mindset, use a 1/8" drill and bore several holes through each web frame. You'll need them later, when you're fastening the dust panel to the top frame and the bottom shelf to the bottom frame.

FIT THE BACK, SHELVES, AND DUST PANEL

12. Lay the cabinet face down on protective pads or a blanket.

13. Use a router and a rabbeting bit to cut a 3/8"-wide x 1/4"-deep rabbet around the inside of the frame (see p. 25).

14. This sort of routing always leaves rounded corners; square them up with a sharp chisel.

15. Cut the back panel to fit the rabbet.

16. Measure and cut the top dust panel. It's screwed to the underside of the top web frame.

17. Measure for the shelves and cut them to size. You'll determine the shelf heights later.

18. Apply veneer tape to the edges of the shelves. Use a hot household iron, and trim them to the proper thickness with a block plane.

19. Sand all the plywood parts with 220-grit paper, and apply three coats of finish to the shelves (both sides) and two coats to the top dust panel and both sides of the back.

Top it off

1. The top is a straightforward biscuited plywood frame and panel. Start by cutting the plywood panel to final length, and follow the sequence of steps described on page 50.

2. A profile softens both the feel and the appearance of the edge. To make the panel appear thinner than it really is, use a handheld router to cut a 30° chamfer around the bottom edge.

3. Round the top edge with a 3/8" roundover bit.

4. Finish sand to 220 grit; carefully sand the profiled edges by hand.

5. Put the top in place and lightly secure it with a couple of clamps.

6. Fasten the top in place with several 2" drywall screws. Drive them upward through the web frame.

7. Attach the bottom shelf to the bottom web frame in the same manner.

The top and back are cut to fit early in construction, but they're not fastened in place until the end. That way, you can easily fit and install the shelves and doors.

Build and fit the doors

The doors are built much like the top. There's one important difference: Since the frame and the panel are flush on the inside of the doors, you must do the layout and biscuit work from the inside (see p. 50). It's easy to forget this and make the common error of working from the more familiar outside, so mark your parts clearly, and keep yourself oriented.

1. Lay out the frames and cut the biscuit slots.

2. Cut the panels and sand them with 220-grit paper.

3. Apply three coats of water-based poly to both sides of the panels.

4. Attach the solid wood frames to the panels.

5. Provide room for the doors to swing by planing a 2° bevel on the inner edge of the right door. Run the door over the jointer with the fence tilted away from the blade (2° off the perpendicular). The back of the door goes against the fence. Don't bevel the left door yet.

6. Set the doors in place, analyze any trouble spots, and trim as necessary.

7. Transfer the mortise locations on the stiles to the doors, then cut those mortises.

8. Sand the doors to 220 grit. Lightly break the arris on the edges by hand sanding.

9. Install hinges on the cabinet frame and doors, leaving the screws slightly loose. Double-check the fit and trim if needed.

DOOR PULL

Now it's time to install the means of opening the doors and keeping them closed. This cabinet has an unusual pull that echoes the curved stiles. It runs the full length of the door and is rabbeted and glued in place. I like to use small but powerful rare earth magnets to make the best stops; they hold well and their placement is not as fussy as other types of stops.

10. Start with a piece of wood that's 1" thick. That's more than you need, but it's easier to make the dado on a thicker piece of wood. Use the table saw and a dado set to cut a $3/16$"-wide by 1"-deep rabbet the length of the pull (see the Door Detail).

11. Replace the standard blade and rip the rabbeted piece to $3/8$".

12. Lay out the curve shown in the Door Pull Detail.

13. Bore the $5/8$" hole for the pull and relieve all the sharp edges, making it smooth to the touch.

14. Cut the curve on the band saw, refine it, and smooth it.

15. Remove the left door and rip $3/16$" from the inner edge.

16. Glue the pull to the inner edge.

17. A 2° bevel on the inner edge (matching that on the right door) makes it easier to open the doors. Run this door through the jointer as you did the right door.

18. Sand the pull smooth with 220-grit paper.

19. Install the hinge pins and check the door in place for fit. When you're satisfied, fully tighten all the hinge screws.

DOOR STOP

20. Make the stop from a piece of solid wood about 1" x 1" x 4" 9see the Door Stop Detail).

21. Bore shallow $3/8$" holes in the face of the stop (their depth should be the same as or slightly less than the thickness of the magnets), about 1 $1/4$" from each end.

22. Bore and counterbore two screw holes for mounting the stop to the cabinet.

23. Round all corners slightly, and smooth the stop with 220-grit sandpaper.

24. Press the magnets into the holes; use a bench vise if the fit is tight. If the fit is loose, glue the magnets in place with epoxy.

25. Special door-catch washers are available, with a countersink area that allows the mounting screw to sit flush with the face of the washer. Alternatively, you can use a standard washer with a $1/2$" O.D., gluing it in place with a quick-setting eoxy. For now, place the two washers on the magnets and center the stop behind the two closed doors. (You can work from the back of the cabinet, if need be.) the outside door faces should sit flush with the outer frame. Mark the stop location and screw it into place.

26. Dab a small amount of toothpaste on the washers and shut the doors and reopen them. The tothpaste will mark the exact locations for correct placement of the washers. Glue or screw them in place.

Close it up

PLACING THE SHELVES AND DUST PANEL

These shelves are fixed in place, supported above and below by $1/2$" x $1/2$" strips of wood glued to the cabinet. Hot-melt glue cures quickly and as a bonus, you can easily pry off the strips and reposition the shelves if need be. If you have a particular function in mind for this cabinet, you'll want to space the shelves accordingly.

1. Rather than working with your head in the cabinet, find a piece of scrap wood and lay out the shelf spacing full size.

2. Cut the lower shelf supports to length and hot-melt glue them into the four corners of the cabinet. Set the lower shelf in place.

3. Install the next set of shelf supports, and then the shelf. Repeat until all four shelves are in place.

OIL THE SOLID WOOD

4. Since the plywood panels were finished in previous steps, most of the finishing work is already done. All that's left is to apply your favorite oil finish to the solid wood parts.

While the oil won't harm the water-based poly on the panels, if you apply it too liberally, it can seep into the end grain of the plywood and discolor the areas where the panel meets the rail. This happened to me, and I simply hid the discoloration with another embellishment. I used more of the $1/4$"-thick solid wood and applied it to both door panels with hot-melt glue.

You can avoid this problem by applying the oil in thin coats, wiping up the excess, and taking care not to flow it into the corners.

5. If you want a little extra protection, you can apply a water-based poly over the oil, but only after the oil has had at least 78 hours to cure.

FASTEN THE BACK

6. Last but not least, screw the back in place with several $5/8$"-long #6 pan head screws.

MALLET

Make a useful tool.

True confession time: I have this thing about lathes—I neither own one, nor derive much pleasure from their use. For the most part, turned objects seem so straightforward and predictable to me. Sometimes the circuitous route may take longer, but often it's much more interesting. At least that's what I discovered many years ago when I needed a round woodworking mallet but had nowhere to turn except to the band saw.

Mallets are striking tools, used to hit other tools (such as chisels) without damage. Hitting chisels and other sensitive tools with a metal hammer is a no-no in my book. It's true that some tools, such as Japanese chisels, are actually supposed to be struck with a metal hammer. No matter—I still prefer the ease and comfort of a well-balanced wood mallet in my hand.

Think dense hardwoods when procuring materials for a mallet. Typical lumberyard choices are hard maple or beech, but you may have access to a more diverse selection. Many exotics are hard and dense, and you can even use logs from your own backyard. Holly, dogwood, and hornbeam are a few of my favorites. Converting a small log into usable wood is not hard (see p. 164).

Mallets are most often tapered and cylindrical—a form that's easy to control and comfortable to use. The band saw is quite adept at creating such a form, assuming a sharp blade and well-tuned machine. With just a few simple steps (knock on wood), your mallet will take shape in no time!

Making a hardwood mallet that fits your hand is a quick and satisfying project. Use any dense hardwood; contrasting colors look especially nice.

Cut List & Supplies

NUMBER OF PARTS	DESCRIPTION	DIMENSIONS IN INCHES			COMMENTS
		Thickness	Width	Length	
Solid wood (any dense hardwood)					
1	Head	2	4 1/2	12	*Cut groove, then cut into two 2" x 4 1/4" x 4 1/4" pieces*
1	Handle	7/8	7/8	10 3/4	*Use a contrasting color wood.*

FROM FIREWOOD TO LUMBER

1. Find a suitable log and use a small axe to create an approximately flat surface.

2. Joint the surface to get it truly flat.

3. Draw a straight line to guide your sawing.

4. Put the flat surface on the band saw table, and proceed to dimension the log as required.

How to Build the Mallet

Cut and shape the head

Cut a groove in the block that will become the head, and then cut the block into two pieces, each 4 1/4" long. Before you can band saw the head round, the two halves need to be joined; but if you glue the handle in place, you can't orient the head on the saw table to make the cut.

Solution: Temporarily glue the halves together with a piece of paper in the joint. Later, they'll pry apart easily. Draw a circle on one end of the block, and cut to the line on the band saw.

Cut and shape the handle

Pry the head apart and plane or sand the handle to fit the groove. Draw lines on the handle to show where it exits the head and shape the exposed portion to fit your hand.

Put it together

Glue the halves together, with the handle in the groove. Clean it up smooth, and shape the head on a stationary belt sander or by hand.

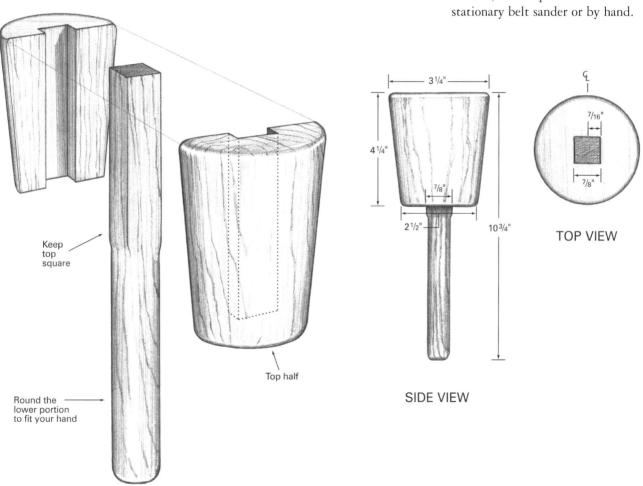

Keep top square

Round the lower portion to fit your hand

Top half

EXPLODED VIEW

3 1/4"

4 1/4"

7/8"

2 1/2"

10 3/4"

SIDE VIEW

7/16"

7/8"

TOP VIEW

Building the Mallet

Cut and shape the head

1. Lay out a $7/8$"-wide groove down the center of the piece that will become the head.

2. Cut the groove $7/16$" deep with a dado blade on the table saw. If your dado set isn't wide enough, make two passes with a $1/2$"-wide blade.

3. Clean out the groove (if necessary) with a chisel.

4. Cut two pieces to a final length of $4\,1/4$".

5. Glue the two pieces together, with a piece of paper between them. This old lathe trick makes it possible to separate the two halves later. Alternately, you could use a little hot-melt glue.

6. Draw a $2\,1/2$"-diameter circle on one end of the head block.

7. Tilt the band saw table to 6° and cut around the circle. The low end of the table tilts toward the band saw's throat.

8. Save the offcuts for gluing cauls.

9. Gently pry apart the halves and scrape away all the paper and glue.

Glue the two halves together for band sawing. Lay a sheet of paper between the two halves so you can separate them later.

Tilt the band saw table, and saw the circular head.

Pry the halves apart, and scrape away the paper and glue residue.

Cut and shape the handle

1. Plane or sand the handle material so it fits snugly in the groove and allows the top halves to make full contact with one another.

2. Cut the handle to final length and mark where it enters the head.

3. Shape the handle below this point to feel comfortable in your hand, using a spokeshave, files, or stationary belt sander.

Shape the handle with a spokeshave and scraper so it fits your hand.

Put it together

1. Apply a small amount of paste wax around the bottom of the mallet head and on the exposed portion of the handle to make glue removal easier.

2. Spread glue on the halves of the head and on the interior part of the handle.

3. Clamp the mallet together, using the band saw offcuts as cauls.

4. Round the head and shape the handle further on a stationary belt sander.

5. Though it may be tempting to sand to perfection, don't bother. Leaving the mallet slightly rough will provide more friction as it strikes a cutting tool.

Round and smooth the head on a stationary belt sander.

FOLDING SCREEN-SHELF

Keep it light with decorative paper and a clever knock-down design.

As winter wanes and the days grow brighter, I am restless for change. Though it provided comfort through the cold months, tending the wood-burning stove starts to feel like more of a chore than a pleasure. Come spring, I am ready for new tasks and projects to enliven the heart and home. The local art store is a good place for inspiration—I head straight for the decorative paper display, where an infusion of color and texture awaits the imagination.

Paper is a quick and inexpensive way to cover a lot of surface area without time-consuming prep work (see p. 171). Most art stores carry a variety of papers from dazzling reds to subtle tones. For many, the most difficult aspect of working with decorative papers is choosing just one. The interplay between wood and paper makes for endless possibilities, so bring along samples of wood to help with the selection process. Lightweight woods such as cypress or clear pine are perfect for this project. Feel free to choose an extravagant paper—it's used to cover only a few square feet of light plywood panels set in solid wood frames.

Three such frame-and-panel assemblies (one large and two smaller) make up the back and ends of the screen. The frames are biscuited, and the paper-covered panels slip into grooves cut in the frame.

A typical folding screen consists of three separate frames joined together with bi-fold hinges, allowing for a freestanding zigzag configuration. Try something different and join the panels with butt hinges. If you configure the panels in a U-shape, you can slip shelves into slots on the end frames and lock them in place with exposed decorative wedges. Built like a screen, it's now a lightweight, knock-down shelving unit.

In use, the bottom shelf, which is stronger than the other shelves, holds heavier items that serve as ballast for the unit. It alone has a stiffener glued to the underside to prevent sagging.

With splashes of color from the papered panels, this shelving unit makes a statement. It's as good-looking from the back as from the front—perfect for dividing a small space. It's just the thing for throwing off the dreary confines of winter and filling almost any void—within or without. Thinking about the next design is just as satisfying as building it.

Decorative papers add new dimensions of color and texture to this knock-down shelf-screen.

Cut List & Supplies

NUMBER OF PARTS	DESCRIPTION	DIMENSIONS IN INCHES			COMMENTS
		Thickness	Width	Length	
Solid wood (choose color to match decorative paper)					
6	Stiles	3/4	2 3/8	36	
12	End rails	3/4	3	9	
1	Top rail	3/4	3 3/4	37 5/8	
1	Center rail	3/4	3	37 5/8	
1	Bottom rail	3/4	4	37 5/8	
2	Bottom shelf stiffeners	3/4	2 15/16	42	
4	Filler pieces	3/4	4	13 3/8	
1	Wedge tenon stock	3/4	2	55	*For 12 wedges total, each 4 1/4" long*
9	Shelves	3/4	4 5/8	46 1/4	*3 boards per shelf, glued to final width of 13 7/8"*
Plywood					
4	End panels	1/4	8 1/2	8 1/2	
2	Back panels	1/4	13 7/8	36 3/4	
Other materials & supplies					
4	Brass butt hinges and screws				*1 3/8" wide x 2 1/2" long. Hinges with loose pins are easier to install.*
	#20 biscuits				
8	Sheets of decorative paper				*Approx. 20" x 20". See Choosing and Using Decorative Papers on the opposite page.*

A few years back, while shopping in an art store, I discovered the wonderful world of decorative papers. At my fingertips, I found an array of colors and textures, with effects from muted and subtle to dazzling. I instantly realized those papers could bring the same effects to my woodworking without a lot of labor or expense.

Art-store papers come from around the world, and my favorites are the handmade artisan papers. Interspersed with the paper's irregular fibers, you'll find surprising tidbits of leaves, flowers, and other organic materials. Every sheet is different, and each has a story. The typical sheet is about 20" x 20", though sizes vary. Thickness varies, too. I find the thinner papers easier to work with.

Yellow woodworking glue is fine for sticking fancy paper to 1/4" plywood panels. Thin it slightly with water and brush it on. Use a sheet that's a little bigger than the panel, and roll out wrinkles with a rolling pin. The moisture in the glue makes the paper wrinkle a bit, but the random effect is pleasing and adds a little texture. Trim the excess with a sharp craft knife.

After the glue dries, but before you do any more woodworking on the panels, brush on three coats of water-based polyurethane for protection. When the project is complete, you can clean up any scuffs and refresh the surface with a light sanding and another coat or two of poly.

Yellow woodworking glue works best for applying papers. Thin it with water so it brushes on easily.

Use a sheet of paper that's a little bigger than the panel, and lower it carefully to avoid wrinkles.

Roll out the big wrinkles; the water in the glue will make it impossible to remove them all.

Trim the edges with a craft knife once the glue dries.

Three coats of water-based polyurethane protect the paper during the rest of the building process.

How to Build the Folding Screen-Shelf

Orient yourself and prepare the frame parts

Lay out all the pieces that make up the frames, and figure out where to put the grooves and biscuit slots. Mark everything clearly and then cut the slots and grooves. Finish the frame edges before the panels go in place.

Decorate the panels

Cut the plywood panels to length and glue down the decorative paper. Trim the paper and apply three coats of protective finish.

Assemble the screen

Glue up the three frame-and-panel assemblies. Mortise for the hinges. Finish the frames. Apply the filler pieces to cover seams in the paper.

Build and install the shelves

Cut the open mortises in the boards that make up the shelves, and then glue them up to width. Cut the notches in the ends of the shelves to fit the slots in the end panels. Add stiffeners to the underside of the bottom shelf. Fine-tune the fit of the shelves. Cut and fit the wedge tenons.

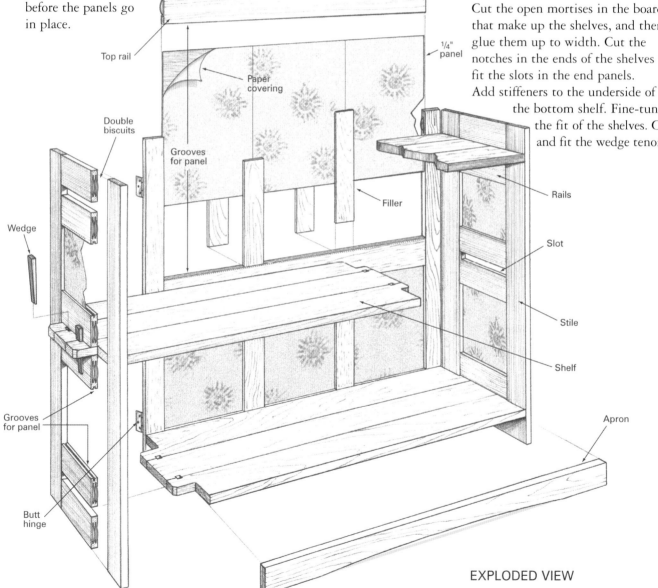

Top rail

Paper covering

Double biscuits

Grooves for panel

Wedge

Grooves for panel

Butt hinge

¼" panel

Filler

Rails

Slot

Stile

Shelf

Apron

EXPLODED VIEW

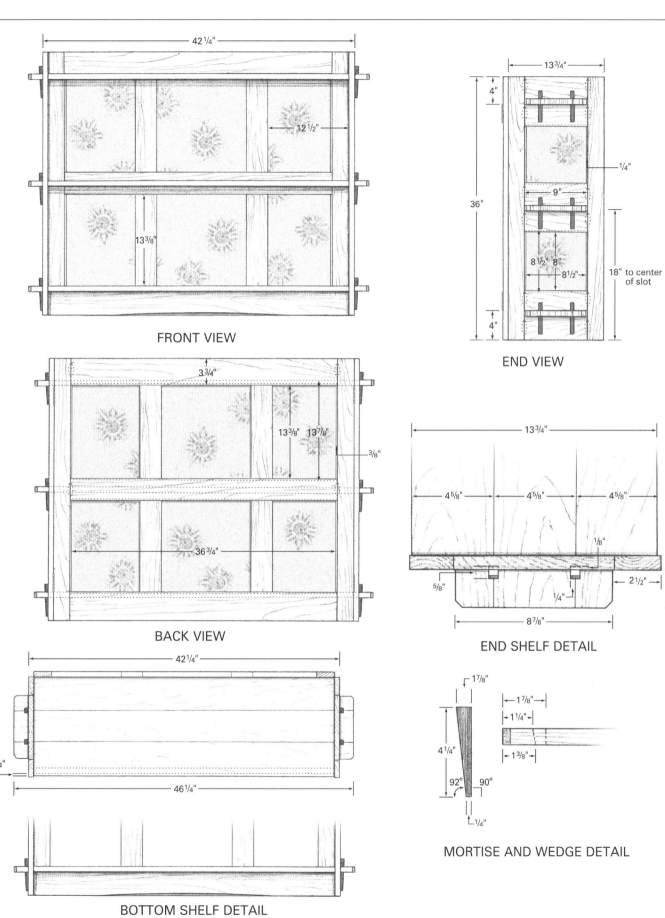

FRONT VIEW

END VIEW

BACK VIEW

END SHELF DETAIL

BOTTOM SHELF DETAIL

MORTISE AND WEDGE DETAIL

Building the Folding Screen-Shelf

Orient yourself and prepare the frame parts

LAY OUT THE PIECES

1. Determine how you want to arrange the stiles and rails for beauty. You'll want to think about each panel and about adjoining panels. Think in terms of symmetry and visual balance, with no jarring color or grain transitions at the joints. Lay out all the pieces in their final positions.

2. The shelf slips through slots in the end panels. Instead of cutting the slots, we'll join two rails to the stiles and leave a slot between. It's crucial that the slots are large enough to accommodate the thickness of the shelves. Rather than trying to measure and leave enough room, make some spacers from scrap material about $13/16$" thick. Set them in place now to locate the rails, and save them for later use when gluing up the frames.

3. With the panel laid out correctly, mark the rail/stile joints for the biscuit slots (see p. 46).

4. Take a close look at the drawings, and mark where to cut the grooves that hold the top and bottom edges of the paper-covered panels. This can get confusing; some rails are grooved on both edges, some on one edge, and the stiles have no grooves at all.

5. Before you move the pieces, make sure each one is clearly marked with its name, orientation, and which cuts to make where.

Prepare the frame parts for assembly. Lay them out, cut all the biscuit slots, and prefinish the inside edges.

CUT THE GROOVES

6. A $1/4$"-wide groove is large enough to accommodate most finished panels, unless the paper is unusually thick.

7. Use a dado blade (see p. 63) to cut a $1/4$"-wide x $1/4$"-deep groove on the rails.

CUT DOUBLE BISCUIT SLOTS

Be sure to use two biscuits per joint for added strength (see p. 49).

8. When cutting the slots for double biscuits, remember to make all cuts with the biscuit joiner's fence resting on the same reference surface. Cut the slots with the frame parts face up or face down; whichever you choose, make sure it's always the same.

9. A spacer about $3/16$" thick makes it easy to raise the biscuit joiner for the second cut.

10. Cut the slots on the rails first, then slot the stiles.

FINISH THE FRAME EDGES

11. Sand all the inside edges of the stiles and rails up to 220 grit.

12. Break the sharp edges of each piece, but not every inch. Note how the pieces go together to make the frame, and be careful not to round the edges where stiles meet rails.

13. Apply two coats of quick-drying shellac (see p. 20). Finish only the inside edges and not at the joints.

14. Once the shellac dries, lightly sand the finished surfaces with 400-grit paper.

Decorate the panels with your choice of paper, and protect them with a couple of coats of water-based clear finish.

Decorate the panels

CUT AND DECORATE THE PANELS

Most sheets of decorative paper aren't large enough to cover the back panel; you'll probably need three. Don't worry about the seams. Make them neat, but you'll hide them later with filler pieces simply glued over the seams.

1. Cut 1/4" plywood panels to finished size. Cut the smaller panels first for practice.

2. Use a sharp craft knife to cut the paper a little long so that it overhangs the edges of the panel by about 1/2" all around.

3. Blow the dust off the panel and wipe it down with a damp cloth. Use a brush to apply an even coat of watered-down glue.

4. Lay the paper on the panel, and use a rolling pin or rubber roller (found in home centers) to roll the paper flat and push excess glue out to the sides.

5. Paper both sides of each panel.

6. Let the panels dry thoroughly before trimming the overhanging paper.

FINISH THE PANELS

7. Lightly sand the panels with 220-grit paper wrapped around a block.

8. Apply three coats of water-based poly (see p. 21). Use a 2" foam brush and allow at least 30 minutes between coats.

Assemble the screen

GLUE UP THE FRAMES WITH THE PANELS IN PLACE

This is a complicated glue-up, so make a dry run of each frame assembly to practice without glue or biscuits. You'll need the 13/16"-thick spacer blocks used when you first laid out the frames to assure consistent slot space for the shelves.

1. Apply glue and insert biscuits in the stile slots.

2. Hold one stile horizontally in the bench vise with the biscuits facing up. Apply glue to the mating rail ends and use a mallet to join them together.

3. Place a panel in the groove and glue the next rail in place. Keep in mind that the panels don't completely fill the spaces between the frames; there's a gap at each side. The gap is 1/4" on the end panels. Place the panels in approximate position and just let them float. Later you can secure them in place with a dollop of hot-melt glue or wood spacers glued in the groove.

4. This step applies only when you're assembling end panels. After gluing all the rails, position the spacer blocks in the shelf slots. Hold the blocks in place with masking tape.

Glue up the frame and panel assemblies, and join them with butt hinges.

5. Remove the entire assembly from the vise and lay it on the bar clamps. Clamp lightly and then add cauls to flatten the ends (see p. 49). Then apply enough pressure to close the joints.

MORTISE THE HINGES

6. Cut hinge mortises on each frame (see p. 76), but don't attach the hinges to the frames just yet.

FINISH THE FRAME ASSEMBLIES

7. Sand all surfaces through 220 grit. Soften the sharp edges and give close attention to visible end grain.

8. Cut the filler pieces that cover the paper seams on both sides of the back frame assembly. Don't try to make them fit perfectly—leave a little breathing room for likely wood movement. Sand them, too.

9. Clean off any dust and wipe the frames down with a damp cloth. Apply a coat of shellac to the fronts of filler pieces and to both sides of each frame. When the shellac is dry, lightly sand the frames with 400-grit paper.

10. Again wipe down with a cloth, and apply three coats of water-based poly, allowing about 30 minutes between coats.

11. When the finish is thoroughly dry, screw the hinges to the frames, but don't tighten down the screws all the way. By leaving them loose initially, you will have a small amount of adjustment when putting the two hinge halves together.

12. Hold the frames together and slip in the hinge pin.

13. Tighten the hinge screws until they seat firmly in the countersinks. Do this slowly—the difference between tight and overtight is tiny.

14. Stand the screen frames upright and rotate the ends into shelf-holding position.

APPLY THE FILLER PIECES TO COVER THE SEAMS

Now I am going to ask you to make what purists might consider a woodworking transgression. Rather than take the time for fancy joinery, this is a good place to be practical. Use hot-melt glue to attach the filler pieces to the back panels.

15. Mark some reference points for positioning the pieces.

16. Let the glue gun reach maximum temperature. Apply the glue and simply press the filler pieces in place.

Build and install the shelves

MORTISE THE SHELVES

1. Decide on the best-looking arrangement of boards for each shelf, and prepare them for assembly as described on page 48. Joint the edges, and lay out and cut the biscuit slots, with no biscuit within 4" of the ends.

2. Using the End Shelf Detail as a guide, lay out the angled mortise locations as shown. For general information on cutting open mortises, see page 59. Follow the method described to cut the mortises with hand tools.

3. Glue up the shelves and leave them in clamps for at least an hour.

CUT THE NOTCHES

4. Remove the shelves from the clamps, scrape off the excess glue, and sand with 220 grit.

5. The shelves are probably a little too wide at this point, so rip the boards to final width. You may want to take a little from each edge just to keep the mortises on center. Clean up edge cuts on the jointer or with a hand plane.

6. Lay out the shoulder notches on each shelf. Mark clearly to facilitate successful cuts. I lightly score the beginning of each cut with a sharp knife. It helps the saw to start exactly on the line.

The finished screen-shelf looks as good from the back as it does from the front.

Fit the shelves to the screen assembly, and wedge them in place.

7. Saw the crosscut portion of the notch first and then the rip cut.

8. Clean up the corners with a sharp chisel if necessary.

9. Use a Japanese saw to crosscut the sharp corners from the ends of the shelves.

10. Clean up the saw cuts with sandpaper wrapped around a block. Work carefully to maintain a crisp line.

STIFFEN THE BOTTOM SHELF

11. Cut the shelf stiffeners to final length, as shown in the illustrations.

12. Cut the curves on the bottom edges. These curves aren't just for beauty—reducing the area that contacts the floor creates more stability on uneven surfaces.

13. Attach the supports to the bottom shelf with biscuits.

FINISH THE SHELVES

14. Sand everything up to 220-grit paper.

15. Apply one coat of shellac to both sides as a sealer. When it's dry, sand lightly with 400-grit paper.

16. Remove any dust from the surface and wipe the shelves down with a damp cloth.

17. Apply three coats of water-based poly.

FIT THE SHELVES

18. You may want to have an extra set of hands for this process. There's some technique to slipping the shelves into the frame. It's a four-handed job and not easy to do solo. You may have to balance the shelves on your leg while you manipulate the ends; just experiment a little to figure out what works best for you.

CUT AND FIT THE WEDGE TENONS

Choose a hardwood for the wedge tenons. Cherry, walnut, or maple work well. If you're feeling bold, this is a great time to consider an exotic wood. Base your choice on the degree of color contrast you want with the wood used in the frame.

19. Mill the tenon material to preliminary thickness and width. From this stock, crosscut 12 individual pieces to final length.

20. Cutting the wedges is easier if you take a few minutes to build the band saw fixture shown in the illustration to the right. Smooth up the cut and slightly round the edges of the hypotenuse side of each tenon.

21. Fit the wedges by tapping them lightly into the shelf mortises with a small hammer or mallet. The wedge tenons need to fit closely in order to exert enough force against

the frame to tie the unit together structurally. But take care: The mortise is less than 2" from the end of the board—potentially weakening the end. If you pound the wedges too tight, they might break the ends right off the shelf.

22. Remove material from the wedges as necessary to get the right fit. You'll know it's right when the wedge slips solidly into place, and it takes a little tug to pull it free. A light tap with a mallet is good, but you shouldn't have to pound it.

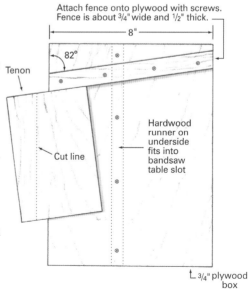

Attach fence onto plywood with screws. Fence is about 3/4" wide and 1/2" thick.

8"

82°

Tenon

Cut line

Hardwood runner on underside fits into bandsaw table slot

3/4" plywood box

BANDSAW JIG FOR WEDGE TENONS

TEA CHAIR

Relax with angles.

We all slouch into the easy chair of complacency, eager to be cushioned from the rough edges of life. As a woodworker, I find I often slip into the easy chair world of 90 degrees, a place where my mind likes to rest. There's nothing wrong with right angles, but so much of life is organized in a square. Like a box. And as comfortable as it seems, it can be hard to get out of the box.

Every so often, I need a new slant on life—a brain teaser to jolt me out of the comfort zone. That's when I know it's time to build a chair!

I first learned chair-making by taking classes, and then from working to other's plans. Occasionally, I run across photos of chairs that interest me, as was the case with this chair. Japanese industrial designer Katsuo Matsumura came up with the design in the 1970s, and for a time the chair was produced and sold commercially. The original frame was made from larch—an inexpensive wood in Japan (at least back then)—and had a woven cattail seat. I have never seen one in person, but have greatly admired its simple beauty and have often wondered how it would feel or look tucked into a cozy niche at home.

With sparse information about the design and only a few available dimensions, I got some 2 x 4s and started playing around with the angles and proportions. Eventually I built a chair that I felt was visually balanced and comfortable. The final version was made of white oak. I simplified the construction, replacing a tricky angled joint with a simple carriage bolt. For a little pizzazz, I sprayed the bolts (and the screws used on the slats) with two coats of copper metallic paint. You could also etch the bolt heads with a file, as in the Platform Bed (see p. 131).

Forgive me, Mr. Matsumura, for naming your chair after my favorite beverage. It's one of my favorite seats. Each morning I settle in to drink my tea and read self-help books. Thus engaged, pondering the profundities of life, woodworking is never far from my thoughts. Exploring angles has once again thrust my heart and mind into new realms.

Though the angles make the tea chair look complex, the joinery is rather simple. This chair is made of white oak.

Cut List & Supplies

NUMBER OF PARTS	DESCRIPTION	DIMENSIONS IN INCHES			COMMENTS
		Thickness	Width	Length	
Solid wood (white oak)					
2	Seat rails	$13/16$	$2\,3/8$	31	*Rough cut to length of 35"*
2	Back seat rail	$13/16$	$2\,3/8$	38	*Rough cut to length of 42"*
2	Runners	$13/16$	$2\,3/8$	29	
4	Seat slats	$3/4$	$3\,1/2$	$17\,3/4$	
8	Back slats	$3/4$	$3\,5/8$	17***	***Rough cut length. Determine final length from the actual chair. It should be about 16 3/4". Cut to final length after bracket center is fitted to vertical.*
Other materials & supplies					
2	$5/16$" carriage bolts with nuts and washers				
	1 $1/2$" drywall screws				*For fastening rails to runners*
	1 $1/4$" drywall screws				*For fastening slats*
	$1/2$" x 1 $1/2$" fluted dowels				
	Epoxy glue				
	Copper metallic spray paint				*For dressing up the screws and bolts (optional)*

How to Build the Tea Chair

Angle the rails

Get into the non-90° frame of mind by cutting the angles on the rail ends. You can cut the back rails on the miter saw (set it at 31°), but the seat rail angle is too acute for most miter saws (you'd need to set the saw at 67°). A simple table-saw jig (see p. 187) solves the problem.

Join the runners and rails

Dowels only work when the holes in the two pieces align perfectly. You'll need careful layout and measurement to get good joints. Bore the dowel holes in the runners on the drill press, then clamp the rails in position to transfer the hole locations from the runners to the rails. Use a doweling jig to position the holes in the rails. Glue the rails to the runners with epoxy glue, and then fasten the intersection with carriage bolts.

Cut and attach the slats

The slats are rabbetted at each end and nicely chamfered all around. Make the seat slats first, and clamp a couple in place for a test fit to determine the final length for the back slats. Prefinish all the chair parts before assembly. Finally, screw the slats in place, with a 1/8" gap between each slat.

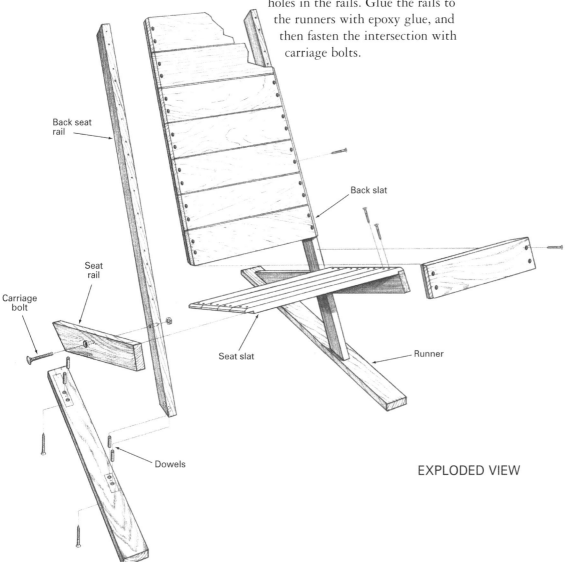

Back seat rail

Seat rail

Carriage bolt

Dowels

Seat slat

Back slat

Runner

EXPLODED VIEW

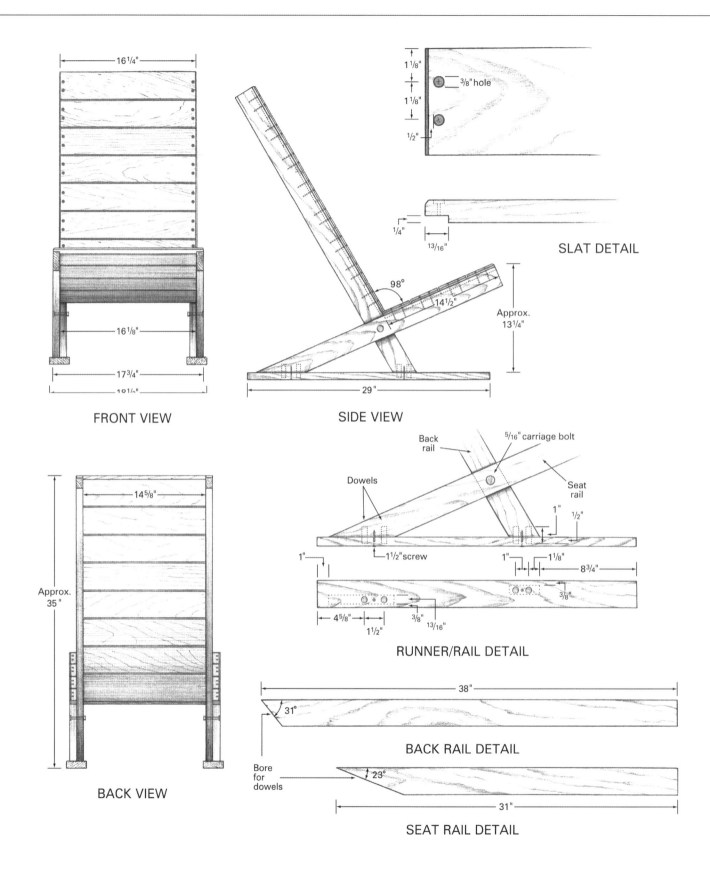

FRONT VIEW

16 1/4"

16 1/8"

17 3/4"

SIDE VIEW

98°

14 1/2"

Approx. 13 1/4"

29"

SLAT DETAIL

1 1/8"

3/8" hole

1 1/8"

1/2"

1/4"

13/16"

BACK VIEW

Approx. 35 "

14 5/8"

RUNNER/RAIL DETAIL

Back rail

5/16" carriage bolt

Seat rail

Dowels

1 "

1/2 "

1 1/2"screw

1"

1 1/8"

8 3/4"

1"

4 5/8"

3/8 "

13/16"

3/8 "

BACK RAIL DETAIL

38"

31°

SEAT RAIL DETAIL

Bore for dowels

23°

31"

Building the Tea Chair

The seat rail angles are too acute to cut on a miter saw. A simple table saw jig solves the problem.

Angle the rails

1. Cut the acute angles on one end of the seat rails, with the angle table-saw sled shown in the Table Saw Sled illustration and in the photos on pp.186–187.

2. Measure from the long point of the seat rail to the other end to get the final length. This will be a 90° cut, so you can cut it on a miter saw set at 0°.

3. Cut the angled end of each back rail on the miter saw set at 31°.

4. Measure from the long point of the back rail, and cut to final length with the saw set at 0° (a 90° cut).

BORE THE RUNNERS

5. Cut the runners to final length.

6. Lay out the dowel locations on the runners (see the Runner/Rail Detail). Square all the lines across the face of the runner so you can see them when the rails are in place.

7. Remember the runners aren't identical—there's a right and a left rail. Orient them on the bench as they are in the chair and lay out and mark them carefully.

8. Bore all the dowel holes in the drill press, making them 1/2" deep.

MORE HOLES

Because of the angles between the rails and runners, it's nearly impossible to clamp the assembly together during glue-up. You can remedy this situation with a few well-placed screws driven from the underside of the runner. They'll pull everything firmly into place while the glue dries.

9. From the top of the runners, bore a 1/8" hole between the dowel holes. Go right through the runner.

10. Flip the runner over, and countersink the underside deeply enough to bury the drywall screw's head.

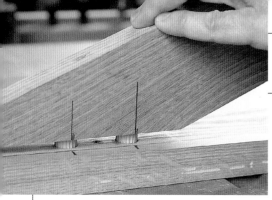

When angles are involved, dowels make good joints.

Join the runners and rails

DOWEL THE SEAT RAILS

1. Hold the angled end of the seat rail in position on the runner, using a spring clamp to keep things steady.

2. Transfer the centerlines of the runner dowel holes to the seat rails (see the photo below).

3. Bore the holes on the seat rails with a doweling jig (see the next page). Make these holes 1" deep.

4. Slip the dowels in the holes (but don't glue them yet), and put the seat rail in place. Hold the runner in the bench vise for stability. Make sure the dowel holes are deep enough for the rail to seat firmly on the runner.

5. Square a line across the seat rail, 14 1/2" from the front end. This is where the seat rail and back rail intersect.

Hold the seat rail in position and mark the centerline of the dowel locations on it, transferring them from the runner.

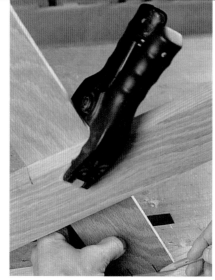

Clamp the back rail to the seat rail and make sure it's seated against the runner before transferring the dowel hole locations from the runner to the rail.

DOWEL THE BACK RAILS

6. Position the back rail on its marks on the runner, and adjust it to intersect with the seat rail in the correct location. Hold it in place with a spring clamp.

7. Transfer the hole locations from the runner to the back rail.

8. Bore the holes in the back rail with the doweling jig.

9. With the dowels in place, test fit the seat rail and back rail. Put a spring clamp at the intersection.

10. Mark the areas where the two pieces overlap so you can leave the edges untouched when sanding in a later step.

SAND AND SMOOTH THE RAILS AND RUNNERS

11. Soften all the edges, except where the rails intersect. You want to leave those edges crisp and untouched.

12. Sand everything up to 220 grit.

GLUE UP THE ANGLES

13. Test fit the parts with the dowels in place. Make sure the joints are tight.

14. Apply paste wax around the joints, but not in them. Epoxy is a tenacious adhesive, and the wax prevents any squeeze-out from sticking. Once the glue has cured, the excess is easy to clean off with a sharp chisel.

15. Secure the runner in the bench vise. Apply epoxy to the runner dowel holes and press the dowels in place.

16. Spread epoxy on the end of the seat rail and in the dowel holes, and press the joint together.

17. Remove the runner from the vise and drive the screw up from below.

18. Repeat the process to glue the back rail in place.

19. Secure the rail intersection with a clamp and let the glue cure overnight.

Rabbets on the ends of the slats make for a stronger joint and a lighter appearance.

Cut and attach the slats

BOLT THE RAILS TOGETHER

20. Bore a $5/16$" hole through the intersection of the rails. Use the drill press. During this operation, support the frame on the table with blocks of scrap wood. Make sure there's some scrap directly beneath the hole to prevent the bit from tearing a ragged edge in the back side of the hole.

21. Install the carriage bolts with the heads on the outsides of the frames.

SEAT SLATS

1. Cut end rabbets on each slat, using a dado blade and a miter gauge.

2. Mark the screw hole locations on each slat.

3. Bore countersunk holes on the drill press to fit the screw heads. To allow for some seasonal wood movement, make the shank holes a little oversize—about $5/32$".

4. Soften the edges and ends of each slat with a slim 45° chamfer. Use a router table or hand plane.

5. Finish sand up to 220 grit.

BACK SLATS

6. Clamp two seat slats in place against both rails.

7. Measure the distance between the back rails, from outside to outside. This is the finished length of the back slats.

8. Cut the back slats to final length.

ON DOWELS AND DOWELING

I don't normally use dowels in furniture construction. Biscuits are easier in most situations. However, there are a few instances where I think dowels are very effective—such as the angles used in this chair. Use fluted dowels instead of cutting dowel rod to length. As the joint is seated, the grooves relieve pressure inside the hole by letting some glue squeeze out. When extra holding power is an issue, use epoxy instead of yellow glue.

Perpendicularity of all the holes is the key to having your dowel joints fit together. The drill press easily bores perpendicular holes in flat square pieces, but is hard to set up for angled pieces. This is where a doweling jig comes in.

The doweling jig clamps over the workpiece and is set up so the holes are automatically centered in the thickness of the piece. It has hardened steel guides to keep the drill bit at 90°. All you have to do is manage the depth. A little too deep is no problem; too shallow and the pieces won't seat, and the dowel will be visible in the gap between the parts.

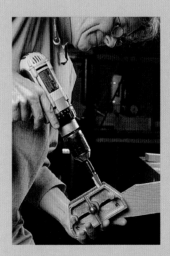
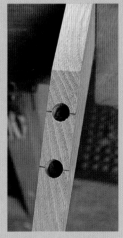

Well-fitted doweled joints require properly drilled and positioned holes. A doweling jig lets you drill perpendicular holes exactly on the centerline.

9. Rabbet the ends and chamfer the edges just as you did for the seat slats.

10. Finish sand up to 220 grit.

PREFINISH

This chair has a lot of nooks and crannies, so you can save a great deal of time and trouble by finishing the pieces before assembly. My own chair has an oil finish. Whatever finish you use, let it dry for at least 24 hours before assembling the chair.

ATTACH THE SLATS

11. Attach the first slat at the back. Clamp both ends and drill pilot holes in the rails.

12. Fasten the slat in place with four drywall screws.

13. Lay a ¹/8" spacer block against the front edge of the slat (it's easier if the spacer is long enough to span the rails), and nestle the next slat against it.

14. Clamp the slat in place and drill pilot holes. Fasten it.

15. Repeat, using the spacer between each slat.

16. Attach the back slats in the same manner, starting at the bottom and working up.

FINISHING TOUCHES

17. A paste wax rubdown adds a nice luster to an oil finish; apply a coat or two after the oil has had at least 78 hours to dry.

For extra comfort, you might like some cushions. Thin high-density foam works best (1" or so in thickness is about right). Add some tie strings to keep them in place.

TABLE SAW SLED, TOP VIEW

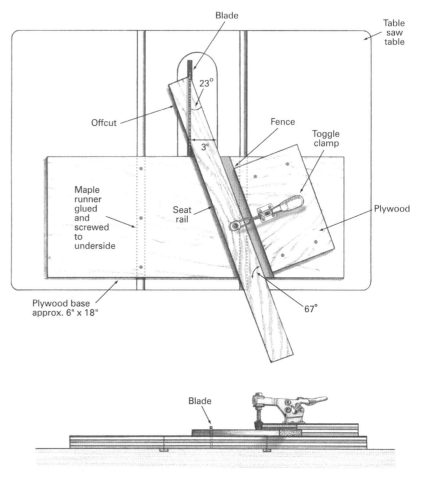

Blade

Table saw table

23°

Offcut

3"

Fence

Toggle clamp

Maple runner glued and screwed to underside

Seat rail

Plywood

Plywood base approx. 6" x 18"

67°

Blade

TABLE SAW SLED, FRONT VIEW

TABLE SAW SLED FOR ACUTE ANGLES

Most miter saws cut only a little more than a 45° angle. The seat rails for this project are at 23°, which would require your miter saw to be set at 67°. You might consider using the table saw and a miter gauge, but it's a little scary for angles this acute. The safest and most accurate way to cut such an angle is with a table saw sled. Running in both miter slots, it supports the workpiece without wobble. Except for the toggle clamp, you can build it from scrap (see the Table Saw Sled illustrations on the opposite page).

1. Cut the plywood base, and center it over the blade slot (blade lowered). Slide the fence up to the right edge to square it to the blade. Lock the fence in place.

2. Mark, countersink, and bore screw holes over the slots.

3. Mill maple runners to fit your table saw's miter slots. They should be tight enough so they don't wobble, but loose enough to slide without binding.

4. Place the runners in the miter slots, and apply a small line of glue to each.

5. Place the plywood base on the plywood runners, using the table saw fence as a guide.

6. Screw the runners to the sled.

7. Move the fence away and slide the sled back and forth to check its

motion. If it's a little hard to move, look for glue squeeze-out in the slots. A little paste wax helps lubricate the runners.

8. Draw the sled back and raise the blade. Turn on the saw, push the sled into the blade, and cut about 2" into the plywood. Turn off the saw and lower the blade.

9. Set an angle finder to 23° and mark this on the front edge of the plywood, about 3" to the right of the kerf.

10. Fasten a strip of wood along this line as a fence.

11. Fasten a larger piece of plywood outboard of the fence to hold a toggle clamp to keep the workpiece from wobbling.

12. Test the jig on some scrap to get a feel for how it works.

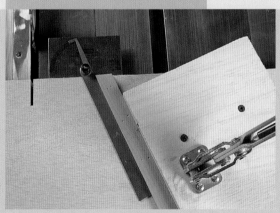

Fasten the fence 23° to the edge of the plywood. Its location is not critical, but make it about 3" to the right of the kerf.

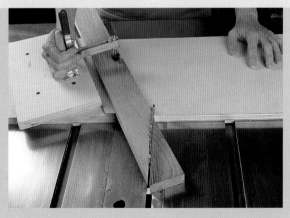

A sled running in both miter slots holds the workpiece securely and is the safest and most accurate way to make angled cuts on the table saw. This photograph was taken from behind the saw.

ELEMENTAL TABLE

Work with, not against, nature.

Sometimes I go to home centers just to look around, but it's not what you think. I am not there for retail therapy, unlike so many others. I visit the home center with the sole intention of seeing something different. I comb the aisles, surf the displays, and let the waves take me where they will. This is apparently unusual because puzzled clerks keep cycling back to me, asking, "May I help you find something?" "No thanks," I reply. "It has to find me."

Inspiration recently found me in the garden center of my local home store. A concrete stepping-stone stopped me in my path. Thunderstruck, I gazed at it, whispering, "All it needs is a little embellishment with spray paint, and there it is: an instant weatherproof tabletop!" I found myself headed to the plumbing aisle as if propelled by a strong sea current, then to the paint department for copper metallic spray paint. I sailed on, first to the local lumberyard for some wood, and then back to my shop, where I was soon building the first Elemental Table.

The stepping-stone set the tone for the design. Only rugged materials would complement it, so I chose white oak for the table base and legs. I built bold but slightly curved mitered legs, painting them with pitch black milk paint for contrast. Paint is always a good finish for wooden furniture that needs to stand up to the elements. It's tougher and more durable than any clear finish, and it does a better job of locking moisture out of the wood.

Instead of building wooden aprons, I joined the legs with spindles cut from copper tubing pressed into holes drilled in the legs. Copper tubing is light and easy to cut with an inexpensive wheel-type tubing cutter. Over time, the copper loses that bright surface and develops a lovely patina. If you prefer the shine or ever wish to restore it, sand the copper tube with 400-grit sandpaper and use a little steel wool to apply a coat or two of paste wax.

Woodworking is so much more than buying tools and materials or spending time in the shop. It's an eternal quest for ideas that can lead you to many places—if you're willing to go with the flow.

Although this table isn't made to withstand direct exposure to the outdoors, its rugged materials and a couple of coats of paint make it perfect for use under a porch roof. The top is a concrete stepping-stone with a little spray paint on it, and the spindles are copper tubing. The splined mitered legs are made of white oak and painted with milk paint.

Cut List & Supplies

NUMBER OF PARTS	DESCRIPTION	DIMENSIONS IN INCHES			COMMENTS
		Thickness	Width	Length	
Solid wood (white oak)					
8	Leg pieces	1 3/8	4 1/2	24	*Cut to finished length of 23 1/2" after rabbeting shoulders*
4	Spline material	1/4	1	24	
Plywood					
2	Clamping forms for tops of legs	3/4	2	16 1/16	*Any scrap material is fine, even plywood.*
1	Clamping form for bottom of legs	3/4	14 1/4	14 1/4	*Any scrap material is fine, even plywood.*
Other materials & supplies					
12	Spindles	5/8	10 1/4		*Use 1/2"-diameter M-type copper tubing.*
1	Concrete stepping-stone	1 1/2	16	16	
1 tube	Construction adhesive				
12	Nylon gliders				*Use three small gliders per foot.*
1 tube	Clear silicone caulk				
	Waterproof glue				

How to Build the Elemental Table

Build the mitered legs

Rip a 45° bevel on one edge of the leg pieces, then cut the spline grooves in the bevel. Rabbet the top ends of each leg piece. Bore the spindle holes in the straight edge of each piece. Cut a template for the curves on the top and inside edges of the legs, and cut the curves on the band saw. Use a router and template-cutting bit to perfect the inner curve. Cut the legs to finished length, and sand and paint them.

Join the legs and add the top

Cut the spindles to length and sand the ends to fit snugly into the holes drilled in the legs. Join two legs with spindles; no gluing is involved—just slip the spindles into the holes. Use a plywood clamping form between the rabbet shoulders to set the distance between the legs and draw the legs together with clamps. Use the same process to join the two leg assemblies together. Seal the bottoms of the legs and install three gliders on each leg.

Run a line of construction adhesive around the shoulders and press the top in place.

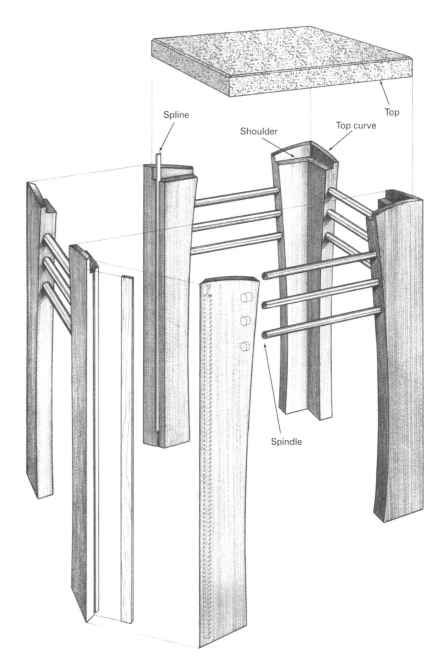

Spline

Shoulder

Top curve

Top

Spindle

EXPLODED VIEW

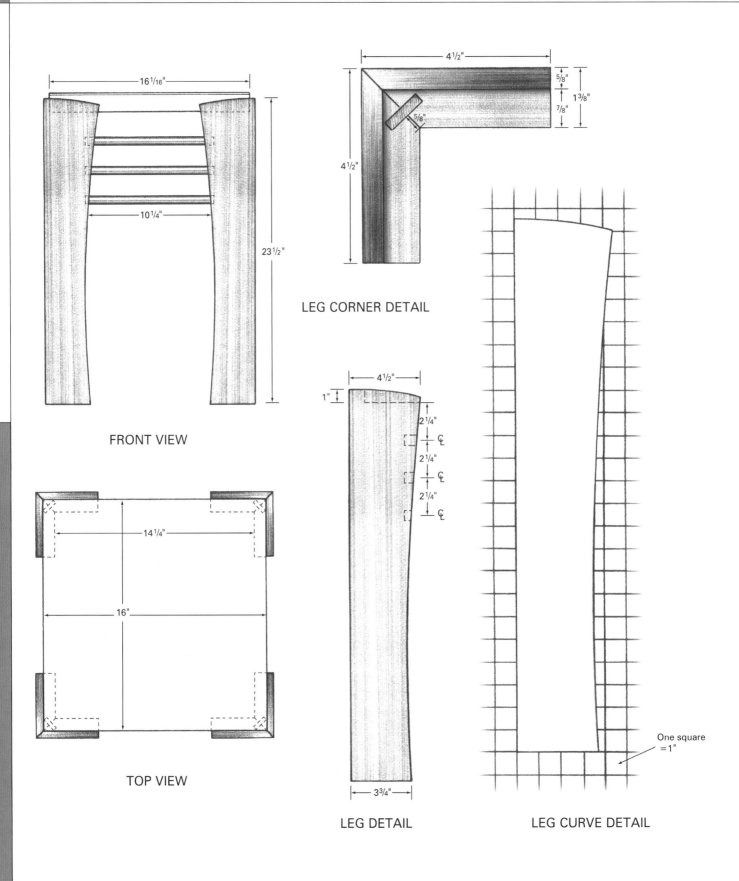

16 1/16"

23 1/2"

10 1/4"

FRONT VIEW

4 1/2"

5/8"

1 3/8"

7/8"

5/8"

LEG CORNER DETAIL

14 1/4"

16"

TOP VIEW

4 1/2"

1"

2 1/4"

℄

2 1/4"

℄

2 1/4"

℄

3 3/4"

LEG DETAIL

One square
= 1"

LEG CURVE DETAIL

Building the Elemental Table

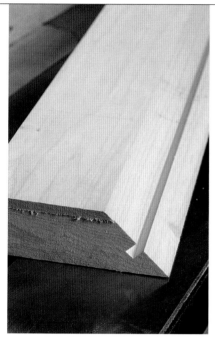

Splined mitered joints in the legs make for a strong joint with no visible end grain.

Build the mitered legs

CUT THE SPLINED MITER AND RABBET THE TOPS

1. Cut the splined miters in the leg pieces (see p. 65).

2. Lay out the rabbet on the top end of one leg piece (see the Leg Corner Detail).

3. Set up the table saw with a dado blade and cut the rabbet in each leg piece.

BORE FOR SPINDLES

4. Lay out the spindle locations on the inner surface of one leg, measuring down from the shoulder (see the Leg Detail). Use this as a pattern to lay out the hole locations on the other leg pieces.

5. Bore 5/8"-diameter x 3/4"-deep holes on the drill press.

SHAPE THE LEGS

6. On a piece of 1/4" plywood, lay out the inner edge curve of the leg (see the Leg Curve Detail). Use the method described on page 74.

7. Use a flexible metal ruler to draw the curve on the top of the template.

8. Cut the template on the band saw, and refine the curve with a sanding drum, files, and/or a hand sander.

9. Use the template to draw the top and inner curves on all the leg pieces.

10. Cut the curves on the band saw, being sure to leave the line for reference. Save the offcuts to use later as cauls.

11. Use a template-cutting bit and a router running against the template to refine the long curve on the inner edge of the leg. See page 74 for details.

12. Shape the top curve with a sander. A stationary belt sander is best, but if you don't have one, you can use a random orbit sander. Don't spend too much time on this—you can't get the curve perfect until the two leg pieces are glued up.

SURFACE PREP

13. Finish sand the inside surfaces up to 150 grit.

14. Apply a thin coat of paste wax along the insides of the miter edges, but keep the wax off the gluing surfaces.

CUT THE SPLINES

15. Resaw the spline material on the band saw. Cut it approximately in half.

16. Plane the splines to final thickness, frequently checking for a snug fit in the groove.

ASSEMBLE THE LEGS

Gluing the legs requires a lot of clamps and is a somewhat awkward process. I suggest enlisting a friend to help. Make a practice run before the glue flows.

17. Lay two clamps on the floor, with the offcut cauls in place.

18. Spread a thin layer of waterproof glue on each mitered surface. Run a thin bead in the grooves.

19. Insert the spline in one piece, then press the two miters together.

20. Place the leg in the clamps. Use the offcuts as cauls on the curved edge, and thin scraps of plywood on the miters.

21. Check that the shoulders align. They must be perfectly flush at the joint.

22. Stand the leg on end and add more clamps in opposing directions.

PREFINISH

23. Perfect the top curve.

24. Final sand the outside surfaces with a random orbit sander, working your way up to 220 grit.

25. Cut the legs to final length, measuring downward from the rabbets.

26. Mix up the milk paint as directed by the manufacturer. Brush two coats on all surfaces of the legs, lightly hand sanding with 400-grit paper between coats.

27. Seal the milk paint with three coats of gel varnish. Lightly hand sand with 400-grit paper between coats.

Join the legs and add the top

TWO LEGS WITH SPINDLES

1. Hold the copper tubing lightly in a metal vise—its thin walls are easy to collapse.

2. Cut the copper to length with a plumber's tubing cutter—an inexpensive home-center item.

3. Test the spindles' fit in the $5/8"$ holes previously drilled in the legs. They must fit tightly enough to hold the table in its assembled position until the top goes on. Sand the ends of the spindles lightly to get the desired fit.

4. Lay a leg on a protective mat spread upon the bench. Tap the three spindles in place with a rubber mallet. Don't hit the tubing directly, or you may dent it. Hold a wood block atop the tubing and strike it.

5. If the spindles fit well, you needn't glue them to the legs. Brush a little oil finish in each hole to help the tubing slip in. If the fit is too loose to hold the table togeth-

The spindles fit snugly in their holes, but they don't really hold the table together. The structural integrity comes from the construction adhesive that joins the top and the legs.

er, you can use glue. Omit the oil and put a little epoxy in the holes. Before the glue cures, make sure the top fits between the shoulders.

6. Tap the other leg onto the ends of the spindles. You needn't seat the spindles in the ends of the holes— just get them started.

7. Place the $16 \ 1/16"$ plywood clamping forms in the rabbets that will later hold the top.

8. Use clamps to draw the legs together. The clamping form establishes the correct distance between the legs, assuring proper alignment.

9. Repeat with the other two legs and the remaining spindles.

FOUR LEGS WITH SPINDLES

10. Slip spindles into the remaining holes in the two subassemblies and join the four legs together.

11. Place the $14\,1/4$"-square plywood clamping form on the bench and move the leg/spindle assembly to the upright position.

12. Place one of the long plywood clamping forms in the rabbets to establish the proper position for this new leg. Draw the two assemblies together with clamps.

13. The spindles should fit tightly enough for the base to hold its position for the remaining steps. Remove the clamps.

GLIDERS

14. Turn the base upside down on the protective mat.

15. Lightly coat the bottom of each leg with silicone caulk to seal the end grain.

16. Tap three small gliders into the bottom of each leg.

GLUE THE TOP IN PLACE

17. Spray paint the concrete top as desired.

18. Load a tube of construction adhesive in a caulking gun, and apply a thin film to the rabbeted shoulders at the top of each leg.

19. Squeeze out an additional little blob of caulk in the mitered corners.

20. Set the top in the adhesive, and push down with all your weight to compress the adhesive and set the joint.

21. Check for adhesive squeeze-out. If you find any, remove it with mineral spirits.

A little spray paint transforms a concrete stepping-stone into a rugged and dramatic tabletop.

SMALL CABINET

Here's an appealing invitation to use hand tools.

As a professional woodworker, I must use machinery and work as efficiently as possible. But when I build something for myself or a friend, I find I use hand-tool methods as often as I can. It's a wonderful way to slow down, put aside any concerns for efficiency or hourly rate, and just pay attention to the details of what's happening now. I enjoy the shavings piling up at my feet and the ryoba's murmur.

But let's not get too carried away. As fun as hand tools are to use, some processes are so much easier to do by machine that it makes no sense to try to do them by hand. For instance, milling the small parts of this cabinet is fun to do by hand. Hand sawing and planing the many parts of a more complex project to thickness is an enormous task that would take so much time and effort to do properly that using machinery instead is only sensible.

This small cabinet uses simple dado/rabbet joinery for the carcase, something you can easily do by hand with planes, saws, and chisels. All the cuts are straightforward, except the stopped rabbet in the back edge of the top. For that, I suggest you use a router and rabbeting bit—they take all the fight out of what would be a fussy hand-tool operation requiring the purchase of several specialized tools to complete.

Simple though it is, this project will add new skills to your repertoire, and you'll be a better woodworker for having built it. You'll learn new ways of doing things, and gain the experience you need to create your own unique blend of hand and machine techniques. Then you'll be in a position to work every step of your projects using the methods best suited to your own situation.

This small cabinet is the ideal project for improving hand-tool skills. It is made from clear pine; the pull is a small branch of mountain laurel.

Cut List & Supplies

NUMBER OF PARTS	DESCRIPTION	DIMENSIONS IN INCHES			COMMENTS
		Thickness	Width	Length	
Solid wood (clear pine, basswood, or cypress)					
1	Top	$5/8$	7	$16\,1/2$	
2	Sides	$5/8$	7	$20\,1/4$	
1	Bottom	$5/8$	7	$11\,1/4$	*Cut to final length to fit carcase*
2	Doors	$5/8$	$5\,3/8$	$16\,7/8$	*Cut to final length and width to fit carcase*
1	Doors	$1/2$	$1/2$	$1\,1/2$	*Dimensions are approximate—just make a stop that looks good.*
1	Apron	$5/8$	$2\,1/2$	$10\,5/8$	*Cut to final length to fit carcase*
2	Shelves	$5/8$	$5\,1/2$	$10\,5/8$	*Cut to final length and width to fit carcase*
8	Shelf posts	$1/4$	$1/4$	$5\,3/8$	
Plywood					
1	Back	$1/4$	$11\,1/4$	$17\,3/8$	*Cut to final length and width to fit carcase.*
Other materials & supplies					
4	8d finishing nails	$1/8$		$1\,1/4$	*Door pivots*
8	Dowel pins	$1/8$		$1\,1/4$	*For fastening apron. Cut slightly longer dowels and round the heads if you want them to protrude.*
10	#6 x $5/8$" pan head screws				
2	Door pulls				*Buy ready-made, or make your own from a small branch*

How to Build the Small Cabinet

Build the carcase

Hand cut the dadoes in the top and the mating rabbets in the sides. Then cut the bottom to fit and rabbet its sides. Rabbet the back edges of all four pieces so the back will be flush when it's installed later. Cut the curves in the bottom edges of the sides, and then carve the embellishments. Spokeshave the low relief curve in the underside of the top. Final sand everything, then glue up the carcase.

Cut and fit the doors

Cut the left door to length and width, with a uniform-width gap all around. Cut a relief on the back edges of the door and install the pivot pins. Cut the right door to length and scribe against the left door for width. Cut the relief on the back edges and install the pivot pins. Fasten the stop in place and install the pulls.

Fit the apron, back, and shelves

Cut the apron to fit, then cut the curve along its bottom edge. Carve embellishments along the curve, and install the apron with 1/8" dowels.

Fit and attach the plywood back. Cut the shelves to fit the inside of the cabinet and support them on small posts glued into the corners.

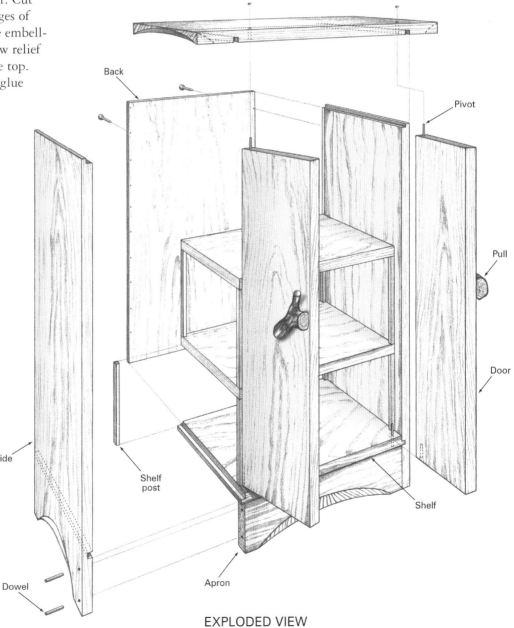

Back

Pivot

Pull

Door

Side

Shelf post

Apron

Shelf

Dowel

EXPLODED VIEW

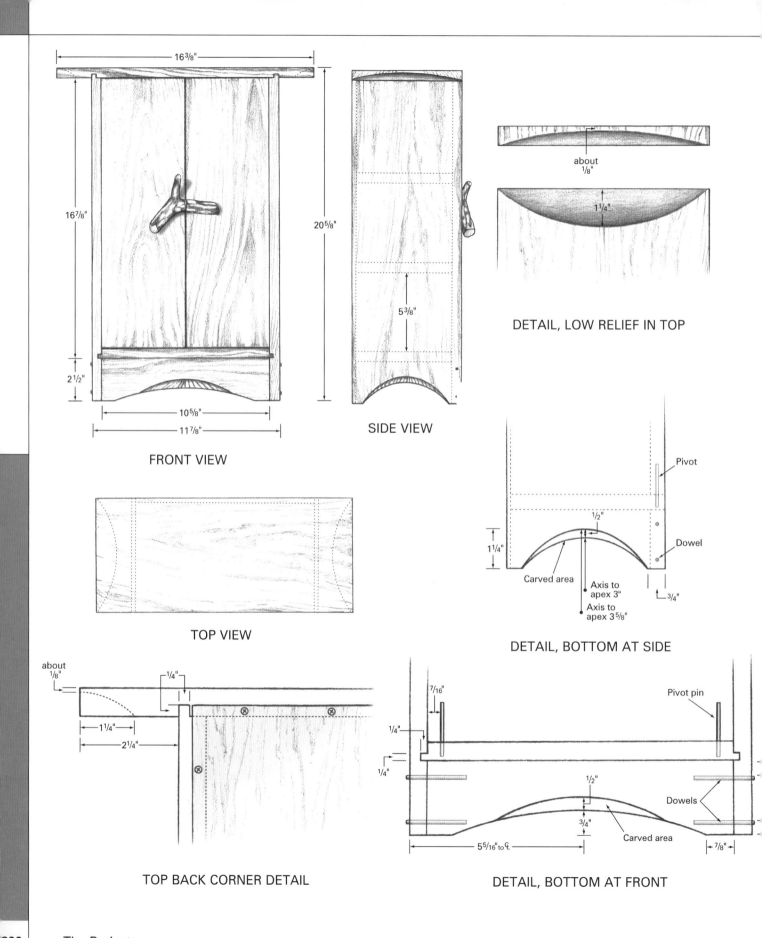

16³⁄₈"

16⁷⁄₈"

20⁵⁄₈"

2¹⁄₂"

10⁵⁄₈"

11⁷⁄₈"

FRONT VIEW

5³⁄₈"

SIDE VIEW

about ¹⁄₈"

1¹⁄₄"

DETAIL, LOW RELIEF IN TOP

Pivot

¹⁄₂"

1¹⁄₄"

Carved area

Axis to apex 3"

Axis to apex 3⁵⁄₈"

Dowel

³⁄₄"

DETAIL, BOTTOM AT SIDE

TOP VIEW

about ¹⁄₈"

¹⁄₄"

1¹⁄₄"

2¹⁄₄"

TOP BACK CORNER DETAIL

⁷⁄₁₆"

¹⁄₄"

¹⁄₄"

Pivot pin

¹⁄₂"

³⁄₄"

Carved area

5⁵⁄₁₆" to ℄

⁷⁄₈"

Dowels

DETAIL, BOTTOM AT FRONT

Building the Small Cabinet

Hand-cut dadoes and rabbets join the carcase.

While you can use machine tools to mill your lumber for this project, this cabinet is small enough so that it's a fun and rewarding exercise to do by hand. For details, see the instructions, right.

Build the carcase

DADO THE TOP AND SIDES
1. Lay out and cut the four dadoes—two on the top and one near the bottom of each side. Use the method described on page 66.

RABBET THE SIDES
2. Lay out and cut the rabbets on the upper and lower ends of the sides.

3. Test fit each joint and adjust as necessary.

4. When a joint fits properly, label the mating parts. Since this is hand joinery, the joints are not interchangeable.

FIT THE BOTTOM
5. Test assemble the top and sides, with the front facing up.

6. Clamp the joints and use a square to make sure the sides are 90° to the top.

7. Measure the distance between the outsides of the dadoes. This is the finished length of the bottom.

8. Cut the bottom to length.

9. Rabbet the ends, using the same method as on the sides.

10. Lay out and bore the 1/8"-diameter holes for the door pivots.

11. Reassemble the carcase with clamps to check the fit and squareness.

RABBET FOR THE BACK
You now have the skills to cut the rabbets along the back edges by hand, but their length makes the process a little more difficult. The top requires a stopped rabbet so it won't be visible in the side view, which is not easily accomplished by

DIMENSIONING LUMBER BY HAND—MOSTLY

LAY OUT THE PARTS
1. To help you get started on the right track, use the power jointer and planer to establish a flat face, a straight edge, and uniform thickness (see p. 44).
2. Lay out each part, avoiding knots and defects in the wood. Each part should have one jointed edge.

CROSSCUT TO ROUGH LENGTH
3. Use a ryoba saw to crosscut (see p. 53).

RIP TO WIDTH
4. Use a combination square or a marking gauge running against the jointed edge to mark the width on both sides of the workpiece.
5. Rip about 1/16" outside your lines with a ryoba. Set one rail of your low workbench at an angle. Ripping takes some getting used to, so keep practicing.
6. Place the board in a bench vise and plane down to the line. Check frequently to make sure the edge is square to the face.

CUT TO FINAL LENGTH
7. It's possible to make truly square crosscuts with Japanese saws, but it takes some time to master. The best way to learn the skill is by frequent practice exercises on scrap. Sooner or later your mind and body will do it right every time. In the meantime, use a miter saw or a table saw—without guilt.

hand. This is a great time to blend the router and rabbeting bit into the tool mix.

12. Rout full-length rabbets along the back edges of both side pieces (see p. 25).

13. Lay out the stopped rabbet on the top piece.

14. Rout the stopped rabbet with a plunge router (see p. 64). Use the same bit setup.

SCALLOPS ON THE SIDES
15. Lay out the upper and lower curves (see the Detail, Bottom at Side illustration).

16. Cut the lower curve on the band saw.

17. Hand sand the curve to smooth out the saw cuts and soften the edges.

18. Carve the scallops from the upper curve downward. Use a 3/4" gouge.

Use a 3/4" gouge to cut scalloped embellishments along the curve at the bottom of the sides.

SHAPE THE TOP
19. Make a light mark on the underside of the top, about 1 1/4" in from the ends.

20. Cut the low relief back to this point (see p. 78).

SURFACE PREP
21. Final sand both the insides and outsides of each piece with a random orbit sander. Work your way up to 220 grit.

22. Lightly soften all edges with a hand plane or by hand sanding.

GLUE-UP
23. Make a final test assembly before applying glue. Follow the steps below, omitting the glue for the test. Double-check the fit and the squareness of the joints. Correct any problems.

24. Start with the sides and bottom. Brush glue into the dadoes and on the inside faces of the rabbets. Don't glue the rabbets at the back—it's not attached until the cabinet is otherwise complete.

25. Fit the joints together with the cabinet facedown on the bench.

26. Brush glue into the dadoes on the top, and then fit it to the sides.

27. Clamp lightly with a web clamp to hold the carcase together while applying other clamps.

28. Clamp as shown in the photo at the top of this page.

Wrap the carcase in a webbing clamp to hold it together until you can apply all the clamps shown here. Be sure the corners are square and the back rabbets are aligned.

29. Check that the back rabbets are all flush. Correct this at the expense of losing flushness in the front— that's easily planed flush later.

30. Check that the corners are all square and adjust the clamps as necessary.

CLEAN UP
31. Gently remove any beads of squeezed-out glue with a chisel.

32. Hand plane the front face of the cabinet so all the joints are flush.

33. Lightly chamfer all the edges.

Cut and fit the doors

SIZE THE LEFT DOOR

1. Measure the inside width of your cabinet and divide it by two.

2. Plane the left door to final width.

3. Measure the inside height of the cabinet at the left corner and at the middle. If they're the same, cut the door to final length with two square ends. If the carcase is slightly out of square, cut the bottom edge at an angle. Use a bevel gauge to transfer this angle from the carcase to the door.

4. Mark the location of the 1/8"-diameter holes for the pivot pins on the top. Bore the holes right through the top. You'll plug them later.

5. Place a couple of credit-card scraps on the cabinet bottom to set the gap between the door and the carcase.

6. Rest the door on the shims. Check that the outer edge is parallel to the carcase and adjust if needed.

7. Hold the door in place and reach inside to scribe along the top. Draw the line on the back of the door.

If despite your best efforts the cabinet isn't square, cut the doors to fit its shape. Use a bevel to transfer the corner angle from the cabinet to the door.

Mark the final length on the back of the left door by setting it in place on shims and then scribing the top.

Build the doors to fit the cabinet perfectly—even to the extent of making them as parallelograms if necessary.

8. Saw along this line and cut the door to final length.

FIT THE LEFT DOOR

9. Shim the bottom, and tape two shims to the left side of the cabinet.

10. Clamp the left door in place.

11. Press a small finishing nail into the doors at the pivot points. Use the pivot holes in the top and bottom as guides. Tap the nail lightly to clearly mark the pivot hole locations in the door.

12. Remove the door and bore the pivot holes.

13. Round the inside left edge of the door with a hand plane so it can swing.

14. Plane a slight bevel (about 2°) on the inside right edge of the door. This allows the two doors to meet closely at the center and still have room to swing open.

15. Lightly soften all the edges and finish sand the door to 220 grit.

HANG THE LEFT DOOR

16. Set the door on the shims and use nails as temporary pivot pins.

17. Check the swing and plane away any material that prevents free movement.

18. Remove the door and place the cabinet on its back.

19. Drive the 1/8" lower pin up through the bottom, exposing only a small amount.

20. With the cabinet upright again, set the door on the pin.

21. Drive the top pin slowly; allow it

to find and go a little way down into the hole bored in the door.

22. Double-check the door swing. If it still moves freely, drive the pins all the way in.

23. Sink the top pin about $1/8"$ below the surface. Use a nail set, but be careful not to damage the wood around the hole.

INSTALL THE RIGHT DOOR
24. Follow the same steps used on the left door to determine the final length (and crosscut angle if it's not 90°).

25. Final sand the door to 220 grit.

26. Transfer the pivot-hole locations as with the left door, and bore the holes in the door.

27. Round the inside right edge with a hand plane to allow smooth operation.

28. Temporarily pivot the door on nails. If the door is still too wide, move the left door out of the way, and swing it to check for freedom of movement.

29. Gently close the doors with the left door overlapping the right and scribe against the right door to mark the final width, as shown in the lefthand photo above.

30. Remove the door and plane to the line, adding a 2° bevel to the inside edge.

31. Hang the right door, using the same process used on the left door.

Mark the final width of the right door when it's hanging on temporary pivot pins. Scribe its left edge from the left door.

STOP
32. Cut and shape a stop as shown in the righthand photo above. The dimensions aren't critical—just make a nice-looking stop.

33. Countersink and bore two screw holes in the stop.

34. Close the doors and make sure they're flush with the front.

35. Go in through the back and scribe along the back edges of the doors, drawing the line on the inside of the cabinet top.

36. Stand the cabinet on the top, and position the stop at the center of the cabinet, with its front edge on the scribed line. Screw it in place.

Cut a small stop and screw it to the underside of the top. Turn the cabinet upside down and work with gravity to make the process easier.

PULLS
A free-form pull made from a small tree branch suits this simple cabinet. I used a small length of branch from a mountain laurel, a common shrub in my area.

37. Flatten the back of the branch on a stationary belt sander.

38. Lay the cabinet on its back, and place the pull in position.

39. Drill right through the branch and the doors, using a $1/32"$ bit. The tiny holes are barely visible on the branch, but clearly mark the locations of the screw holes in the door.

40. Countersink and bore screw holes in the back sides of the doors.

41. Fasten the pull in place.

42. Slip a dozuki into the gap between the doors and saw the branch in two.

Fit the apron, back, and shelves

CUT AND CARVE THE APRON

The apron adds a nice finishing touch to the cabinet, closing the front and keeping the lower pivot pins in place.

1. Measure the width of the cabinet just below the bottom piece and cut the apron to length, using the undercut method described below.

2. Lay out the curves on the bottom edge (see p. 74).

3. Cut the lower curve on the band saw, and smooth the saw cuts and soften the edges by hand sanding.

4. Use a small V-gouge to carve the embellishments.

5. Final sand the outside surface up to 220 grit. Soften the top and bottom edges.

INSTALL THE APRON

6. Apply a small amount of glue to the top edge only, and clamp the apron in place.

Once the carcase is built and the doors hung, fit the apron, back, and shelves to the cabinet.

7. Bore two $1/8$"-diameter x $1 1/4$"-deep holes through the sides and into the apron.

8. Drive $1/8$" wooden dowels through the holes. These fit tightly, so only a small drop of glue is necessary.

9. Cut the dowels flush or let them protrude slightly. If you do the latter, lightly round the heads with a piece of sandpaper.

BACK

10. Measure the length and width to the outsides of the rabbets.

11. Cut the back to fit (plywood is hard to cut by hand; use machines for this).

12. Bore pilot holes, and fasten the back in place with pan head screws.

SHELVES

13. Cut the shelves to length and width so they fit snugly inside the cabinet.

Carve the embellishments on the apron with a small V-gouge.

14. Final sand to 220 grit and soften the front edges of the shelves.

15. Apply a small amount of glue to the posts, and use hand pressure to press them in place in the bottom corners of the cabinet.

16. Lay the lower shelf atop the posts.

17. Glue the next set of posts in place atop the lower shelf.

18. Lay the upper shelf in place.

FINISHING

19. Cut two small dowels and fit them into the top door pivot holes.

20. Lightly hand sand the outside of the cabinet with 220-grit paper to clean it up.

21. Apply a coat of oil to the outside only, being sure to wipe the excess off the surface before it dries.

22. After 78 hours of drying time, rub on a coat or two of paste wax for sheen.

UNDERCUTTING JOINTS FOR A TIGHT FIT

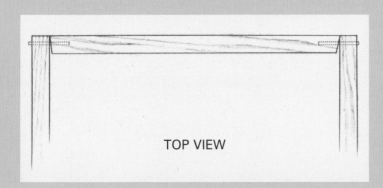

TOP VIEW

There are some cases in woodworking where the outward appearance of a joint is more important than its strength. The small cabinet apron is a good example. The cabinet is plenty strong without the apron, yet without it, the cabinet doesn't look right. Since appearance is the issue, you can save the trouble of making a perfectly fitted apron by undercutting the joint so the front fits perfectly, but there's a gap at the back. It's a technique commonly used when installing crown molding. Just cut the apron a tiny bit long and pare away at the back corners with a sharp chisel or block plane until it fits. (See the illustration at left).

Acknowledgments

I suppose the apex of any woodworker's career is the opportunity to write a book, and I am grateful to Lark Books for seeking me out. It has been a wonderful experience in every way, even the really hard parts. Though after all is said and done, I would rather cut wood than mince words any day!

Special thanks to Pat (Barney) Bernarding for sticking with me through thick and thin—'til glue and screw us do part!

Thanks to all my friends for listening. Where would I be without my sounding boards?

To Bo Smith for those first few words that got the process going.

Thank you to Barb Berwernitz for building the Furniture from a Box table (shown on page 117).

Finally, I give many thanks to Drew Langsner and Country Workshops for instilling my appreciation for hand tools, and for the opportunity to teach other women.

Last but not least, Sassy and Arlo—my canine support team—who stood by me all the way.

To the empowerment of women everywhere!

Suggested Reading

TECHNICAL WOODWORKING BOOKS

Flexner, Bob. *Understanding Wood Finishing.* Emmaus: Rodale Press, 1994.

Lee, Leonard. *The Complete Guide to Sharpening.* Newtown: Taunton Press, 1995.

Odate, Toshio. Japanese *Woodworking Tools: Their Tradition, Spirit and Use.* Fresno: Linden Publishing, 1998.

Rae, Andy. *Choosing and Using Hand Tools.* Asheville: Lark Books, 2002.

Rogowski, Gary. *The Complete Illustrated Guide to Joinery.* Newtown: Taunton Press, 2002.

RELATED SUBJECTS

Edwards, Betty. *Drawing on the Right Side of the Brain.* Los Angeles: J.P. Tarcher, 1979.

Norbury, Betty. *Furniture for the 21st Century.* New York: Viking, 1999.

Stem, Seth. *Designing Furniture: From Concept to Shop Drawing.* Newtown: Taunton Press, 1989.

PERIODICALS

Fine Woodworking. Taunton Press

Woodwork: A Magazine for All Woodworkers. Ross Periodicals

ORGANIZATIONS

The Furniture Society, 111 Grovewood Road, Asheville, NC 28804.
Tel: (828) 255-1949
Web site: www.furnituresociety.com

Metric Conversion Chart

INCHES	METRIC (MM/CM)	INCHES	METRIC (MM/CM)	INCHES	METRIC (MM/CM)
1/8	3 mm	8 1/2	21.6 cm	23	58.4 cm
3/16	5 mm	9	22.9 cm	23 1/2	59.7 cm
1/4	6 mm	9 1/2	24.1 cm	24	61 cm
5/16	8 mm	10	25.4 cm	24 1/2	62.2 cm
3/8	9.5 mm	10 1/2	26.7 cm	25	63.5 cm
7/16	1.1 cm	11	27.9 cm	25 1/2	64.8 cm
1/2	1.3 cm	11 1/2	29.2 cm	26	66 cm
9/16	1.4 cm	12	30.5 cm	26 1/2	67.3 cm
5/8	1.6 cm	12 1/2	31.8 cm	27	68.6 cm
11/16	1.7 cm	13	33 cm	27 1/2	69.9 cm
3/4	1.9 cm	13 1/2	34.3 cm	28	71.1 cm
13/16	2.1 cm	14	35.6 cm	28 1/2	72.4 cm
7/8	2.2 cm	14 1/2	36.8 cm	29	73.7 cm
15/16	2.4 cm	15	38.1 cm	29 1/2	74.9 cm
1	2.5 cm	15 1/2	39.4 cm	30	76.2 cm
1 1/2	3.8 cm	16	40.6 cm	30 1/2	77.5 cm
2	5 cm	16 1/2	41.9 cm	31	78.7 cm
2 1/2	6.4 cm	17	43.2 cm	31 1/2	80 cm
3	7.6 cm	17 1/2	44.5 cm	32	81.3 cm
3 1/2	8.9 cm	18	45.7 cm	32 1/2	82.6 cm
4	10.2 cm	18 1/2	47 cm	33	83.8 cm
4 1/2	11.4 cm	19	48.3 cm	33 1/2	85 cm
5	12.7 cm	19 1/2	49.5 cm	34	86.4 cm
5 1/2	14 cm	20	50.8 cm	34 1/2	87.6 cm
6	15.2 cm	20 1/2	52 cm	35	88.9 cm
6 1/2	16.5 cm	21	53.3 cm	35 1/2	90.2 cm
7	17.8 cm	21 1/2	54.6 cm	36	91.4 cm
7 1/2	19 cm	22	55 cm	36 1/2	92.7 cm
8	20.3 cm	22 1/2	57.2 cm	37	94.0 cm

Index